WHERE TO STAY
IN ITALY
& Switzerland

ANWB

Produced by the Publishing Division of The Automobile Association

Directory taken from the accommodation database of the ANWB (Royal Dutch Touring Club), compiled by the AA's Hotel and Touring Services Department, and generated by the AA's establishment database

Maps prepared by the ANWB (Royal Dutch Touring Club) ©ANWB

Editor: Virginia Langer

Copy Editor: Christopher Staines

Hotel descriptions translated by Bernadette Hickman

Cover designed by The Paul Hampson Partnership, Southampton

Cover illustration by Diana Ledbetter

Preliminary pages designed by Peter C Gibbons

Head of Advertisement Sales:
Christopher Heard, telephone 0256 20123 (ext 21544)

Advertisement production:
Karen Weeks, telephone 0256 20123 (ext 21545)

Typeset by Gardata BV, Leersum, Netherlands

Printed by BPCC Hazell Books, Member of BPCC Ltd, Aylesbury

Colour supplement produced by Sussex Litho Ltd, Chichester

Every effort is made to ensure accuracy, but the publishers do not hold themselves responsible for any consequences that may arise from errors or omissions. While the contents are believed correct at the time of going to press, changes may have occurred since that time or will occur during the currency of this book.

A CIP catalogue record for this book is available from the British Library.

Published by The Automobile Association, Fanum House, Basingstoke, Hampshire RG21 2EA

ISBN 0 7495 0598-2

Contents

WHERE TO STAY

A new series of European hotel guides from two of Europe's leading motoring associations: the Automobile Association of Britain (AA), and the Royal Dutch Touring Club (ANWB)

Your complete guides to accommodation in Europe; the whole series lists over 5000 hotels, with nearly 1500 that have been specially recommended by the AA and ANWB.

❏ Up-to-date details of facilities, prices and opening times

❏ An ABC of Contintental motoring and touring information

❏ Route maps and town plans to help you find your hotel

Foreword

The Automobile Association (AA) and the Royal Dutch Touring Club (ANWB), the two leading motoring clubs in Britain and the Netherlands, have joined forces to launch a brand new series of guides to hotel accommodation in Europe's most popular holiday destinations. Both the AA and the ANWB are highly regarded, not only for their expert knowledge of all aspects of motoring, but also for the reliability of their touring information, their hotel inspection and classification schemes and the quality of their road maps. It has seemed a logical step, therefore, and one which will benefit members of both associations and users of their guides, for the two clubs to pool resources and expertise to produce the *Where to Stay* guides. Currently there are four titles available in the series:

Where to Stay in France, Belgium and Luxembourg

Where to Stay in Spain, Portugal and Andorra

Where to Stay in Germany and Austria

Where to Stay in Italy and Switzerland

All the accommodation listed in the books is regularly visited by ANWB inspectors to ensure that acceptable standards are maintained. Those hotels that are particularly recommended are highlighted in the directories by printing the AA and ANWB symbols alongside their entries to enable the reader to identify them at a glance. These hotels are sent a special door/window sticker, as pictured below, and whenever you see this symbol you will know that the hotel has been specially recommended.

All the books contain a wide range of accommodation, at all prices, from quite simple guesthouses to deluxe hotels, but because of popular demand, we have weighted our selection towards the budget end of the market, without, however, compromising our standards of quality. We have also tried to concentrate on providing the greatest choice in those regions of the countries that are most popular with tourists.

We send out questionnaires every year so that we can, wherever possible, give up-to-date prices and details. Please note that although establishments provide this information in good faith, it is often difficult for them to forecast prices accurately in advance over a 12-month period, so the information should be regarded as a guide only.

We are always grateful to have comments and recommendations from users of our guides, so please use the report form you will find at the back of the book to let us know of your findings, and send any comments to the ANWB at the address given on the form. As the guides are updated every year, it is important to make sure that you are using the current editions.

⚫

Finally, a request to our readers: the owners of the hotels in our guides have, by responding to our questionnaires or placing an advertisement, taken the trouble to provide you with accurate information about their establishments. They would appreciate knowing if the time and money they have spent has been worth it, so we should be grateful if you could mention that you obtained your information about their hotels from the AA/ANWB *Where to Stay* guides.

⚫

HOTEL DREI KÖNIGE CHUR

1793-1993 • 200 years of traditional hospitality

Reichsgasse 18, CH-7002 Chur • Telephone 081-22 17 25 • Telefax 081-22 17 26

HOLIDAY IN CHUR

Chur, the capital of the holiday canton of Graubünden, is the ideal starting point for numerous walks in an enchanting mountain landscape. Hotel Drei Könige has dreamed up something special for you: experience unforgettable hours in a still unspoilt natural environment for three, five or seven days. It is still possible to eat and sleep here in a traditional hotel situated in a charming and exceedingly hospitable provincial. town at very favourable rates. We look forward to welcoming you.

7-day adventure holiday
'Steinbock'
Swiss Fr. **598,—** per person.

INCLUDED

The price of all three adventure holidays – 'Steinbock', 'Adler' and 'Murmeli' – includes:
- Rooms with shower/WC, TV, telephone, radio alarm, mini bar and hair dryer.
- Half board with choice of two menus each day.
- Buffet breakfast.
- Information on walks.
- Guided walks to 'Churer Adlerhorst' (an eagle hewn out of the rock on the Mittenberg), including lunch.
- (Hire of) binoculars and walking stick.
- A gift of a beautiful, light rucksack for walking.

5-day adventure holiday
'Adler'
Swiss Fr. **498,—** per person.

COUPON FOR INFORMATION

Yes, I'm interested in adventure holidays in Chur. Please send further information free of charge to:

Surname/Christian name

Adress

Postcode/Town/Country

Complet coupon, cut out and send to:
Hotel Drei Könige, Reichsgasse 18, CH-7002 Chur
Telephone: (+41) 81 22 17 25, fax: (+41) 81 22 17 26

3-day adventure holiday
'Murmeli'
Swiss Fr. **298,—** per person.

P&O European Ferries

Cruising you to the Continent

In the year which sees us 'officially' embracing Europe, it's fitting that trends show British travellers are becoming more 'Continental' in their approach to holidays.

Sun and sangria no longer satisfy the adventurous spirit of today's holidaymakers who are switching from traditional air packages to independent motoring holidays.

This trend is reflected in the growing numbers opting for the freedom of a Continental motoring holiday, where they can go where they want, when they want!

After a successful year in 1992, the leading car ferry operator P&O European Ferries forecasts a bumper 1993 as more people than ever take their cars across the Channel for a European-style holiday.

In addition, the company has carried most of the British travellers to the new EURO DISNEY® Resort near Paris, as its first official travel partner in the UK.

To meet this demand, P&O European Ferries has invested heavily in its fleet – improving facilities and levels of service afloat and ashore to match the expectations of today's sophisticated travellers.

Facilities on Board

Four superferries will be in operation by the start of the peak season on P&O European Ferries premier route from Dover to Calais following the £20 million lengthening and refurbishment of the 'Pride of Kent' – bringing her up to the same standards as the 'Pride of Dover' and the 'Pride of Calais'.

Joining the fleet of superferries from the Spring is the new 'Pride of Burgundy'. Fully equipped to the P&O European Ferries high standard this new superferry will carry 1300 passengers and 600 cars from Dover to Calais in style.

With up to five ships operating in peak periods, the company will have the facility to carry over 85,000 passengers and more than 25,000 cars in just one 24-hour period on its 75-minute Dover to Calais route alone.

This level of investment ensures that the company keeps one or more steps ahead of its competitors. It does this by providing unmatched facilities on board which makes passengers choose P&O European Ferries first, time and time again.

Wining and dining

A touch of P&O cruise-style glamour has been added to all ships operating from Dover – to Calais and Boulogne – with luxurious Peninsular Lounges. On services to Calais, stylish POSH (port out,

starboard home) bars complete the picture.

New coffee shops now give an additional choice on sailings from Portsmouth to Le Havre, supplementing self-service and buffet restaurants.

On all sailings, passengers can enjoy excellent food at value-for-money prices in self-service, smart à la carte or buffet-

style restaurants – many of which have recently been re-styled.

Club Class

Club Class travel is yet another innovation from P&O European Ferries, which sets them apart from the rest.

The ultimate experience in car ferry travel, Club Class is available on all P&O European Ferries sailings for a small supplement.

It brings the bonus of guaranteed seats in exclusive Club Class lounges with steward service and complimentary tea, coffee and newspapers – all in stylish surroundings and a peaceful haven away from the crowds, even during the busiest holiday periods.

And for business travellers who need to work on their way across the Channel, Club Class also provides desks in quiet corners for paperwork and telephones. Fax and photocopying facilities are also available on most ships.

On short sea crossings, Club Class lounges feature luxurious but informal furnishings, with free standing easy chairs and coffee tables as well as a bar for the exclusive use of Club Class travellers.

Lounges on Portsmouth crossings have a duty-free trolley service provided by stewards while wide reclining seats with extending footrests give Club Class passengers the chance for a cruise-style snooze!

which the whole family will find both informative and entertaining.

Special menus are also provided – at special prices – in self-service and waiter-service restaurants.

And for parents with babies, there are nursing and changing facilities.

Shopping

Every P&O European Ferries ship has spacious duty-free shopping areas boasting an enormous range of wines, spirits and tobacco at special shipboard prices.

Department store-style tax free gift

The Felixstowe service also boasts reclining seats and an in-cruise entertainment audio system.

Fun for youngsters

P&O European Ferries likes to keep all the family happy during a crossing – not just the grown-ups. Colourful play areas are therefore provided for youngsters on most sailings, or they can laugh away their crossing watching cartoons or films in video lounges. Exclusive EURO DISNEY features on board every ship,

shops now offer far more than just perfume and jewellery. Clothing, travel accessories, photographic and audio goods as well as gifts mean that no-one need panic if vital holiday items have been left at home.

Currency exchange bureaux are also available on every sailing.

NO-ONE OFFERS YOU MORE ACROSS LA MER.

This year, we've put even more pleasure into cruising with P&O European Ferries.

As well as more sailings to more destinations, we've introduced the added comfort and relaxed style of our unique Club Class on every route.

And with the introduction of a fourth new superferry, The 'Pride of Burgundy', to the Dover-Calais service in 1993, we can now offer up to fifty crossings a day on this route alone.

We still offer unbeatable value with the extension of our Family Bonus Fares and Short Stay Excursions.

And, with our unique computerised tickets on most routes you can simply sail through the check-ins.

This year, we also offer you the biggest selection of Holiday by Car ideas we've ever had. Helping you cruise even further into Europe, with a choice of high quality accommodation.

You can even cruise right into the heart of the Euro Disney® Resort with P&O European Ferries, Euro Disney's Preferred Travel Partner.

When you cruise with P&O European Ferries, we make it easy to take it easy. Who could ask for more?

For further information, see your local travel agent or call P&O European Ferries direct on (0304) 203388.

P&O
European Ferries

DON'T JUST GET ACROSS. CRUISE ACROSS

Caring for the disabled

P&O European Ferries prides itself on its caring attitude to its passengers generally, and in particular to disabled and handicapped travellers for whom it reserves an especially warm welcome.

Lifts and wheelchair-accessible toilets and cabins are provided on most ships to ensure disabled passengers have a relaxed and enjoyable crossing.

Some ships are more suited to the disabled passenger than others and with notice, P&O European Ferries will give advice on the best sailings to choose as well as make arrangements for cars to be parked close to lifts to allow easy access to passenger decks.

Registered disabled travellers who are also members of the DDA (Disabled Drivers Association) or DDMC (Disabled Drivers Motor Club) can take their cars across free with P&O European Ferries by booking with either association.

Which route across?

With six convenient routes to the Continent, P&O European Ferries leads the field when it comes to choice. It has

more routes and more sailings than any other operator, all ideally placed to get you off to the right start when you reach the other side.

The 75-minute sailing from Dover to Calais is the fastest cross-Channel route by ship and is consistently the number one choice for the majority of passengers. Calais and its near neighbour Boulogne provide direct links to most parts of Europe and getting away speedily on the other side is now easier thanks to the extension of the A26 motorway to the French coast and right into the port of Calais.

But if you are heading for the Benelux countries, or perhaps to Germany and Scandinavia, P&O European Ferries sailings from Felixstowe to Zeebrugge could be a better option – with a longer sea crossing giving more time to relax and a

shorter drive on arrival.

Sailings from Dover to Ostend are operated by RMT, P&O European Ferries Belgian partners. They have recently introduced a new superferry onto the route, together with Club Class travel on most sailings. They also provide a 100 minute Jetfoil service for foot passengers from Dover to the Belgian port, which links up with rail connections on both sides of the Channel.

A favourite option for those heading for the sun – Brittany, Normandy, the south of France or beyond – are sailings from Portsmouth to Le Havre and Cherbourg. Day and night crossings are available to both ports – with comfortable cabins available for a good night's rest. Excellent motorway links from Le Havre to Paris also make this route a good choice for trips to the French capital.

Motorists should carefully weigh up which route is best – look at your starting point in the UK, the distance to your port of departure, sailing time and length of drive to your destination. Remember that the shortest crossing may not be the cheapest once you take overnight stops, motorway tolls and petrol costs into consideration.

Long and short trips across

P&O European Ferries isn't just about getting you from A to B. The company also offers a wide range of inclusive holidays from five days to a fortnight or more in their 'Holidays by Car' brochure. You can choose from hotels, seaside apartments, rural gîtes and holiday villages in France, Belgium, Holland, Germany and Austria, or a go-as-you-please touring programme which gives the freedom of exploring by car with the security of pre-booked hotel accommodation.

P&O European Ferries also offers themed breaks away as part of its 'BreakAway to the Continent' programme – varying from the sheer indulgence of a gastronomic weekend to the thrill of a ballooning trip. While for the health conscious, there's everything from a cycling treasure hunt in Picardy to a real tonic in a Normandy spa to golfing in Northern France.

And as part of its partnership with

EURO DISNEY, an exciting programme of short breaks is available offering exclusive holidays by car ferry from the 'BreakAway to Dreamland 1993' brochure, available from AA Shops or direct from P&O European Ferries.

In addition, for the independent traveller, there are discounted car ferry fares available on every route for trips of three and five days, as well as for ten days via Portsmouth.

Before you go

Take advantage of the many other services offered by P&O European Ferries.

◆ Every year 350,000 motorists travel overseas with the backing of the AA, who have 85 years' experience in helping motorists.

◆ Motorail –
P&O European Ferries can arrange rail travel to Southern France, Spain and Italy.

◆ Through fares – via agreements with other car ferry operators. P&O European Ferries can offer special through fares from Italy to Greece and some of the Greek Islands as well as from Denmark to Sweden and Finland.

◆ Customer information – an around-the-clock service for P&O European Ferries passengers gives up-to-date details of sailings from Dover to France and Belgium, together with weather reports. Telephone 0304 223603 (French routes) or 0304 223604 (Belgian route).

◆ Further information on P&O European Ferries services or copies of its brochures are available from AA Shops or direct from P&O European Ferries, Channel House, Channel View Road, Dover. Kent CT17 9TJ. Telephone 0304 203388.

How to
use this guide

MAPS

The maps begin on page 1. There is a separate map section for each country in this guide. The first page for each country is the key map; this is divided into boxes, and numbers in the top corners indicate page numbers of the detailed maps which follow.

The maps indicate regions, main roads and rivers.

The following symbols are used for towns.
■ A large town with one or more hotels
□ A large town included for location purposes
● A small town with one or more hotels
○ A small town included for location purposes

DIRECTORY

A short introduction to each country has a description of the hotel classification system, plus general information on motoring, accident procedures, currency, telephones, etc.

Finding a hotel

To find a hotel in a certain area, refer to the map sections, where towns with hotels are indicated by solid squares and circles.

To find a hotel in a specific town, refer to the directory of hotels for each country. The directories are arranged in alphabetical order according to towns; hotels are listed alphabetically under each town.

Directory of hotels

AA/ANWB selected hotels

If a hotel name appears in red, it means that it has been specially recommended by the AA and ANWB. These hotels are entitled to display the sticker with the AA and ANWB symbols, indicating that it reaches the appropriate standards of quality.

All hotels in this guide receive a sticker with the year 1993 printed on it. *This is different from the joint recommendation badge described above.*

Hotel classification

Many countries in Europe have hotel classification schemes. This is sometimes done by national authorities, as in France, and sometimes by a national motoring organisation, as in Britain. The classification system used for each country is explained in the country introduction. In the directory of hotels, the classification precedes the establishment name.

Hotel charges

Unless otherwise indicated, prices are in the local currency. These charges are indications of the lowest room price (without bath/shower etc) to the highest room price (with bath/shower etc). Prices may vary according to season, and some establishments may have special group rates.

Please regard these prices as guidelines. Although every effort is made to publish current charges, these may change without notification at short notice. The prices in this guide are based mainly on 1992 charges; where the prices reflect increases for 1993, they are preceded by an asterisk.

If there is a dash in front of the symbol for single room, this indicates that there are no special single rooms in the hotel, and the price given is for single occupancy of a double room. If no prices are given, the hotel did not publish price information.

To avoid misunderstanding it is always best to check prices when booking, or on arrival at the hotel.

Continental breakfast is usually included in the room price. In some hotels half-board is obligatory, and if the extra meal service is ignored, the price may be increased.

Symbols

Symbols indicating the facilities and services offered by the hotels are listed on page *xvii*. Facilities listed as being in the room (showers, toilets, televisions, etc) are available in some rooms, not necessarily in *every* room. Note that televisions can often be hired at the reception desk.

Abbreviations for types of establishment

Following each establishment name, an abbreviation for the type of establishment is given in brackets:

Hotel-café-restaurant (HCR) An establishment built and furnished for accommodation, which also has a licence for a café and restaurant

Hotel-restaurant (HR) As HCR above, but with restaurant only

Motel (MT) An HR or HCR beside or near a motorway, adapted to the special requirements of motorists

Hotel-garni (HG) An establishment which provides bed-and-breakfast accommodation only

Hotel-pension (HP) An establishment which is similar to a hotel, but which caters mainly for longer-staying guests

Hotel-apartment (HA) An establishment which lets flats for certain periods, and which also provides meals

Pets

Some hotels do not allow pets for hygiene reasons. Although the information about pets has been checked for this guide, the policy of individual hotels can change at short notice without notification. Therefore the AA and ANWB cannot take responsibility for information about pets. It is best to confirm the policy of each hotel in writing when booking, or on arrival.

Symbols & Abbreviations

HCR	hotel-café-restaurant		in a wooded area		lift
HR	hotel-restaurant		beside a river		rooms on the ground floor
HP	hotel-boarding house		beside a lake		rooms with bath
HG	bed-and-breakfast (no restaurant for non-residents		within 500 metres of the seafront		rooms with shower
HA	apartment hotel		in the town centre	WC	rooms with toilet
*	1993 price		outside the town	TV	rooms with television
	single room		situated on a main road		special diets on request
	double room	P	car park on hotel premises		half-board only
AE	American Express		hotel garage		permission required to bring pets
	Diners Club		terrace		no pets
E	Eurocard		indoor terrace		
VISA	Visa		outdoor swimming pool		
	in a quiet area		indoor swimming pool		

Example of a directory entry

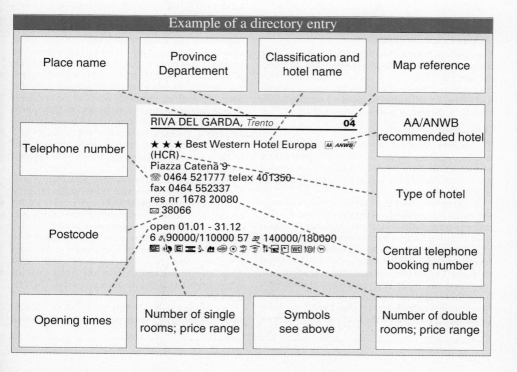

- Place name
- Province Departement
- Classification and hotel name
- Map reference
- Telephone number
- AA/ANWB recommended hotel
- Type of hotel
- Postcode
- Central telephone booking number
- Opening times
- Number of single rooms; price range
- Symbols see above
- Number of double rooms; price range

RIVA DEL GARDA, *Trento*   04

★ ★ ★ Best Western Hotel Europa AA ANWB
(HCR)
Piazza Catena 9
☎ 0464 521777 telex 401350
fax 0464 552337
res nr 1678 20080
✉ 38066

open 01.01 - 31.12
6 90000/110000 57 140000/180000
AE E VISA ⚐ ⌖ ⚑ ⚓ WC ○○

Continental ABC
Motoring and general information

The ABC provides a general background of motoring information, and should be read in conjunction with the country introductions.

Familiar international road signs are generally used, but in every country there are a few exceptions. Watch particularly for signs indicating crossings and speed limits. For British motorists, probably the most unfamiliar aspect of motoring abroad is the rule giving priority to traffic coming from the right, and unless this priority is varied by signs, it must be strictly observed.

Make sure that you have clear all-round vision. See that your seat belts are securely mounted and not damaged, and remember that in most European countries their use is compulsory. If you are carrying skis, remember that their tips should point to the rear.

Give serious consideration to preparing your vehicle for a holiday abroad. We recommend that you have a franchised dealer service your car shortly before you holiday or tour abroad. You should also carry out your own general check for any audible or visible defects.

A

AA service overseas

The AA does not maintain any offices outside Great Britain and Ireland, but it is represented by allied motoring clubs and other organisations throughout Europe. European motoring clubs allied to the AA will extend a courtesy service to AA members, insofar as their facilities will allow.

Accidents

The country introductions give specific regulations and information on summoning the emergency services. The international regulations are similar to those in the UK; the following action is usually required or advisable:

If you are involved in an accident you must stop. Place a warning triangle on the road at a suitable distance to warn following traffic of the obstruction (see *Warning triangle/hazard warning lights*, page *xxx*). The use of hazard warning lights in no way affects the regulations governing the use of warning triangles. Obtain medical assistance for anyone injured in the accident. If you need to call the police, leave the vehicle in the position in which it came to rest; if it seriously obstructs other traffic, mark the position of the vehicle on the road and get the details

confirmed by independent witnesses before moving it.

The accident must be reported to the police if it is required by law, if the accident has caused death or bodily injury, or if an unoccupied vehicle or property has been damaged and there is no one present to represent the interests of the party suffering damage. Notify your insurance company (by letter, if possible), within 24 hours of the accident; refer to the conditions of your policy. If a third party is injured, the insurance company or bureau whose address is given on the back of your Green Card should be notified; the company or bureau will deal with any claim for compensation to the injured party.

Make sure that all the essential details are noted, especially those concerning third parties, and co-operate with police or other officials taking on-the-spot notes by supplying your name, address or other personal details as required. It is also a good idea to take photographs of the scene; try to get good shots of other vehicles involved, their registration plates and any background which might help later enquiries. This record may be useful when completing the insurance company's accident form.

If you are not involved in the accident but feel your assistance as a witness or in any other useful capacity would be helpful, then stop and park your car carefully, well away from the scene. If you cannot assist at the scene, then do not stop out of curiosity or park your car at the site.

Automatic gearboxes

When towing a caravan, the fluid in an automatic gearbox becomes hotter and thinner, so there is more slip and more heat generated in the gearbox. Many manufacturers recommend the fitting of a gearbox oil cooler. Check with the manufacturer as to what is suitable for your car.

Automatic transmission fluid is not always readily available, especially in some of the more remote areas of Western Europe, and tourists are advised to carry an emergency supply.

B

BBC World Service

The BBC World Service transmits English-language broadcasts which can be heard in many European countries. A full programme including current affairs, sport and music is available, with world news every hour. Most car radios operate on medium and long wave, so to hear BBC World Service programmes in north-western Europe refer to the following frequencies and times.

KHz	Metres	Summer broadcasting times GMT	
1296	231	02.00–03.30, 06.00–06.30,	04.45–05.00, 22.00–23.30
648	483	05.00–5.30, 11.00–15.15,	06.00–10.30, 16.00–16.15
198	1515	20.00–03.30,	23.45–04.45

Brakes

Car brakes must always be in peak condition. Check both the level in the brake fluid reservoir, and the thickness of the brake lining/pad material. The brake fluid should be completely changed in accordance with the manufacturer's instructions, or at intervals of not more than 18 months or 18,000 miles.

However, it is always advisable to change the brake fluid before starting a Continental holiday, particularly if the journey includes travelling through a hilly or mountainous area.

Breakdown

If your car breaks down, try to move it to the side of the road, or to a position where it will obstruct the traffic flow as little as possible. Place a warning triangle at the appropriate distance on the road behind the obstruction. Remember that hazard warning lights may not be effective, since they cannot be seen around bends or over rises in the road, and warning lights may not function if your car has an electrical fault. So make sure your warning triangle is at an appropriate place to warn oncoming traffic. Having first taken these precautions, seek assistance if you cannot deal with the fault yourself.

Motorists are advised to take out AA Five Star Service, the overseas motoring emergency cover, which includes breakdowns and accident benefits, and personal travel insurance. Details and brochures are available from AA shops, or telephone 0256 55295.

Note   Members who have not purchased AA Five Star Service prior to departure, and who subsequently require assistance, may request spare parts or vehicle recovery, but the AA will require a deposit to cover estimated costs and a service fee prior to providing the service. All expenses must be reimbursed to the AA in addition to the service fee.

British Embassies/Consulates

In most European countries, there is usually more than one British Consulate, and degrees of status vary. The functions and office hours of British Vice-Consulates and Honorary Consuls are naturally more restricted. Generally, consulates (and consular sections of the embassy) are ready to help British travellers overseas, but there are limits to what they can do. A consulate cannot pay your hotel, medical or any other bills, nor will they do the work of travel agents, information bureaux or police. Any loss or theft of property should be reported to the local police, not the consulate, and a statement obtained confirming the loss or theft. If you still need help (such as the issue of an emergency passport or guidance on how to transfer funds), contact the consulate. See respective country introductions for addresses/locations of British Embassies and Consulates.

C

Camping and caravanning

Information is given separately in the AA guide *Camping and Caravanning in Europe*, on sale at most AA shops and good bookshops.

Caravan and luggage trailers

Take a list of contents, especially if any valuable or unusual equipment is being carried, as this may be useful. A towed vehicle should be readily identifiable by a plate in an accessible position showing the name of the maker of the vehicle, and the production or serial number. See also *Identification plate* page *xxiv.*

Claims against third parties

The law and levels of damages in foreign countries are generally different to our own. It is important to remember this when considering making a claim against another motorist arising out of an accident abroad. Certain types of claims invariably present difficulties, the most common probably relate to the recovery of car-hire charges. Rarely are they fully recoverable, and in some countries they may be drastically reduced or not recoverable at all. General damages for pain and suffering are not recoverable in certain countries, but even in countries where they are, the level of damages is usually lower than our own.

The negotiation of claims against foreign insurers is extremely protracted, and translation of all documents slows down the process. A delay of three months between sending a letter and receiving a reply is not uncommon.

Compulsory equipment

All countries have different regulations on how vehicles should be equipped, but generally these domestic laws are not enforced on visiting foreigners. However, where a country considers that aspects of safety or other factors are involved, they will impose some regulations on visitors.

Crash, or safety helmets

Both countries in this guide require visiting motorcyclists and their passengers to wear crash, or safety helmets.

Credit/charge cards

Credit/charge cards may be used abroad, subject to the 'conditions of use' set out by the issuing company who, on request, will provide full information. Establishments display the symbols of cards they accept; hotels which accept credit/charge cards are indicated in the *Directory* – see page *xvii* for further information. See also country introductions under *Petrol/diesel* for information on using credit cards to purchase fuel.

Currency and banking hours

There is no limit to the amount of sterling notes you may take abroad, but it is best to carry only enough currency for immediate expenses.

As some countries have regulations controlling the import and export of currency, you are advised to consult your bank for full information before making final arrangements.

Customs regulations for European countries *(other than the UK)*

The completion of the European single market on 1 January 1993 abolishes temporary importation, permitting free movement between member states. Consequently, persons travelling from one member state to another are free to take not only their personal belongings, but a motor vehicle, boat, caravan or trailer, across the internal frontiers without being subject to any Customs control or formality.

Bona fide visitors to non-EC countries may generally assume that they can *temporarily* import *personal articles* duty free, providing the following conditions are met:

  a that the articles are for personal use, and are not to be sold or otherwise disposed of;
  b that they may be considered as being in use and in keeping with the personal status of the importer;
  c that they are taken out when the importer leaves the country; or
  d that the goods stay for no more than 6 months in any 12-month period, whichever is the earlier.

All dutiable articles must be declared when you enter a country, otherwise you will be liable to penalties. If you are taking a large number of personal effects with you, it would be wise to prepare an inventory to present to the Customs authorities on entry. Customs officers may withhold concessions at any time, and ask the traveller to deposit enough money to cover possible duty, especially on portable items of apparent high value such as television sets, radios, cassette recorders, pocket calculators, musical instruments, etc, all of which must be declared. Any deposit paid (for which a receipt must be obtained) is likely to be high; it is recoverable (but only at the entry point at which it was paid) on leaving the country and exporting the item. Alternatively, the Customs may enter the item in the traveller's passport; if this happens, it is important to remember to get the entry cancelled when the item is exported. Duty and tax-free allowances may not apply if the traveller enters the country more than once a month, or is under 17 years of age (other ages may apply in some countries). EC allowances do not apply to residents of the Channel Islands and the Isle of Man.

A temporarily imported motor vehicle, boat, caravan, or any other type of trailer is subject to strict control on entering a country. They are subject to Customs duty and a variety of taxes, depending upon the circumstances and the period of the import, and also upon the status of the importer. Non-resident tourists entering a country, with a private vehicle for holiday or recreational purposes who intend to export the vehicle within a short period enjoy special privileges, and the normal formalities are reduced to an absolute minimum in the interests of tourism. A temporarily imported vehicle, etc, should not:

a be left in the country after the importer has left;
b be put at the disposal of a resident of the country;
c be retained in the country longer than the permitted period;
d be loaned, sold, hired, given away, exchanged or otherwise disposed of.

Customs regulations for the United Kingdom

If, when leaving Britain, you *export* any items which look very new, for example, watches, items of jewellery, cameras, etc, particularly of foreign manufacture, which you bought in the UK, it is a good idea to carry the retailer's receipts with you, if they are available. In the absence of such receipts, you may be asked to make a written declaration of where the goods were obtained.

The exportation of certain goods from the United Kingdom is prohibited or restricted. These include: controlled drugs; most animals, birds and some plants; firearms and ammunition; strategic and technological equipment (including computers); and items manufactured more than 50 years before the date of exportation.

When you enter the United Kingdom you will pass through Customs. You must declare everything in excess of the duty and tax-free allowance (see page *xxii*) which you have obtained outside the EC, or on the journey, and everything previously obtained free of duty or tax in the United Kingdom. Additionally, although the limits on duty and tax paid goods purchased within the EC ended on 31 December 1992, the import of tobacco goods, wines and spirits have the following guide levels to differentiate between personal and commercial importations: tobacco goods to 800 cigatrettes, 400 cigarillos, 200 cigars and 1.0 kg pipe and hand rolling tobacco; wines and spirits to 10 litres of spirits, 20 litres of fortified wines, 90 litres wine (of which not more than 60 litres are sparkling) and 110 litres of beer.

You must also declare any prohibited or restricted goods, and goods for commercial purposes. Do not be tempted to hide anything or to mislead the Customs! The penalties are severe and articles which are not properly declared may be forfeit. If articles are hidden in a vehicle, that too becomes liable to forfeiture. Customs officers are legally entitled to examine your luggage. Please co-operate with them if they ask to examine it. You are responsible for opening, unpacking and repacking your luggage.

The importation of certain goods into the United Kingdom is prohibited or restricted. These include:

a controlled drugs: under the Misuse of Drugs Act 1971, the importation and exportation of certain drugs such as diamorphine (heroin), cocaine, cannabis, lysergide (LSD), opium, barbiturates and amphetamines are prohibited. Only controlled drugs covered by an appropriate Home Office licence may be brought into or taken out of the UK. However, the Home Office has issued an Open General Licence (OGL) which allows ordinary travellers to import and export small quantities of certain controlled drugs, when in medicinal form, for the personal use of themselves or a member of household travelling with them. The OGL also allows doctors to import and export a different range of drugs for administration to a patient under their care. Full details of the OGL can be obtained from Customs Division 2 Branch A, New King's Beam House, Upper Ground, London SE1 9PJ, telephone 071 865 4904. It is a serious matter to smuggle controlled drugs as the offence carries very heavy penalties on conviction. Where passengers are unaware as to whether or not the drugs they intend to bring into or take out of the UK are controlled under the Misuse of Drugs Act they should contact a Customs Officer. You should be aware the *possession* of drugs controlled under the Misuse of Drugs Act 1971 is an absolute offence ie liability for prosecution is not dependent on knowledge thereof. You should therefore be on your guard if anyone asks you to carry anything through a Customs control on their behalf;

b counterfeit currency, counterfeit goods and goods infringing a copyright;

c firearms (including gas pistols, gas canisters, electric shock batons, stun guns and similar weapons), ammunition, explosives (including fireworks) and flick knives, swordsticks, knuckle-dusters, butterfly knives and certain other offensive weapons;

d horror comics, indecent or obscene books,

magazines, films, video tapes and other articles;

e animals and birds, whether alive or dead (including stuffed); certain articles derived from endangered species, including fur skins, ivory, reptile leather and goods made from them (cats, dogs and other mammals must not be landed unless a British import licence (rabies) has previously been issued; birds also require an import health licence);

f meat and poultry and their products (including ham, bacon, sausage, pâté, eggs, milk and cream), but 1kg per passenger (aged 17 or over) of fully cooked meat/poultry products in hermetically sealed containers, which include cans, glass jars and flexible pouches, is allowed – the fully cooked products must have been heat treated in the hermetically sealed containers and be capable of being stored at room temperature;

g plants, parts thereof and plant produce, including trees and shrubs, potatoes and certain other vegetables, fruit, bulbs and seeds. *Note* There is a concession specifically for travellers who are returning from Europe or other countries bordering the Mediterranean who wish to bring in plant material for their personal use. The following may be imported as passenger baggage without a plant health certificate:
2kg (total) of tubers, bulbs or corms free from soil excluding potatoes. One bouquet of cut flowers excluding gladiolus and chrysanthemum. Five retail packets of seeds excluding fodderpea seed and beet seed. Two kg (total) of fruit and vegetables excluding potatoes. Five plants for planting including cuttings excluding plants of the beet family, grasses, chrysanthemums, fruit trees, grapevine and forest trees and bonsais;

h wood with bark attached;

i certain fish and fish eggs (whether live or dead) and bees;

j radio transmitters (*eg* citizens' band radios, walkie-talkies, cordless telephones, etc) not approved for use in the United Kingdom.

Customs Notices No. 1 and *No. 9* are available to all travellers at the point of entry, or on the boat, and contains useful information of which returning tourists should be aware. Details for drivers going through the red and green channels are enclosed in *Notice No. 1*. Copies of this can be obtained from any office of Customs and Excise.

Duty and tax-free allowances

Goods obtained duty and tax-free on a ship or aircraft, or obtained outside the EC

TOBACCO PRODUCTS	
200	Cigarettes
	or
100	Cigarillos
	or
50	Cigars
	or
250g	Tobacco

ALCOHOLIC DRINKS	
2 litres	Still table wine
1 litre	Over 22% vol (*eg* spirits and strong liqueurs)
	or
2 litres	Not over 22% vol (*eg* low strength liqueurs or fortified wines or sparkling wines)
	or
2 litres	Still table wine

PERFUME
50g/60cc

TOILET WATER
250cc

OTHER GOODS	
£32	but no more than: 50 litres of beer 25 mechanical lighters

Note
Persons under 17 are not entitled to tobacco and drinks allowances.

D

Dimensions and weight restrictions

For an ordinary private car, a height limit of 4 metres and a width limit of 2.50 metres are generally imposed. Apart from a laden weight limit imposed on commercial vehicles, every vehicle, private or commercial, has an individual weight limit. For information on how this affects private cars, see *Overloading* page *xxvi*. If your route involves using one of the major road tunnels through a mountainous area, there may be additional restrictions. If you have any doubts, consult the AA.

Direction indicators

All direction indicators should be working at between 60 and 120 flashes per minute. Most standard car-flasher units will be overloaded by the extra lamps of a caravan or trailer, and a special heavy-duty unit or a relay device should be fitted.

Drinking and driving

There is only one safe rule: *If you drink, don't drive.* The laws are strict and the penalties severe.

Driving licence

You should carry your national driving licence with you when motoring abroad. A driving licence issued in the UK or Republic of Ireland is generally acceptable, subject to the minimum age requirements of the country you visit, but see country introductions for further information. If you plan to drive a hired or borrowed car in the country you are visiting, make local enquiries.

If your licence is due to expire before your anticipated return, it should be renewed in good time prior to your departure. The Driver and Vehicle Licensing Agency (in Northern Ireland the Department of the Environment for Northern Ireland) will accept an application two months before the expiry of your old licence.

E

Electrical information
General The public electricity supply in Europe is predominantly AC (alternating current) of 220 volts (50 cycles), but can be as low as 110 volts. In some isolated areas, low voltage DC (direct current) is provided. European circular two-pin plugs and screw-type bulbs are usual. Useful electrical adapters (not voltage transformers) which can be used in Continental shaver points and light bulb sockets are available in the UK from larger electrical retailers.
Vehicle Check that all connections are sound and that the wiring is in good condition. If problems arise with the charging system, you must obtain the services of a qualified auto-electrician.

Emergency messages to tourists
In emergencies, the AA will help pass messages to tourists whenever possible. AA members wishing to use this service should telephone the AA Information Centre, 0345 500600.

The AA can arrange for messages to be published in overseas editions of the Daily Mail and, in an extreme emergency (death or serious illness concerning next-of-kin), undertake to pass on messages for possible broadcast on overseas radio networks. Obviously the AA cannot guarantee that messages will be broadcast, nor can the AA or the Daily Mail accept any responsibility for the authenticity of messages.

Emergency SOS messages concerning the dangerous illness of a close relative may be broadcast on BBC Radio 4 long wave on 1515m/198KHz at 06.59 and 17.59hrs BST (see *BBC World Service*, page *xix*). Messages should be arranged through the local police or hospital authorities.

If you require further information, contact the tourist office or motoring club of the country you are staying in. Before you leave home, make sure your relatives understand what to do if an emergency occurs.

Engine and mechanical
Consult your vehicle handbook for servicing intervals. Unless the engine oil has been changed recently, drain and refill with fresh oil and fit a new filter. Deal with any significant leaks by tightening up loose nuts and bolts and renewing faulty gaskets and seals.

Brands and grades of engine oil familiar in Britain are usually available in Western Europe, but may be difficult to find in remote country areas. When available, they will be much more expensive than in the UK and generally packed in 2-litre cans (3.5 pints). It is sensible to assess the normal consumption of your car and carry what oil you will need for the trip.

If you suspect that there is anything wrong with the engine, however insignificant, deal with it immediately. Even if everything seems in order, do not neglect such common-sense precautions as checking valve clearances, sparking plugs and contact breaker points where fitted, and making sure that the distributor cap is sound. Check the fan belt for fraying and slackness. If any of these items show signs of wear, replace them.

Attend to obvious mechanical defects. Look particularly for play in steering connections and wheel bearings and, where applicable, ensure that they are adequately greased. A car that has covered many miles will have absorbed a certain amount of dirt into the fuel system, and as breakdowns are often caused by dirt, it is essential that all filters (fuel and air) should be cleaned or renewed.

Owners should seriously reconsider towing a caravan with a car that has already given appreciable service. Hard driving on motorways and in mountainous country puts an extra strain on ageing parts, and replacing items such as a burnt-out clutch can be very expensive.

The cooling system should be checked for leaks, the correct proportion of anti-freeze ascertained and any perished hoses or suspect parts replaced.

Eurocheques
The Eurocheque scheme is a flexible money-transfer system operated by a network of European banks. All the major UK banks are part of the Uniform Eurocheque scheme, and they can provide a multi-currency chequebook enabling you to write cheques in the currency of the country you are visiting. Most European banks will cash Eurocheques, and retailer acceptance is widespread (over 5 million throughout Europe). Contact your bankers well in advance of your departure for further information.

F

Ferry crossings

From Britain, the shortest sea crossing from a southern port to the Continent is the obvious but not always the best choice, depending on how the Continental port is serviced by main roads leading to your destination. Seek advice before making bookings so that your journey is as economic and as comfortable as possible.

The AA can book your sea crossing (ferry or Sea-Cat). For advice on availability and instant confirmation, call in at your local AA shop.

Fire extinguisher

It is sensible (compulsory in Greece) to equip your vehicle with a fire extinguisher when motoring abroad. A Spares Pack, which can include a fire extinguisher, can be hired from the AA.

First-aid kit

It is best (compulsory in Austria and Greece) to equip your vehicle with a first-aid kit when motoring abroad. A Spares Pack, which can include a first-aid kit, can be hired from the AA.

G

Garages

In most European countries, garage business hours are 08.00 – 18.00hrs Monday to Saturday; on Sundays and public holidays, repairs, breakdown service and petrol are often unobtainable. In many countries, especially France, it may be difficult to get a car repaired during August, because many garages close down for the annual summer holidays. A complete list of service agencies for your make of car is generally available through your own dealer.

Some garages in Europe occasionally make extremely high charges for repairing tourists' cars; always ask for an estimate before authorising a repair. *You must settle disputes with Continental garages on the spot*. It has been the AA's experience that subsequent negotiations can seldom be brought to a satisfactory conclusion.

H

Holiday traffic

For information relating to holiday traffic, see *Road conditions*, page *xxviii*. AA members can obtain fur-

ther information on holiday traffic by ringing the AA Information Centre on 0345 500600. All travellers can telephone the AA's recorded information service (see page *xxxii*), or refer to Teletext.

I

Identification plate

If a boat, caravan or trailer is taken abroad, it must have a unique chassis number for identification purposes. If your boat, caravan or trailer does not have a number, an identification plate may be purchased from an AA port shop. Boats registered on the Small Ships Register are issued with a unique number which must be permanently displayed.

Insurance *(vehicles and boats)*

Vehicle insurance is compulsory in all Western European countries. Although policies issued in the UK provide cover in all these countries, this usually automatically reduces to satisfy only the minimum requirements of the compulsory third party insurance law of other countries.

Before taking a vehicle overseas, it is important to contact your broker or insurer to arrange an extension of your full home cover to apply in the countries you intend visiting. This will be agreed by your own insurer usually upon payment of an additional premium, although some insurers do provide extensions at no extra charge to existing policy holders. This extension should be acknowledged by the insurers issuing an International Motor Insurance Certificate or Green Card. The Green Card must be signed on receipt, as it will not be accepted without the signature of the insured. Although a Green Card is not compulsory in Italy and Switzerland; the AA recommends that, wherever possible, you always carry one when motoring outside the UK. Internationally recognised by the police and other authorities, it could save considerable inconvenience in the event of an accident.

If you are towing a caravan or trailer it will need separate insurance and mention on your Green Card. Remember the cover on a caravan or trailer associated with a Green Card is normally limited to third-party towing risks, so a separate policy is advisable to cover accidental damage, fire and theft. If you are taking a boat, third-party insurance is compulsory in Italy and Switzerland.

Motorists can get expert advice from AA Insurance Services for all types of insurance. Full details are available from any AA shop or direct from AA Insurance Services Ltd, PO Box 2AA, Newcastle upon Tyne NE99 2AA.

Finally, make sure that you are covered against damage in transit (eg on the ferry or motorail). Most comprehensive motor insurance policies provide adequate cover for transit between ports in the UK, but need to be extended to give this cover if travelling outside the UK. You should check this aspect with your insurer before setting off on your journey.

International distinguishing sign

An international distinguishing sign of the approved pattern (oval with black letters on a white background) and size (GB – at least 6.9in by 4.5in), must be displayed on a vertical surface at the rear of your vehicle (and caravan or trailer if you are towing one). These distinguishing signs indicate the country of registration of the vehicle. On the Continent vehicles are checked for a correct nationality plate; and fines are imposed for a missing or incorrect nationality plate. See *Police fines*, page *xxviii*.

L

Level crossings

Almost all level crossings are indicated by international signs. Most guarded ones are the lifting barrier type, sometimes with bells or flashing lights to warn of an approaching train.

Lights

For driving on the Continent, headlights should be altered so that the dipped beam does not dazzle oncoming drivers. The alteration can be made by fitting headlamp converters (PVC mask sheets), on sale at AA shops. However, it is important to remove the headlamp converters as soon as you return to the UK.

Dipped headlights should also be used in conditions of fog, snowfall, heavy rain and when passing through a tunnel, irrespective of its length and lighting. In some countries, police will wait at the end of a tunnel to check this requirement.

Headlight flashing is used only as a warning of approach or as a passing signal at night. In other circumstances, it is accepted as a sign of irritation, and should be used with caution to avoid misunderstanding. It is sensible in Western Europe – compulsory in Spain and recommended in France, Germany and Italy – to carry a set of replacement bulbs. A Spares Pack, which includes the bulbs, may be hired from the AA.

Note   Remember to have the lamps set to compensate for heavy loads being carried.

M

Medical treatment

Travellers who normally take certain medicines should take enough to last the trip, since they may be difficult to get abroad.

Those with certain medical conditions (diabetes or coronary artery diseases, for example) should get a letter from their doctor giving treatment details. Some Continental doctors will understand a letter written in English, but it is better to have it translated into the language of the country you intend to visit.

Travellers who, for legitimate health reasons, carry drugs (see also *Customs regulations for the United Kingdom*) or appliances (eg a hypodermic syringe) may have difficulty with Customs or other authorities. Similarly, people with special dietary requirements may have difficulty in making them understood to hotel and restaurant staff. People with special conditions should carry translations of specific requirements to facilitate appropriate treatment and passage through customs.

The National Health Service is available in the United Kingdom only, and medical expenses incurred overseas cannot generally be reimbursed by the UK Government. There are reciprocal health agreements with most Western European countries, but you should not rely exclusively on these arrangements, as the cover provided under the respective national schemes is not always comprehensive. (For instance, the cost of bringing a person back to the UK in the event of illness or death is never covered.) The full costs of medical care must be paid in Andorra, Liechtenstien, Monaco, San Marino and Switzerland. Therefore, as facilities and financial cover can vary considerably, you are strongly advised to take out comprehensive and adequate insurance cover before leaving the UK (such as that offered under AA Five Star Personal).

Urgent medical treatment for accidents or unforeseen illness can be obtained by most visitors, free of charge or at reduced costs, from the health care schemes of those countries with whom the UK has health-care arrangements. Details are in the Department of Health booklet T4 which also gives advice about health precautions and vaccinations. Free copies are available from main post offices, the Health Publications Unit, No. 2 Site, Manchester Road, Heywood, Lancs OL10 2PZ or by telephoning 0800 555777. In some of these countries, visitors can obtain urgently needed treatment by showing their UK passport, but in others an NHS medical card must be produced, and in most European Community countries a Certificate of Entitlement (E111) is necessary. The E111 can be obtained over the counter of the post office on completion of the forms incorporated in booklet T4. However, the E111 must be stamped and signed by the post office clerk to be valid. Residents of the Republic of Ireland must apply to their Regional Health Board for an E111.

Mirrors

When driving abroad on the right, it is essential (as when driving on the left in the UK and Republic of Ireland) to have clear all-round vision. Ideally, external rear-view mirrors should be fitted to both sides of your vehicle, but certainly on the left, to allow for driving on the right.

Motorways

All Western European countries have motorways, varying from a few short stretches to a comprehensive system. Tolls are payable on many of them. A motorway leaflet (containing information on tolls, etc, for France, Italy, Portugal and Spain, is available as part of the AA European Routes Service.

O

Orange badge scheme for disabled drivers

Some European countries which operate national schemes of parking concessions for the disabled, have reciprocal arrangements whereby disabled visitors get the concessions of the host country by displaying the badge of their own scheme. In some countries, responsibility for introducing the concessions rests with individual local authorities, and in some cases they may not be generally available. Enquire locally to be certain of specific requirements. As in the UK, special arrangements apply only to badge holders themselves, and the concessions are not for the benefit of able-bodied friends or relatives. A non-entitled person who seeks to take advantage of the concessions in Europe by wrongfully displaying an orange badge will be liable to whatever local penalties apply.

Overloading

This can create safety risks, and in most countries committing such an offence can involve on-the-spot fines (see *Police fines*, page *xxviii*). If your car is stopped because of overloading you will not be allowed to proceed until the load has been reduced. The maximum loaded weight, and its distribution

between front and rear axles, is decided by the vehicle manufacturer, and if your owner's handbook does not give these facts you should contact the manufacturer direct. There is a public weighbridge in all districts, and when the car is fully loaded (including the driver and passengers), use this to check that the vehicle is within the limits. Load your vehicle carefully so that no lights, reflectors, or number plates are masked, and the driver's view is not impaired. Any luggage loaded on a roof rack must be tightly secured, and should not upset the stability of the vehicle. Any projections beyond the front, rear, or sides of a vehicle, that might not be noticed by other drivers, must be clearly marked. Specific limits apply to projections and may vary from country to country.

Overtaking

When overtaking on roads with two lanes or more in each direction, always signal your intention in good time, and after the manoeuvre, signal and return to the inside lane. Do *not* remain in any other lane. Failure to comply with this regulation, particularly in France, will incur an on-the-spot fine (immediate deposit in France) – see *Police fines*, page *xxviii*.

Always overtake on the left and use your horn to warn the driver of the vehicle being overtaken (except in areas where the use of a horn is prohibited). Do not overtake while being overtaken or when a vehicle behind is preparing to overtake. Do not overtake at level crossings, intersections, the crest of a hill or at pedestrian crossings. When being overtaken, keep well to the right and reduce speed if necessary – *never increase speed*.

P

Parking

Parking is a problem everywhere in Europe, and the police are extremely strict with offenders. Heavy fines are imposed, and unaccompanied offending cars can be towed away. Heavy charges are imposed for the recovery of impounded vehicles. Find out about local parking regulations and try to understand all relative signs. As a rule, always park on the right-hand side of the road or at an authorised place. As far as possible, park off the main carriageway, but not on cycle or tram tracks.

Passengers

It is an offence in all countries to carry more passengers in a car than the vehicle is constructed to seat, but some have regulations as to how the passengers should be seated, particularly in the case of young children. See *Children in cars* in the country introductions for full details.

For passenger-carrying vehicles constructed and equipped to carry more than 10 passengers, including the driver, there are special regulations .

Passports

Each person must hold, or be named on, an *up-to-date* passport valid for all the countries through which he or she intends to travel. Passports should be carried at all times and, as an extra precaution, a separate note kept of the number, date and place of issue. There are various types of British passport, including the standard or regular passport and the limited British Visitor's Passport.

Standard UK passports are issued to British Nationals, *ie* British Citizens, British Dependent Territories Citizens, British Overseas Citizens, British Nationals (Overseas), British Subjects, and British Protected Persons. Normally issued for a period of 10 years, a standard UK passport is valid for travel to all countries in the world. A related passport may cover the holder and children under 16. Children under 16 may be issued with a separate passport valid for five years, and renewable for a further five years on application. Full information and application forms for standard UK passports are available from a main post office or from one of the Passport Offices in Belfast, Douglas (Isle of Man), Glasgow, Liverpool, London, Newport (Gwent), Peterborough, St Helier (Jersey) and St Peter Port (Guernsey). Application for a standard passport should be made to the appropriate Passport Office, enclosing the necessary documents and fees. Allow at least one month for the Passport Office to deal with an application. Between February and June, when the demand for passports is higher, it could take longer and travellers are advised to apply outside of these months if at all possible.

British Visitor's Passports are issued to British Citizens, British Dependent Territories Citizens or British Overseas Citizens over the age of eight, resident in the UK, Isle of Man or Channel Islands. Valid for one year only, they are acceptable for travel in Western Europe including unified Germany. A British Visitor's Passport issued to cover the holder, spouse and children under 16 may only be used by the first person named on the passport to travel alone. Children under eight cannot have their own Visitor's Passport. Full information and application forms are available from main post offices in Great Britain (England, Scotland and Wales) or Passport Offices in the Channel Islands, Isle of Man and Northern Ireland.

Visitor's Passports or application forms for Visitor's Passports are *not* obtainable from Passport Offices in Great Britain. All applications for a Visitor's Passport must be submitted *in person* to a main post office or Passport Office. Provided the documents are in order and the fee is paid, the passport is issued immediately.

Irish citizens resident in the Dublin metropolitan area or in Northern Ireland should apply to the Passport Office, Dublin; if resident elsewhere in the Irish Republic, they should apply through the nearest Garda station. Irish citizens resident in Britain should apply to the Irish Embassy in London.

Petrol/diesel

In Western Europe, grades of petrol compare favourably with those in the UK. Internationally known brands are usually available on main tourist and international routes, but in remote districts familiar brands may not be readily available. The minimum amount of petrol which may be purchased is usually five litres (just over one gallon). You should keep the petrol tank topped up, particularly in remote areas or if you want to make an early start when garages may be closed; use a lockable filler cap for security. Some garages may close between 12.00 and 15.00hrs for lunch. Generally petrol is readily available and petrol stations on many motorways provide a 24-hour service.

Make sure you know the fuel requirement of the vehicle before you go (*eg* leaded petrol, unleaded premium, unleaded super, or diesel) and whether or not the car has an exhaust catalyst. Catalyst-equipped petrol cars will usually have a small fuel filler neck to prevent the use of the standard-sized nozzle dispensing leaded petrol. If in doubt, check with your vehicle dealer or the AA.

Overseas both unleaded and leaded petrol is graded as *Normal* and *Super* and the local definitions are given in the respective country introductions, together with the octane ratings. Some countries are supplying 98 octane unleaded petrol either in addition to or instead of 95 octane. The name may be *Super Plus* or *Premium* but look for the octane rating 98. You should be careful to use the recommended type of fuel, particularly if your car has a catalytic converter, and the octane grade should be the same or higher. If you accidentally fill the tank of a catalyst-equipped car with leaded fuel, the best course, to avoid any possible reduction in the effectiveness of the catalyst, will be to have the tank drained and refilled with unleaded. However, if your car does not have a catalyst but is designed or converted for unleaded petrol, an accidental filling with leaded fuel will do no harm; use it up and go back to unleaded at the next fill. If your car requires leaded fuel and you fill with unleaded by mistake, avoid hard use of the engine until about half the tank is used, then fill with leaded. Ask the vehicle manufacturer or his agent about the suitability of a vehicle for the different fuels.

Petrol prices on motorways will be higher than elsewhere; self-service pumps will be slightly cheaper. Approximate petrol prices for different countries can be checked with the AA. Petrol price concessions in the form of petrol coupons are available for Italy. Check with the AA for the latest position.

If you intend to carry a reserve supply of fuel in a can in your vehicle, check the country introductions for restrictions; moreover, all operators (ferry, motorrail, etc) will either forbid fuel in cans or insist that spare cans are empty. Remember that a roof rack laden with luggage increases petrol consumption, so take this into consideration when calculating mileage per gallon.

Diesel fuel is generally available, but it is probably more inconvenient to run out of diesel, and the above advice on keeping the tank topped up should be followed. If petrol is put into the tank of a diesel car (or vice versa) the tank must be drained and refilled with the correct fuel before the engine is started.

Police fines

Some countries impose on-the-spot fines for minor traffic offences, which vary according to the offence and the country. Other countries, for example France, impose an immediate deposit, and subsequently levy a fine which may be the same, greater or less than this sum. Fines are normally paid in cash in the local currency, either to the police or at a local post office against a ticket issued by the police. The amount can vary from £3 to £600 (approximately). The fines penalise and also help to keep minor motoring offences out of the courts. Disputing the fine usually leads to a court appearance, delays and additional expense. If the fine is not paid, legal proceedings will usually follow. Some countries immobilise vehicles until a fine is paid, and may sell it to pay the penalty imposed.

Once paid, a fine cannot be recovered, but a receipt should always be obtained as proof of payment. AA members who need assistance in any motoring matter involving local police should apply to the legal department of the relevant national motoring organisation.

Priority, including roundabouts

The general rule is to *give way to traffic entering a junction from the right*, but this is sometimes varied at roundabouts (see below). This is one aspect of European driving which may cause British drivers the most confusion. Tourists must become familiar with road signs indicating priority or loss of priority.

Be very careful at intersections, and never rely on receiving the right of way, particularly in small towns and villages where local traffic, often slow moving, such as farm tractors etc, will assume right of way regardless of oncoming traffic. Always give way to public service and military vehicles. Blind or disabled people, funerals and marching columns must always be allowed right of way. Vehicles such as buses and coaches carrying large numbers of passengers will expect, and should be allowed, priority.

Generally, priority at roundabouts is given to vehicles *entering* the roundabout unless signposted to the contrary. This is a reversal of the United Kingdom and Republic of Ireland rule, so be very careful when manoeuvring in an anti-clockwise direction on a roundabout. If possible, keep to the outside lane on a roundabout to make your exit easier.

R

Radio telephones/Citizens' band radios and transmitters

Many countries exercise controls on the temporary importation and subsequent use of radio transmitters and radio telephones, So if your vehicle contains such equipment, whether fitted or portable, you should contact the AA for guidance before departure. The use or possession of devices to detect police radar speed traps, whether inside or outside of vehicles, is illegal in most countries. Penalties are severe, including confiscation of the equipment, payment of an immediate deposit against any subsequent fine and/or a driving ban. If the case is viewed as sufficiently serious, confiscation of the vehicle and even imprisonment may result.

Registration document

You must carry the original vehicle registration document with you. If you do not have your registration document, apply to a Vehicle Registration Office (in Northern Ireland a Local Vehicle Licensing Office) for a temporary certificate of registration (V379) to cover the period away. For the address of your nearest Vehicle Registration Office ask at a post office for leaflet V100. Apply well in advance of your journey as there could be delays of up to two weeks in issuing the certificate if you are not already recorded as the vehicle keeper. Proof of identity (*eg* driving licence) and proof of ownership (*eg* bill of sale), should be produced for the Vehicle

Registration Office. Residents of the Republic of Ireland should contact the local Taxation Office.

If you plan to use a borrowed, hired or leased vehicle, be aware that:

a for a borrowed vehicle, the registration document must be accompanied by a letter of authority to use the vehicle from the registered keeper;

b for a UK registered hired or leased vehicle, the registration document will normally be retained by the hiring company. Under these circumstances, a Hired/Leased Vehicle Certificate (VE103A), which may be purchased from the AA, should be used in its place.

Road conditions

Main roads are usually in good condition, but often not finished to British standards. The camber is often steeper than in the UK, and edges may be corrugated or surfaces badly worn. In France, such stretches are sometimes signposted *'Chausée déformée'*. However, there are extensive motorway systems in France, Germany and Italy, and many miles of such roads in other countries. When roads under repair are closed, you must follow diversion signs – often inadequate – such as *'déviation'* (French) and *'Umleitung'* (German). To avoid damage to windscreens or paintwork, drive slowly over loose grit, and take care when overtaking.

July and August are the peak touring months, particularly in Austria, Belgium, France and Germany when the school holidays start, and during this period motorways and main roads are heavily congested. AA members can obtain further information by ringing the AA Information Centre, telephone 0345 500600. All travellers can consult the Teletext 'Oracle', or the AA's recorded information service (see page *xxxii*).

Throughout the summer, there is a general exodus from the cities, particularly at weekends, when tourists should be prepared for congested roads and hold-ups. See also *Switzerland – Roads* and *Italy – Motorways* .

Road signs

Most road signs throughout Europe conform to familiar international standards. Watch for road markings – do not cross a solid white or yellow line marked on the road centre.

S

Seat belts

Both countries in this guide require wearing of seat belts. If your car is fitted with belts, in the interests of safety, wear them; you also avoid the risk of a police fine.

Spares

The spares you should carry depends on your vehicle and how long you are likely to be away. Spares Packs are available for hire from the AA; full information about this service is available from any AA shop.

In addition to the items contained in an AA Spares Pack, the following are useful:

a a pair of windscreen wiper blades;
b a torch;
c a length of electrical cable.

Remember that when ordering spare parts for dispatch abroad, you must be able to identify them as clearly as possible (by the manufacturer's part numbers if known). When ordering spares, always quote the engine and chassis numbers of your car. (See also *Lights*, page *xxv*.)

Speed limits

It is important to observe speed limits at all times, and remember, it can be an offence to travel without good reason at so slow a speed as to obstruct traffic flow. Offenders may be fined, and driving licences confiscated on the spot. The legal limits may be varied by road signs and where such signs are displayed the lower limit should be accepted. National limits may be temporarily varied at certain times – information should be available at the frontier.

T

Telephones

In most Continental countries, the dialling tone is a continuous tone or a combination of short and long tones. In Italy and Switzerland, cardphones are in use. The cards to operate them are generally available from a post office, shop or tobacconist in the vicinity.

Tolls

Tolls are charged on most motorways in France, Italy, Portugal and Spain. Over long distances, the toll charges can be quite considerable, and it is sometimes worth using some of the all-purpose roads, which are often fast. Always have some local currency ready to pay the tolls, as travellers' cheques etc, are not accepted at toll booths. Credit cards are accepted at toll booths in France. Also see *Motorways*, page *xxvi*.

Note   In Switzerland the authories charge an annual motorway tax. See *Switzerland – Roads* for further information.

Tourist information

National tourist offices are well equipped to deal with enquiries relating to their countries. They are particularly useful for information on current events, tourist attractions, car hire, equipment hire and specific activities such as skin-diving, gliding, horse-riding, etc.

The offices in London are helpful, but local offices at your destination may have information not available elsewhere. Hotels etc, will be able to supply the local address.

Traffic lights

In principal cities and towns, traffic lights are similar to those in the UK, although they are sometimes suspended over the roadway. The density of some lights is poor and can be easily missed – especially those overhead. There is usually only one set on the right-hand side of the road some distance before the road junction, and if you stop too close to the corner, the lights will not be visible. Watch out for 'filter' lights which will enable you to turn right at a junction against the main lights. If you wish to go straight ahead, do not enter a lane leading to 'filter' lights or you may obstruct traffic wishing to turn. See also the country introduction for *Switzerland*.

Trams

Trams take priority over other vehicles. Always give way to passengers boarding and alighting. Never position your vehicle so that it impedes the free passage of a tram. Trams must be overtaken on the right, except in one-way streets.

Tyres

Inspect your tyres carefully; if you think they are likely to be more than three-quarters worn before you get back, replace them before you leave. If you notice uneven wear, scuffed treads, or damaged walls, seek advice. The UK regulations require a minimum tread depth of 1.6mm over the central three quarters of the tyre width around the whole circumference. Western European countries have similar or stricter requirements; the AA recommends at least 2mm of tread.

If your car is heavily loaded, the recommended tyre pressures may have to be raised; this may also be required for high-speed driving. Check the recommendations in your vehicle handbook, but remember pressures can only be checked accurately when the tyres are cold. Remember to check the spare tyre.

V

Valuables

Tourists should pay particular attention to the security of their money and valuables. Whenever possible, excess cash and travellers' cheques should be left with the hotel management *against a receipt*. In some areas, children and youths cause a diversion to attract tourists' attention while pickpockets operate in organised gangs. Avoid stopping to watch unusual incidents, which are more likely to occur in crowded markets or shopping centres.

Note   Valuables should always be removed from a parked car, even if it is parked in a supervised car park or lock-up garage.

Visas

EC citizens travelling within the EC do not require visas. A visa is not normally required by United Kingdom and Republic of Ireland passport holders when visiting non-EC countries within Western Europe for periods of three months or less. However, if you hold a passport of any other nationality, a UK passport not issued in this country, or are in any doubt at all about your position, check with the embassies or consulates of the countries you intend to visit.

W

Warm-climate touring

In hot weather and at high altitudes, excessive heat in the engine compartment can cause carburation problems. If you are taking a caravan, consult the manufacturers of your towing vehicle about the limitations of the cooling system, and the operating temperature of the gearbox fluid if automatic transmission is fitted (see also *Automatic gearboxes* page *xix*).

Warning triangle/hazard warning lights

The use of a warning triangle is compulsory in most European countries, and is always a wise precaution. It should be placed on the road behind a stopped vehicle to warn traffic approaching from the rear of an obstruction ahead. The triangle should be used when a vehicle has stopped for any reason – not just breakdowns. It should be placed in such a position as to be clearly visible up to 100m (110yds) by day and by night, about 60cm (2ft) from the edge of the road, but not in such a position as to present a danger to oncoming traffic. See country introductions for details, but note that on motorways the triangle should be placed about three times as far behind the obstruction as on ordinary roads. A warning triangle is not required for two-wheeled vehicles. An AA warning triangle, which complies with the latest international and European standards, can be purchased from AA shops. Alternatively, a warning triangle can form part of the Spares Pack which may be hired from the AA.

Although four flashing indicators are allowed in the countries covered by this guide, they in no way affect the regulations governing the use of warning triangles. Generally, hazard warning lights should *not* be used in place of a triangle, although they may complement it in use; see *Switzerland* country introduction. See also *Breakdown*, page *xix*.

Weather information and winter conditions

UK regional weather reports (followed by a two-day forecast) and European weather forecasts are provided by the AA Weatherwatch recorded information service. The AA Roadwatch service also provides UK weather reports with its traffic and roadworks information. Continental Roadwatch provides ferry news, road conditions to and from the ferry ports and details of any adverse Continental weather. See page *xxxii* for numbers and charges.

AA members abroad can contact the nearest office of the appropriate national motoring club for weather details (see country introductions). It is advisable to check on conditions ahead as you go along, and hotels and garages are often helpful in this respect.

Winter conditions   Motoring in Europe during the winter months is restricted because of the vast mountain ranges. Reports on the accessibility of mountain passes in Austria, France, Italy and Switzerland are received by the AA from the European Road Information Centre in Geneva. The AA can provide routes avoiding roads which are known to be closed during winter (see *Overseas Routes Application* at the end of this guide for details). Additionally, during the winter months, and also under certain weather conditions, the AA collects information regarding the state of approach roads to the Continental Channel ports, which AA members can obtain by ringing the AA Information Centre or enquiring at the AA port shop before embarking.

AA members can obtain general information on weather conditions by ringing the AA Information Centre, telephone 0345 500600. All travellers can obtain weather information from Teletext, or the AA's recorded information service (see page *xxxii*).

Phone before you go

 Motoring Information

CONTINENTAL ROADWATCH

Traffic conditions to and from ferry ports,
ferry news, major European events and other useful information for the Continental motorist
0336 401 904

MOTORING ABROAD – EUROPE, COUNTRY BY COUNTRY

Taking your car overseas? Be prepared for different
laws, paperwork and driving conditions
Dial **0336-401** plus 3 digits for country

Austria	**866**	**875**	Luxembourg
Belgium	**867**	**876**	Netherlands
France	**869**	**878**	Portugal
Germany	**870**	**879**	Spain
Italy	**874**	**881**	Switzerland

FRENCH MOTORWAYS

Toll information **0336 401 884**

EUROPEAN FUEL

Prices and availability **0336 401 833**

PORT INFORMATION

Hampshire/Dorset Ports **0336 401891**
Kent Ports **0336 401 890**

AIRPORT INFORMATION

Birmingham	**935**	**940**	Heathrow
Edinburgh	**939**	**937**	Luton
Gatwick	**941**	**938**	Manchester
Glasgow	**936**	**942**	Stanstead

 Roadwatch

Ring our famous Roadwatch service for the very latest traffic reports

Dial 0336 401

followed by the 3 digits for the appropriate service

GB NATIONAL TRAFFIC, ROADWORKS AND WEATHER

For the latest reports on traffic hold ups and roadworks
dial **0336-401** plus 3 digits for area (see map)

LONDON & THE SOUTH-EAST – TRAFFIC AND ROADWORKS

Central London	0336 401 122
Between M4 &M1	0336 401 123
Between M1 & Thames Estuary	0336 401 124
Between Thames Estuary & M23/A23	0336 401 125
Between M23/A23 & M4	0336 401 126
M25 orbital motorway	0336 401 127
National motorways	0336 401 110

Calls are charged at 36p per minute cheap rate, 48p per minute at all other times

Italy $\boxed{\text{I 1}}$

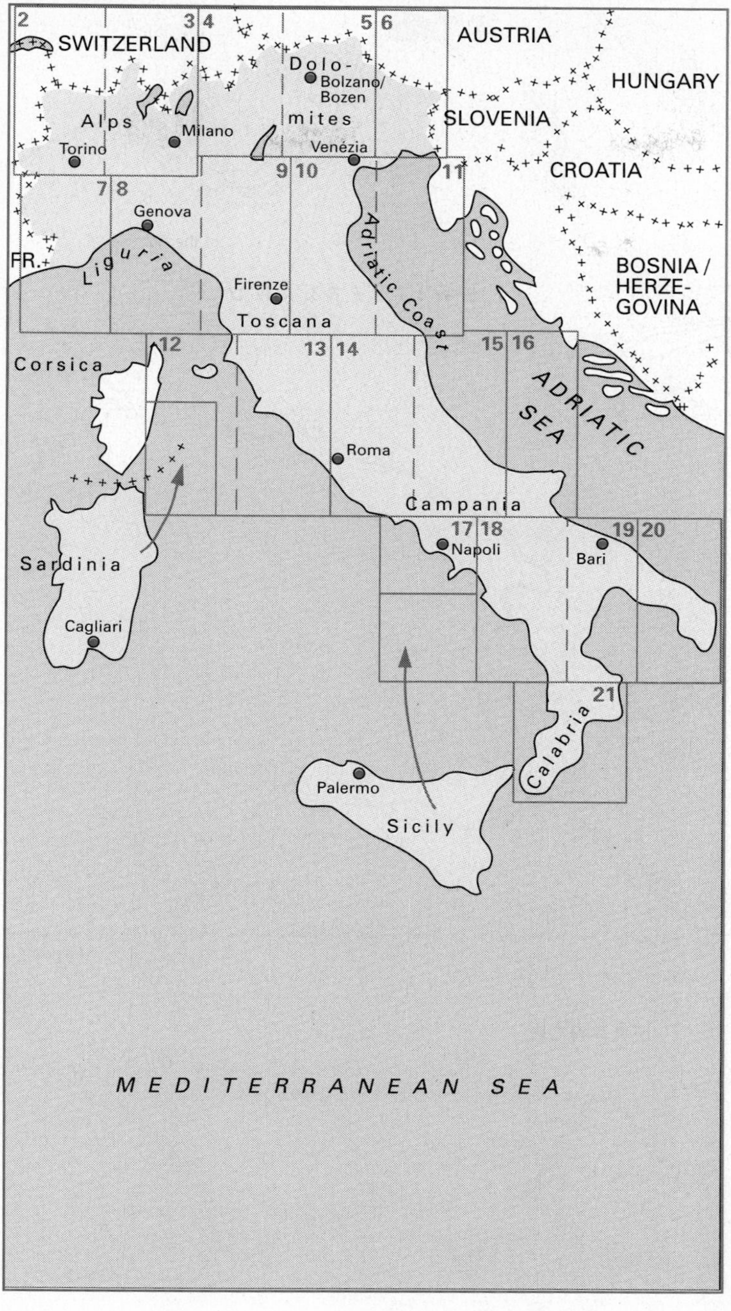

2 | 3 | 4 | 5 | 6
SWITZERLAND

AUSTRIA

HUNGARY

Do-lo-
Bolzano/
Bozen

Alps

mites

SLOVENIA

Milano

Torino

Venézia

CROATIA

7 | 8

9 | 10

11

Genova

BOSNIA /
HERZE-
GOVINA

FR.

Ligur**i**a

Firenze

Toscana

12

13 | 14

15 | 16

Corsica

ADRIATIC
SEA

Roma

Campania

17 | 18

19 | 20

Sardinia

Napoli

Bari

Cagliari

21

Calabria

Palermo

Sicily

MEDITERRANEAN SEA

Italy 12

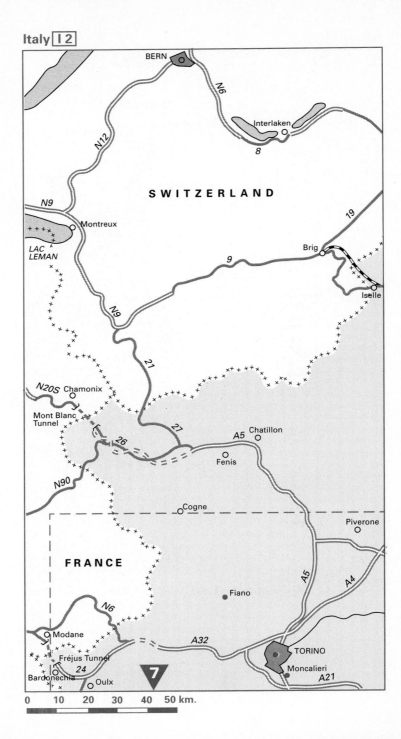

BERN

N6

N12

Interlaken

8

S W I T Z E R L A N D

N9

19

Montreux

Brig

LAC
LEMAN

9

Iselle

N9

21

N20S Chamonix

Mont Blanc
Tunnel

27

A5 Chatillon

26

Fenis

N90

Cogne

Piverone

FRANCE

Fiano

A5

A4

N6

Modane

A32

Fréjus Tunnel

24

TORINO

Bardonechia

Oulx

Moncalieri

A21

7

0   10   20   30   40   50 km.

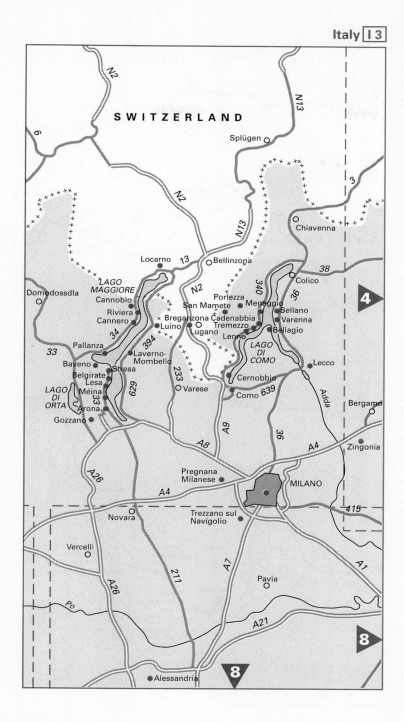

SWITZERLAND

N2

6

Splügen

N13

N2

N13

3

Chiavenna

Locarno 13

Bellinzona

38

LAGO MAGGIORE

N2

Colico

340

36

Domodossdla

Cannobio

Porlezza

Menaggio

Bellano

Riviera

San Mamete

Cannero

Breganzona Cadenabbia

Varenna

Luino

Tremezzo

Ballagio

34

394

Lugano

Lenno

Pallanza

LAGO DI COMO

33

Laverno-Mombello

Lecco

Baveno

233

Belgirate

629

Cernobbio

Adda

Lesa

Méina

Varese

Bergamo

LAGO DI ORTA

33

Arona

Como 639

Gozzano

A9

36

Zingonia

A8

A4

A26

Pregnana Milanese

MILANO

A4

415

Novara

Trezzano sul Navígolio

A1

Vercelli

A7

A26

211

Pavia

Po

A21

4

8

8

Alessandria

ITALY

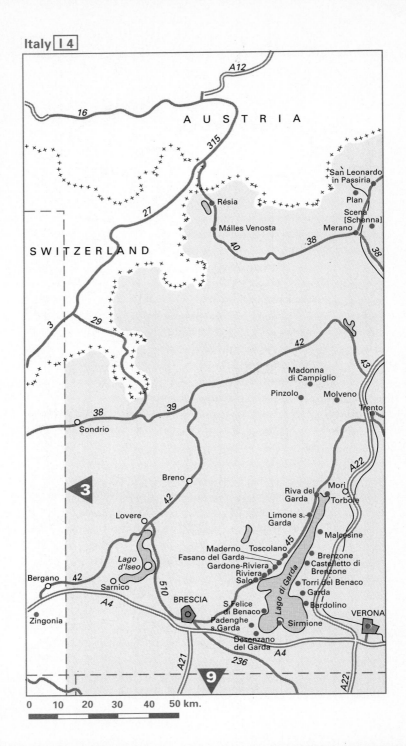

0 10 20 30 40 50 km.

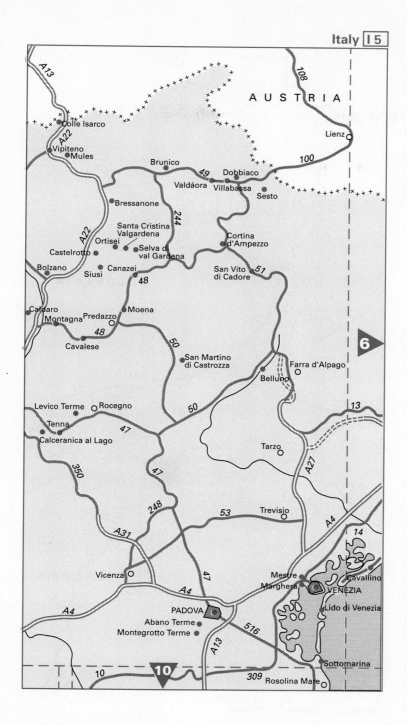

AUSTRIA

A13

108

Colle Isarco

A22

Lienz

Vipiteno
Mules

100

Brunico

49
Dobbiaco

Valdáora
Villabassa

Bressanone
Sesto

244

Santa Cristina
Valgardena
Cortina
d'Ampezzo

A22
Ortisei
Selva di
val Gardena

Castelrotto

Bolzano
Canazei
San Vito
di Cadore
51

Siusi
48

Caldaro
Moena

Montagna
Predazzo

48
50

Cavalese

San Martino
di Castrozza
Farra d'Alpago

Belluno

Levico Terme
Rocegno

13

Tenna
50

Calceranica al Lago

A27

350
Tarzo

47

47

248
53
Trevisio

A31
A4

14

Vicenza

A4

47

Mestre
Cavallino

Marghera
VENEZIA

PADOVA
Lido di Venezia

Abano Terme
A13

Montegrotto Terme
516

Sottomarina

10
309
Rosolina Mare

6

10

ITALY

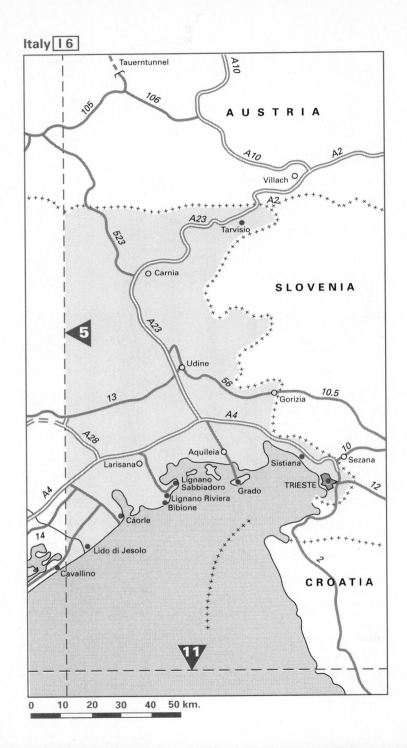

Tauerntunnel

A10

AUSTRIA

105

106

A10

A2

Villach

A2

A23

Tarvisio

523

SLOVENIA

Carnia

A23

5

Udine

56

10.5

13

Gorizia

A4

A28

10

Larisana

Aquileia

Sistiana

Sezana

A4

Lignano
Sabbiadoro

Grado

TRIESTE

12

Lignano Riviera
Bibione

14

Cáorle

Lido di Jesolo

2

Cavallino

CROATIA

11

0   10   20   30   40   50 km.

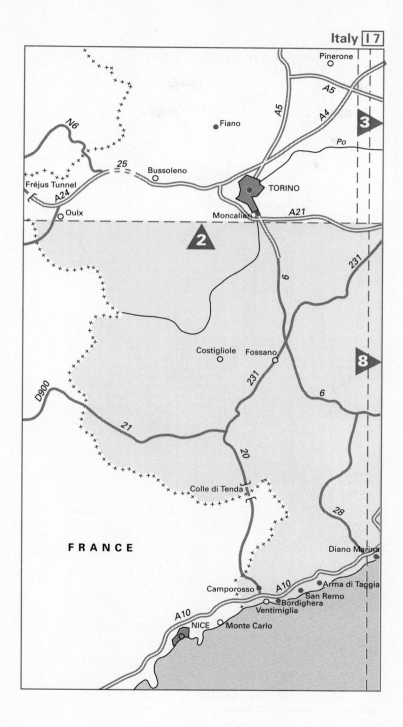

Pinerone

A5

A5

A4

Fiano

Po

3

N6

25

Bussoleno

Fréjus Tunnel

A24

TORINO

Oulx

Moncalieri

A21

2

6

231

Costigliole

Fossano

231

8

6

D900

21

20

Colle di Tenda

28

FRANCE

Diano Marina

Camporosso

A10

Arma di Taggia

San Remo

Bordighera

Ventimiglia

A10

NICE

Monte Carlo

ITALY

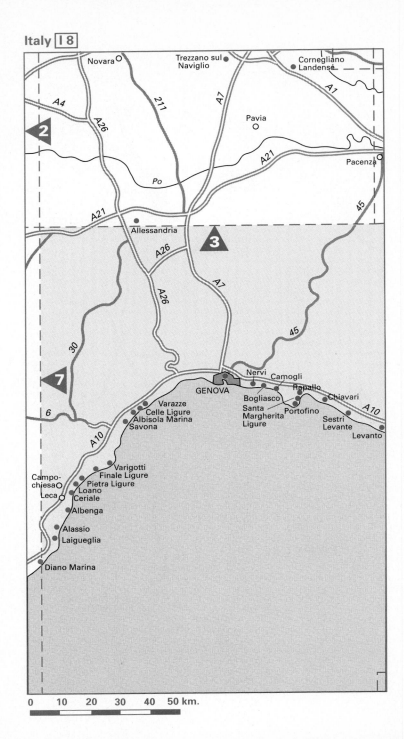

Italy 18

Novara

Trezzano sul Naviglio

Cornegliano Landense

A4

211

A7

A1

A26

2

Pavia

A21

Pacenza

Po

45

A21

Allessandria

A26

3

A26

A7

A7

30

45

7

6

GENOVA

Nervi

Camogli

Rapallo

Bogliasco

Chiavari

Santa
Margherita
Ligure

Portofino

A10

Sestri
Levante

Varazze

Celle Ligure

Albisola Marina

Savona

Levanto

A10

Varigotti

Finale Ligure

Pietra Ligure

Campo-
chiesa

Loano

Ceriale

Leca

Albenga

Alassio

Laigueglia

Diano Marina

0   10   20   30   40   50 km.

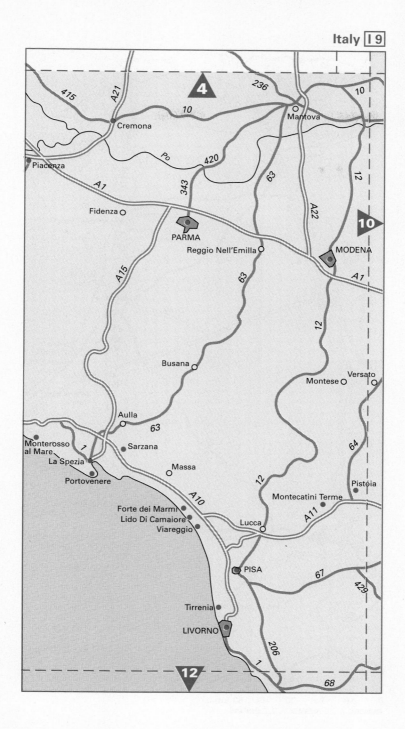

ITALY

Italy I 10

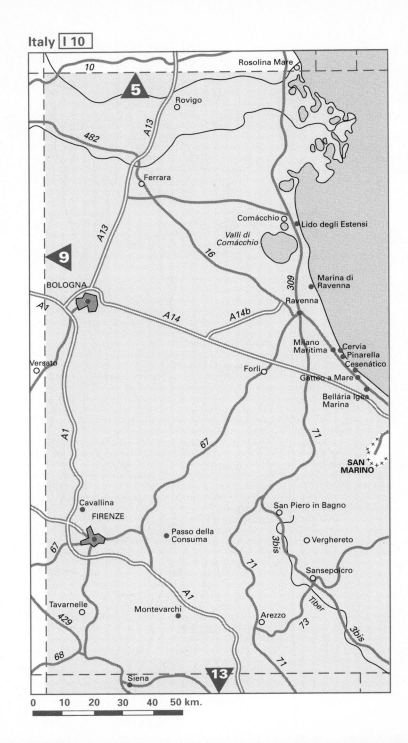

10

5

Rosolina Mare

Rovigo

A13

482

Ferrara

A13

Comácchio

Lido degli Estensi

Valli di
Comácchio

16

9

309

Marina di
Ravenna

BOLOGNA

Ravenna

A7

A14

A14b

Milano
Maritima

Cervia
Pinarella
Cesenático

Versato

Forlí

Gatteo a Mare

Bellária Igea
Marina

A1

67

71

SAN
MARINO

Cavallina

FIRENZE

San Piero in Bagno

Passo della
Consuma

3bis

Verghereto

67

71

Sansepolcro

A1

Tavarnelle

Montevarchi

Tiber

429

Arezzo

73

3bis

68

71

Siena

13

0   10   20   30   40   50 km.

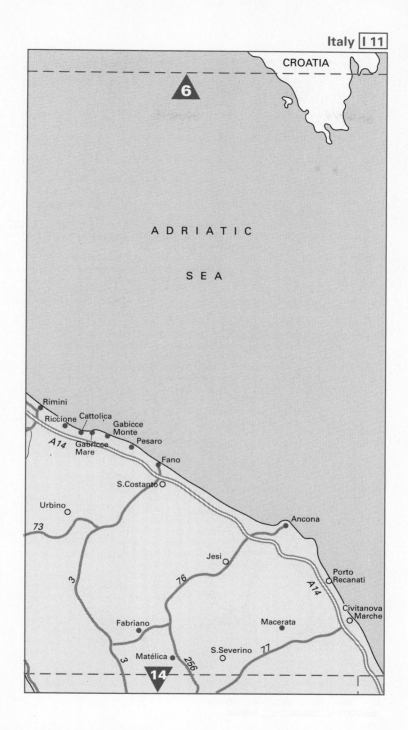

CROATIA

6

A D R I A T I C

S E A

Rimini
Riccione Cattolica
Gabicce
Monte
A14 Gabicce Pesaro
Mare
Fano
S.Costanto

Urbino

73

Ancona

Jesi

3 76

Porto
Recanati

A14

Civitanova
Marche

Fabriano Macerata

3 S.Severino 77
Matélica 256

14

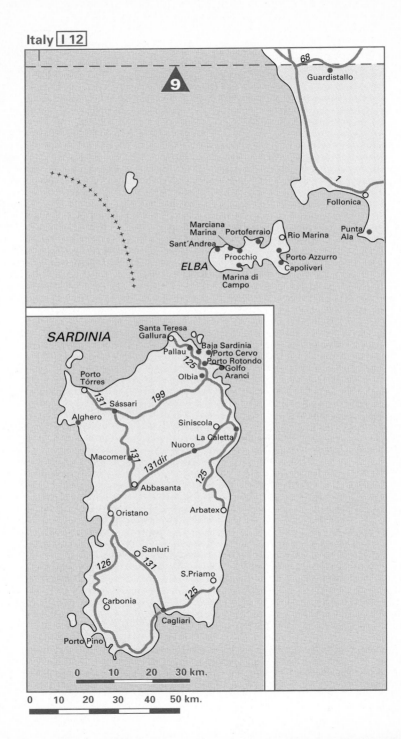

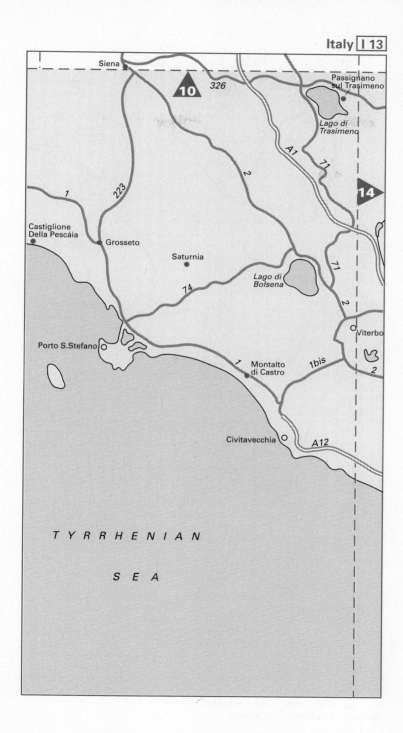

Siena

10 326

Passignano
sul Trasimeno

Lago di
Trasimeno

A1

71

223

2

1

Castiglione
Della Pescáia

Grosseto

Saturnia

Lago di
Bolsena

14

71

74

2

Porto S.Stefano

Viterbo

Montalto
di Castro

1

1bis

2

Civitavecchia

A12

T Y R R H E N I A N

S E A

Italy I 14

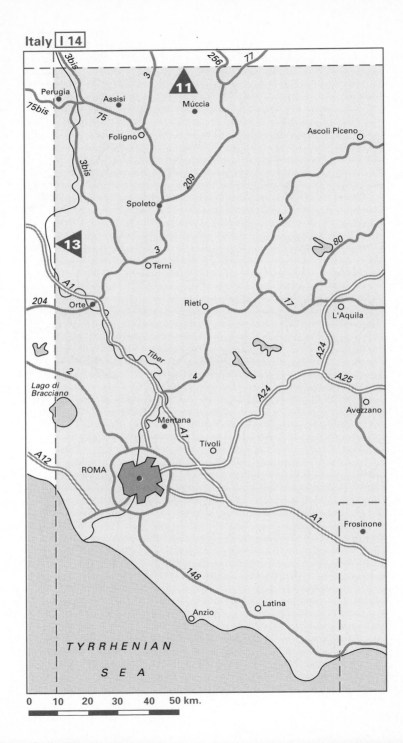

Perugia

75bis

Assisi

3bis

75

256

77

3

11

Múccia

Ascoli Piceno

Foligno

3bis

209

Spoleto

4

80

13

3

Terni

204

A1

Orte

Rieti

17

L'Aquila

Tiber

A24

A25

2

4

A24

Avezzano

Lago di
Bracciano

Mentana

A1

Tívoli

A12

ROMA

A1

Frosinone

148

Latina

Anzio

T Y R R H E N I A N

S E A

0   10   20   30   40   50 km.

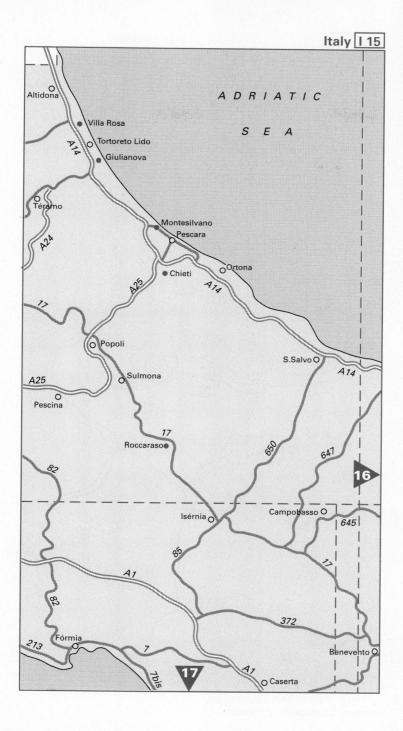

Altidona

Villa Rosa
Tortoreto Lido
A14
Giulianova

Téramo
A24

ADRIATIC
SEA

Montesilvano
Pescara
Ortona
A25
Chieti
A14

17

Popoli
S.Salvo
A14
A25
Sulmona
Pescina

17
Roccaraso
650
647
82
16

Isérnia
Campobasso
645
85
17
A1
82
372
Fórmia
213
7
Benevento
17
7bis
A1
Caserta

Italy I 16

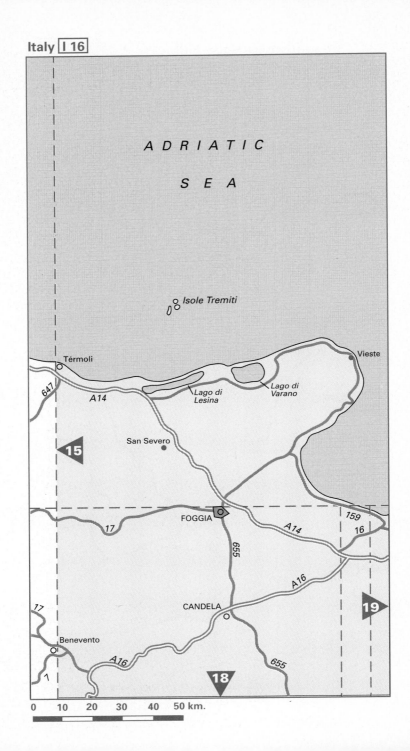

A D R I A T I C

S E A

Isole Tremiti

Térmoli

Vieste

647

A14

Lago di
Lesina

Lago di
Varano

15

San Severo

159

FOGGIA

17

A14

16

655

A16

17

CANDELA

19

Benevento

A16

655

1

18

0   10   20   30   40   50 km.

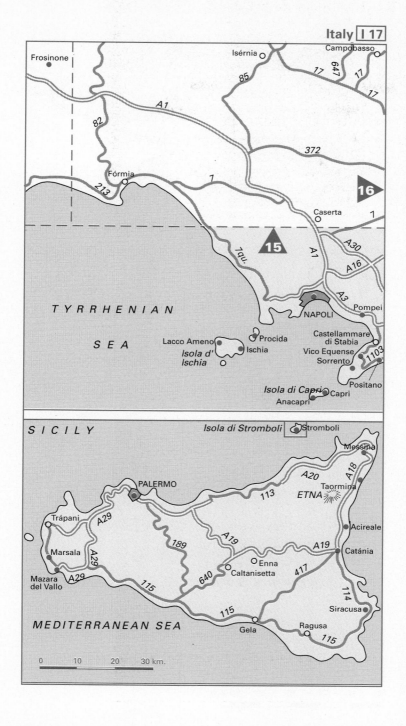

Italy | I 17

ITALY I 17 map details:

Frosinone, Isérnia, Campobasso

85, 647, 17, 17, 17

A1, 82, 372

16

Fórmia, 213, 7

Caserta, 1

15, 7qu., A1, A30, A16, A3

TYRRHENIAN SEA

Pompei, NAPOLI

Lacco Ameno, Procida, Castellammare di Stabia

Isola d' Ischia, Ischia, Vico Equense, Sorrento, 1103

Isola di Capri, Capri, Positano

Anacapri

SICILY, Isola di Stromboli, Stromboli

Messina, A18, A20, 113, Taormina, ETNA

PALERMO, Trápani, A29

Acireale, 189, A19, Catánia, A19

Marsala, A29, Enna, Caltanisetta, 417, 114

Mazara del Vallo, A29, 640, 115, Siracusa

115, Gela, Ragusa, 115

MEDITERRANEAN SEA

0 10 20 30 km.

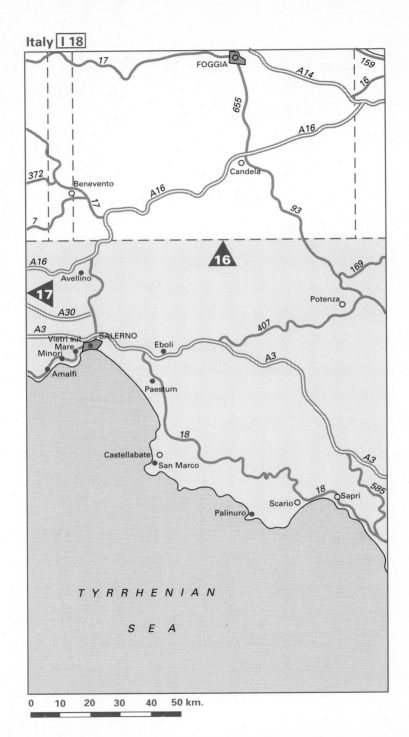

ITALY

Italy I 18

17

FOGGIA

A14

159

16

655

A16

372

Benevento

A16

Candela

7

17

93

A16

169

Avellino

16

Potenza

17

A30

407

A3

Vietri sul Mare

SALERNO

Eboli

Minori

A3

Amalfi

Paestum

18

Castellabate

San Marco

A3

18

585

Scario

Sapri

Palinuro

T Y R R H E N I A N

S E A

0   10   20   30   40   50 km.

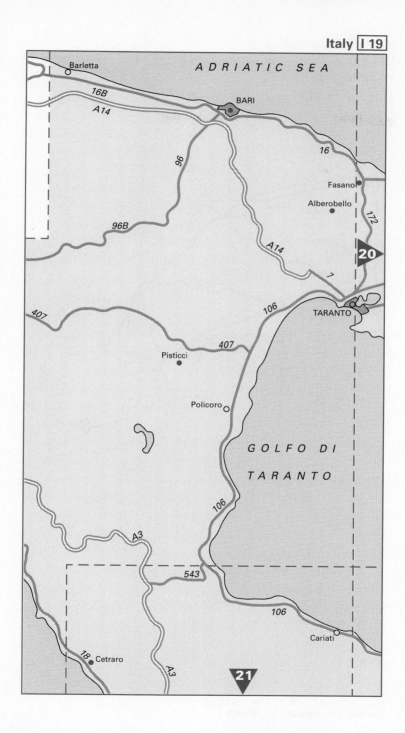

ITALY

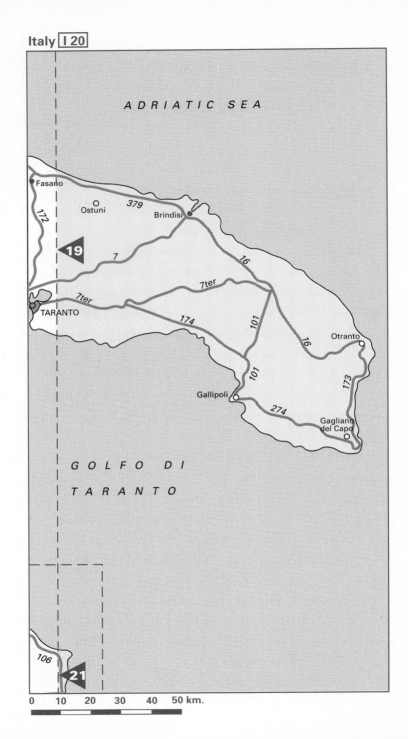

ADRIATIC SEA

Fasano
172
Ostuni
379
Brindisi
19
7
16
7ter
7ter
TARANTO
174
101
16
Otranto
101
173
Gallipoli
274
Gagliano del Capo

GOLFO DI

TARANTO

106
21

0   10   20   30   40   50 km.

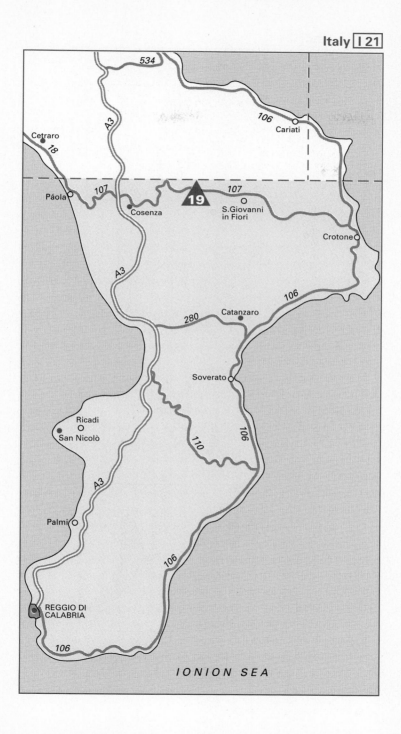

IONION SEA

Switzerland [CH 1]

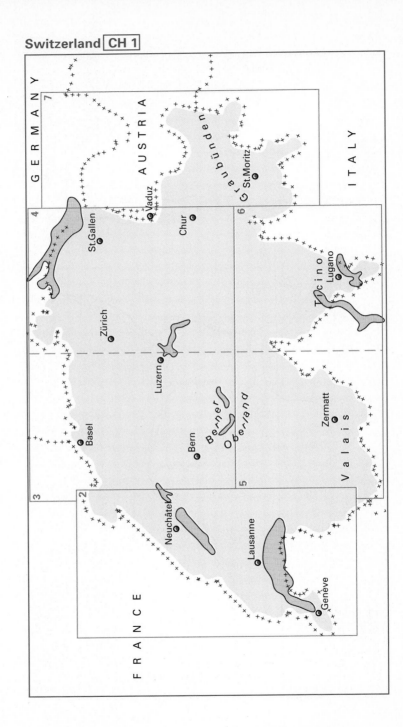

SWITZERLAND

GERMANY

AUSTRIA

ITALY

FRANCE

Graubünden

Ticino

Valais

Berner Oberland

7

4

3

2

6

5

St.Gallen

Vaduz

Chur

St.Moritz

Lugano

Zürich

Luzern

Basel

Bern

Zermatt

Neuchâtel

Lausanne

Genève

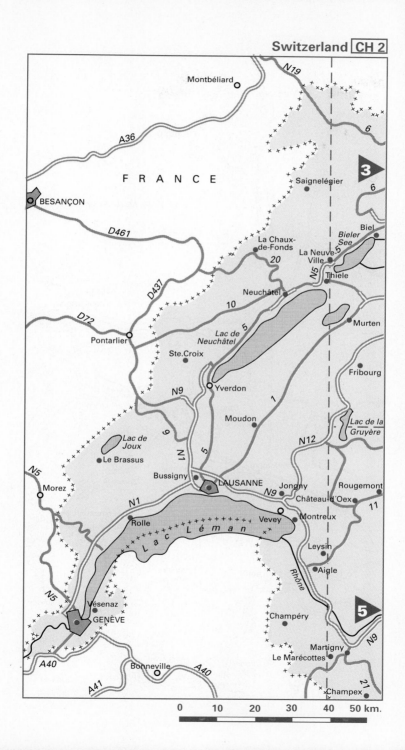

Montbéliard

N19

A36

FRANCE

BESANÇON

D461

Saignelégier

3

6

6

La Chaux-
de-Fonds

20

Biel

Bieler
See

La Neuve-
Ville

Thiele

N5

D437

D72

Neuchâtel

10

Murten

Pontarlier

Ste.Croix

Lac de
Neuchâtel

5

Fribourg

N9

Yverdon

1

Lac de Joux

Le Brassus

9

Moudon

N12

Lac de la
Gruyère

N1

5

Bussigny

LAUSANNE

Jongny

Rougemont

N5

Morez

N1

N9

Château-d'Oex

11

Rolle

Lac Léman

Vevey

Montreux

Leysin

Aigle

Rhône

N5

Vésenaz

GENÈVE

Champéry

5

N9

A40

Bonneville

A40

Martigny

Le Marécottes

21

A41

Champex

SWITZERLAND

0   10   20   30   40   50 km.

24

Switzerland CH 3

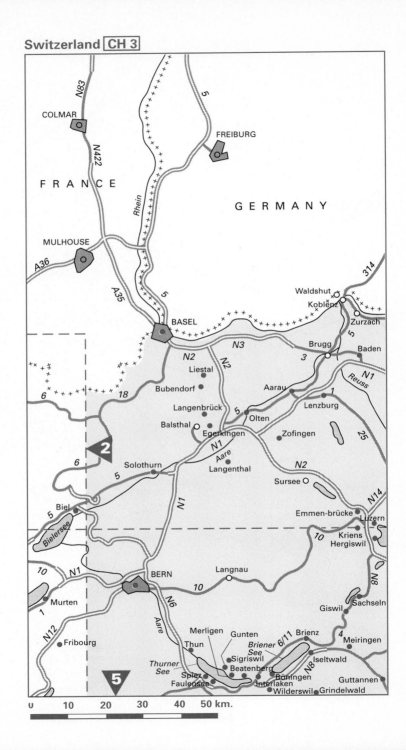

SWITZERLAND

COLMAR

N83

N422

F R A N C E

Rhein

5

FREIBURG

G E R M A N Y

MULHOUSE

A36

A35

5

314

Waldshut

Koblenz

Zurzach

BASEL

N2

N3

N2

Brugg

Baden

3

Liestal

5

N1

Reuss

6

18

Bubendorf

Aarau

Langenbrück

5

Lenzburg

1

Balsthal

Olten

25

Egerkingen

Zofingen

N1

Aare

2

Langenthal

N2

6

Solothurn

Sursee

5

N1

N14

Biel

Emmen-brücke

Luzern

5

Bielersee

10

Kriens

Hergiswil

10

N1

N8

Murten

BERN

Langnau

10

Giswil

Sachseln

N12

N6

Fribourg

Aare

Merligen

Gunten

Brienz

4

Meiringen

Thun

Briener
See

6/11

Iseltwald

Thurner
See

Sigriswil

N8

5

Spiez

Beatenberg

Böningen

Guttannen

Faulensee

Interlaken

Grindelwald

Wilderswil

0   10   20   30   40   50 km.

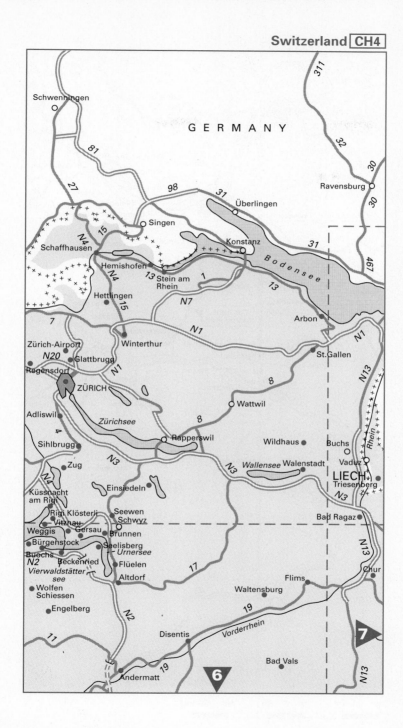

Schwenningen

G E R M A N Y

311

81

32

30

27

98

31

Ravensburg

30

Überlingen

Singen

15

N4

Konstaz

31

467

Schaffhausen

B o d e n s e e

Hemishofen

N4

13

Stein am Rhein

1

13

Hettlingen

15

N7

Arbon

7

N1

N1

Zürich-Airport

Winterthur

St.Gallen

N13

N20

Glattbrugg

N1

8

Regensdorf

ZÜRICH

Adliswil

Zürichsee

8

Wattwil

Rhein

Sihlbrugg

Rapperswil

Wildhaus

Buchs

4

N3

Zug

Wallensee

Walenstadt

Vaduz

N4

Einsiedeln

N3

LIECH.

Küssnacht am Rigi

Triesenberg

Rigi Klösterli

Seewen

N3

Vitznau

Schwyz

Bad Ragaz

Weggis

Gersau

Brunnen

Bürgenstock

Seelisberg

Urnersee

N13

Buochs

N2

Beckenried

Fluelen

Vierwaldstätter see

Altdorf

17

Flims

Chur

Wolfen Schiessen

Waltensburg

Engelberg

N2

19

11

Vorderrhein

N13

Disentis

▼7

Bad Vals

▼6

Andermatt

19

Switzerland $\boxed{\text{CH 5}}$

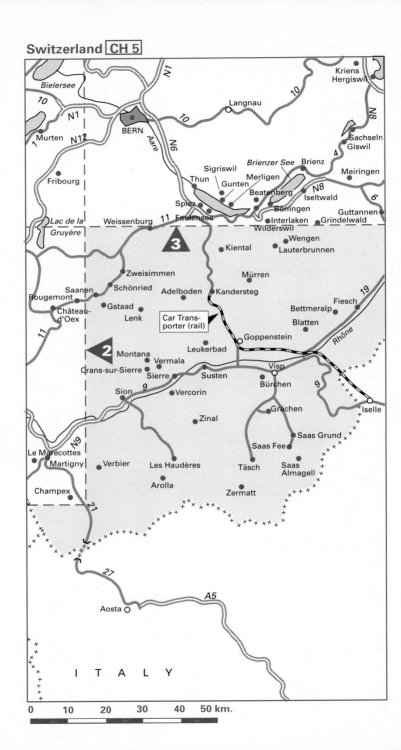

0   10   20   30   40   50 km.

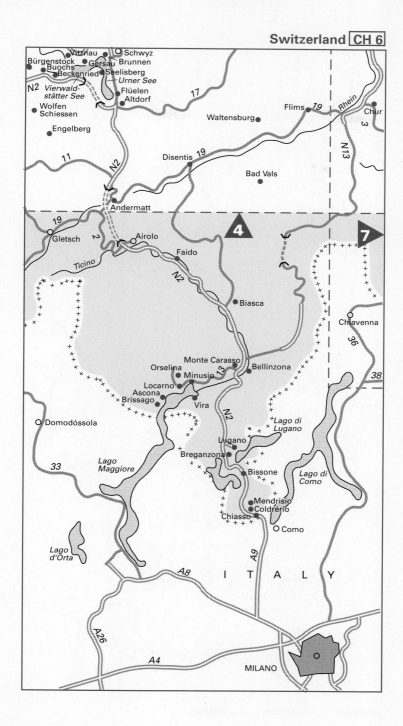

SWITZERLAND

28

Switzerland CH 7

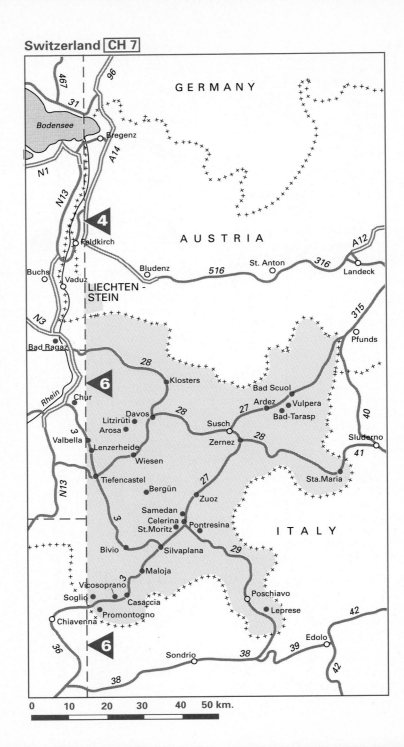

SWITZERLAND

0   10   20   30   40   50 km.

Italy

Capital: Rome

Language: Italian

Currency: Italian lira

Emergency numbers: Fire, police, ambulance, telephone 113. (For *carabinieri*, telephone 112)

Information in Britain: Italian State Tourist Office (ENIT), 1 Princes Street, London W1R 8AY, telephone 071-408 1254

Motoring and general information

Additional information is in the Continental ABC *at the front of the book.*

Accidents: A report must be made to the insurance company. If the accident involves personal injury, obtain medical assistance and report the incident to the police. On motorways there are emergency telephones every 2km (1.25 miles). See also *Warning triangle* below.

Breakdown: Try to move the car to the side of the road to minimize obstruction and place a warning triangle behind the vehicle. The Italian motoring club, Automobile Club d'Italia (ACI), provides a breakdown service, which visiting motorists driving a foreign registered vehicle can use. Towing from the breakdown location to the nearest ACI affiliated garage is free, but a charge is made if the vehicle is towed elsewhere and for any additional services. To get assistance, use the emergency telephones on the motorway, or dial 116 for service on ordinary roads. See also *Warning triangle* below.

British Embassy/Consulates: The British Embassy together with its consular section is located at 00187 Roma, Via XX Settembre 80A, telephone 06 4825441/06 4825551. Other British consular offices are in Florence (Firenze),

Genoa (Genova), Milan, Naples (Napoli), Turin (Torino), Venice (Venezia), Bari, Brindisi and Trieste.

Children in cars: Children under four are required to be in a seat fitted with a child restraint system; children between four and 12 are not permitted as front-seat passengers unless they are using special seats or seat belts suitable for children.

Driving licence: A pink EC type UK or Republic of Ireland driving licence is acceptable. The older all-green UK licence must be accompanied by an official Italian translation which may be obtained free from the AA. The minimum car-driving age for visitors is 18 years; for using a motorcycle of up to 125cc, without a passenger, 16 years; to carry a passenger, or use a motorcycle over 125cc, 18 years.

Horn: Do not sound your horn in built-up areas except in cases of immediate danger. At night, flashing headlights may be used instead. Outside built-up areas, it is compulsory to use the horn when warning of approach is necessary.

Hotels: Establishments are classed into five star categories as follows:
★★★★★ luxury hotel
★★★★ first-class hotel
★★★ very comfortable hotel
★★ comfortable hotel
★ modest but comfortable hotel

Lights: Full-beam headlights are prohibited in cities and towns. Dipped headlights are compulsory when passing through tunnels, even if they are well lit. Fog lamps must be used in pairs, and only when visibility is restricted in fog or snow.

Motoring clubs: There are two motoring organisations: the Touring Club Italiano (TCI), with its head office at 20122 Milan, 10 Corso Italia, telephone 02 85261; and the Automobile Club d'Italia (ACI), head office at 00185 Rome, 8 Via Marsala, telephone 06 49981, or 06 4477 for a 24-hour information and assistance service. Both have branch offices in leading cities and towns.

Motorways: Tolls are charged on most sections: on most motorways (*autostrade*), you can pay with a Viacard, available from ACI offices, motorway toll booths and service areas, some banks, some tourist offices and some tobacconists. The Viacard cannot be used on the A18 and A20 motorways. A leaflet entitled *Motorway Tolls in Europe* is available as part of the AA European Routes Service (see the end of this guide for details).

Parking: Parking is forbidden in the following places: on a main road or a road with fast-moving traffic; opposite another stationary vehicle; on or near tram lines; on or within 12 metres (39ft 6in) of a bus or tram stop; and in specific places in some cities.

If you park in a blue zone (*zona disco*) between 08.00 and 09.30hrs on a working day, you have to display a disc on the windscreen. Discs are available from petrol stations and automobile organisations. Set at the time of parking, they show when the parking time expires according to the limits of the area concerned.

In green zones (*zona verde*) parking is prohibited 08.00–09.30hrs and 14.30–16.00hrs. Vehicles parked illegally will be towed away at the owner's expense, even if they are not causing an obstruction.

Petrol/diesel: Petrol stations do not generally accept credit cards. Leaded petrol is available as *benzina normale* (85–88 octane) and *benzina super* (98–100 octane) grades. Unleaded petrol (*super senza Pb95 NO-RM / super bleifrei*) is sold as *super senza piombo* (95 octane). Pumps dispensing unleaded petrol are marked in English with `super unleaded'. Only one grade of diesel (*gasolio*) is sold for automotive use. Neither petrol nor diesel fuel may be carried in cans in a vehicle.

Priority: Traffic on state highways (*strade statali*), which are all numbered and indicated by signs, has right of way, as do postal buses on special marked routes and public service

vehicles. If two vehicles are travelling in opposite directions and the drivers of each vehicle want to turn left, they must pass in front of each other (not drive round as in the UK).

Speed limits: All vehicles are limited to 50kph (31mph) in built-up areas and 90kph (55mph) outside built-up areas; on motorways the limit is 130kph (80mph) for vehicles over 1100cc and motorcycles over 349cc and 110kph (68mph) for vehicles up to 1099cc and motorcycles between 150cc and 349cc. Motorcycles under 150cc are not allowed on motorways. For cars towing a caravan or trailer the speed limits are 50kph (31mph), 80kph (49mph) and 100kph (62mph) respectively.

Telephone: To call Britain from Italy, you can use either a cardphone or a call-box with a yellow or red sign showing a telephone dial and receiver. Insert coins before lifting the receiver. Listen for the short and long dialling tones, then dial 0044 (international and country codes), the area code without the first 0, and then the number.

To call Italy from Britain, dial 010 (international), 39 (country code), the area code without the 0, and then the number.

Warning triangle: These are compulsory in the event of accident or breakdown. A triangle must be placed on the road not less than 50 metres (55yds) behind a stationary vehicle which is parked in fog, near a bend, on a hill or at night when the rear lights have failed.

Wheel chains: Chains are compulsory on roads marked by a national sign; they can be purchased at garages or vehicle accessory shops. Drivers of vehicles without wheel chains on roads where they are compulsory are liable to prosecution. Spiked tyres may be used on these roads, provided they are fitted to all four wheels.

SAN MARINO

The official information office in the UK is the Italian State Tourist Office (address and telephone number given above). The laws, motoring regulations and emergency telephone numbers are the same as for Italy.

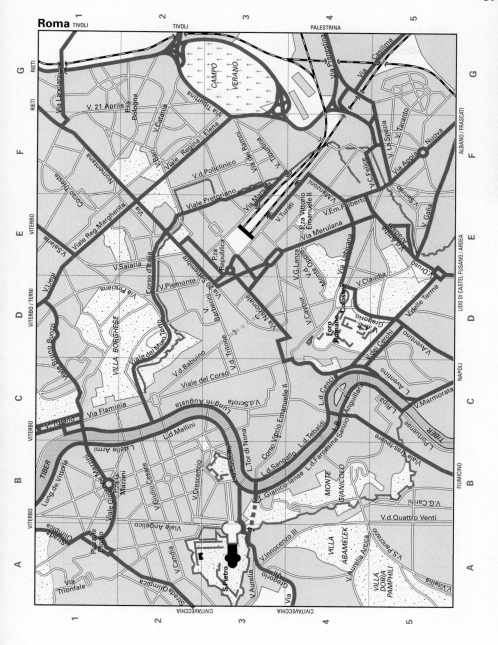

Roma TIVOLI

Firenze

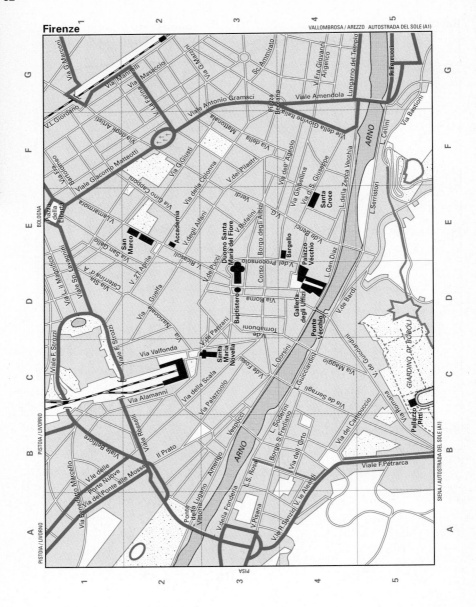

VALLOMBROSA / AREZZO   AUTOSTRADA DEL SOLE (A1)

PISTOIA / LIVORNO

BOLOGNA

SIENA / AUTOSTRADA DEL SOLE (A1)

PISA

PISTOIA / LIVORNO

ARNO

Via G. Marconi

Via Mannelli

Via Masaccio

Via G. La Pira

Via G. Mazzini

Viale Antonio Gramsci

V. L. Giordano

Via degli Artisti

Viale Giacomo Matteotti

Via della Mattonaia

Via della

Via dell'Agnolo

Scr. Ammirato

V. Fra. Giovanni Angelico

Lungarno del Tempio

Viale Amendola

Piazza Beccaria

Viale della Giovine Italia

Via G. Giusti

Via della Colonna

V. del Pilastri

Verdi

Via Ghibellina

Via di S. Giuseppe

L. della Zecca Vecchia

L. Serristori

L. Cellini

Via Bastioni

L. Ferrucci

ARNO

Piazza della Libertà

Via Gino Capponi

Accademia

Via degli Alfani

Via de' Ricasoli

Duomo Santa Maria del Fiore

Borgo degli Albizi

V. G. Giraldi

V. dell'Oriuolo

Santa Croce

San Marco

Via San Gallo

V. 27 Aprile

V. degl Pucci

Bargello

Palazzo Vecchio

V. de Benci

V. della Zecca Vecchia

V.le Spartaco Lavagnini

Via Santa Caterina d'A.

Via L. Il Magnifico

Via Guelfa

Via Nazionale

Battistero

Corso

V. del Proconsolo

Galleria degli Uffizi

V. Gen. Diaz

V.le Bardi

V.le Strozzi

V.le F. Strozzi

Via della Scala

V.le Fratelli Rosselli

Via Valfonda

Santa Maria Novella

V.le Fossi

Via Roma

V.le Tornabuoni

Ponte Vecchio

V. de Guicciardini

Via Alamanni

Via Palazzuolo

Vespucci

L. Gorsini

Via de' Serragli

Via Maggio

GIARDINO DI BOBOLI

Via Romana

Palazzo Pitti

Viale Belfiore

Via Benedetto Marcello

Il Prato

Ponte della Vittoria

Lugano

Armento

V.le delle Porte Nuove

Via del Ponte alle Mosse

V. della Fonderia

V. Pisana

V. R. Stanzial

V. le Ariosto

L. S. Rosa

Borgo S. Frediano

Via dell'Orto

L. Soderini

L. Guicciardini

Via del Campuccio

Viale F. Petrarca

ÁBANO TERME, *Padova*   **05**

★ ★ ★ ★ **Best Western Hotel Due Torri Terme**
(HR)
Via Pietro D'abano 18
☎ 049 8669277 telex 430460 fax 049 8669927
res nr 1678 20080
✉ 35031
open 20.03 - 05.01
* 39 ♨ 95000/105000 41 ♨ 145000/165000
🅰🅴 🕩 📧 ⚒ ⅄ ⊙ ◈ 🅿 ⅋ ⚔ ⅀ ⇅ 🔲 📠 🆆🅲 📺 🍴 ☺

★ ★ ★ ★ **Park** (HCR)
Via Valerio Flacco 31
☎ 049 669671 telex 431516 fax 049 667299
✉ 35031

40 ♨ -/- 60 ♨ -/-
⅄ ⊙ 🅿 ⅋ ⚔ ⅀ ⇅ 🔲 📠 🆆🅲 🍴 ☺

★ ★ ★ ★ **Best Western Hotel Ritz Terme** (HCR)
Via Monteortone 19
☎ 049 8669990 telex 430222 fax 049 8667549
res nr 1678 20080
✉ 35031

* 75 ♨ 100000/125000 excl. breakfast
72 ♨ 138000/173000 excl. breakfast
🅰🅴 🕩 📧 ⚒ ⅄ ♢ 🅿 ⅋ ⅋ ⚔ ⅀ ⇅ 🔲 📠 🆆🅲 📺 🍴 ☺

★ ★ ★ ★ **Terme Internazionale** (HCR)
Viale Mazzini 5
☎ 049 8600300 telex 430039 fax 049 8600322
✉ 35031

60 ♨ -/108000 excl. breakfast 80 ♨ -/189000 excl.
breakfast
⅄ ⊙ 🅿 ⅋ ⅋ ⚔ ⅀ ⇅ 🔲 📠 🆆🅲 📺 🍴 ☺

★ ★ ★ **Terme Italia** (HCR)
Viale Mazzini 7
☎ 049 8600400 telex 430039 fax 049 8600322
✉ 35031

70 ♨ -/76000 excl. breakfast 74 ♨ -/112000 excl.
breakfast
⅄ ⊙ 🅿 ⅋ ⅋ ⚔ ⅀ ⇅ 🔲 📠 🆆🅲 📺 ☺

ACIREALE, *Catania*   **17**

★ ★ ★ ★ **Aloha d'Oro** (HP)
Via A E Gasperi 20
☎ 095 604344 telex 970331
✉ 95024

21 ♨ -/- 100 ♨ -/-
🅿 ⅋ ⚔ 🔲 📠 🆆🅲

ÁLASSIO, *Savona*   **08**

★ ★ ★ **Columbia** (HCR)
Passeggiata Cadorna 12
☎ 0182 640329 fax 0182 642893
✉ 17021

open 23.12 - 15.10
* 2 ♨ 60000/70000 excl. breakfast 24 ♨ 100000/
130000 excl. breakfast
🕩 📧 ⚒ ♨ ⊙ ⅋ 🔲 📠 🆆🅲 ✈

★ ★ ★ ★ **Diana Grand Hotel** (HCR)
Via Garibaldi 110
☎ 0182 642701 fax 0182 640304
✉ 17021

open 24.12 - 20.11
* 14 ♨ 70000/160000 64 ♨ 130000/250000
🅰🅴 🕩 📧 ⚒ ♨ ♢ 🅿 ⅋ ⅋ ⚔ ⅀ ⇅ 🔲 📠 🆆🅲 📺 🍴 ☺
See advertisement on page 35

★ ★ **Firenze** (HG)
Via Dante 10
☎ 0182 43239

3 ♨ 68000/- 21 ♨ 112000/-
⅄ ⊙ 🅿 ⇅ 🔲 📠 🆆🅲

★ ★ **Lido** (HP)
Via 4 Novembre 9
☎ 0182 40158

20 ♨ -/- 30 ♨ -/-
⚔ ⇅ 🔲 📠 🆆🅲 ✈

★ ★ ★ **Majestic** (HP)
Corso L Da Vinci 98
☎ 0182 642721
telex 272032
✉ 17021

This modern hotel
offers a panoramic view
over the sea and also
has its own private
beach. There is ample
opportunity for water-
sports of all kinds. The
restaurant has a choice of international dishes on
the menu, and guests can enjoy an apéritif in the
American bar. The comfortable rooms all feature
a balcony.

17 ♨ 52000/- 58 ♨ 88000/-
⚔ ⅋ ⇅ 🔲 📠 🆆🅲 🍴

Monti Mare (HA)
Via Aurelia
☎ 0182 43036

- *a* -/- 30 *a* -/-
🛇 🏨 �"" 🅿 ⚴ 🄿 🆆🅲

★ ★ ★ **Spiaggia** (HR)
Via Roma 78
☎ 0182 43403 telex 271617

10 *a* -/100000 excl. breakfast 73 *a* -/160000 excl.
breakfast
🛇 �"" 🅿 ⚴ ⵌ 🄳 🄿 🆆🅲 🆃🆅 🍽 ⬥

ALBENGA, *Savona*   08

★ ★ ★ **Sole e Mare** (HCR)
Lungomare Colombo 15
☎ 0182 51817
🖃 17031

10 *a* -/- 18 *a* -/-
🄳 🄿 🆆🅲 🐾

ALBEROBELLO, *Bari*   19

★ ★ ★ ★ ★ **Dei Trulli** (HCR)
Via Cadore 32
☎ 080 9323555 fax 080 9323560
🖃 70011

- *a* 120000/150000 33 *a* 200000/250000
🄰🄴 🄴 ⚒ 🛇 🏨 ☉ 🅿 ⚴ 🄳 🄿 🆆🅲 🆃🆅 🍽 ⬥

ALBISOLA MARINA, *Savona*   08

★ **Coralla** (HCR)
Via Repetto 116
☎ 019 41784
🖃 17012

4 *a* -/- 22 *a* -/85000 excl. breakfast
🅿 🄳 🄿 🆆🅲 🐾

ALESSÀNDRIA, *Alessandria*   03

★ ★ ★ ★ **Best Western Hotel Alli Due Buoi
Rossi** (HCR)
Via Cavour 32
☎ 0131 445252 telex 211397 fax 0131 445255
res nr 1678 20080
🖃 15100

15 *a* 100000/165000 38 *a* 140000/240000
🄰🄴 ⓪ 🄴 ⚒ 🛇 ☉ ⵌ ⴸ 🄳 🄿 🆆🅲 🆃🆅 🍽

ALGHERO, *Sassari*   12

★ ★ ★ **La Margherita** (HR)
Via Sassari 70
☎ 079 979006 fax 079 976417
🖃 07041

3 *a* 57750/63000 excl. breakfast 60 *a* 73500/
78750 excl. breakfast
☉ 🅿 ⚴ ⵌ 🄳 🄿 🆃🆅 🐾

★ ★ ★ **Mediterraneo** (HCR)
Via Fratelli Kennedey 67
☎ 079 979201
🖃 07041

2 *a* -/- 37 *a* -/-
�"" ◐ ◈ ⚴ ⵌ 🄳 🄿 🆆🅲 🍽 ⬥ ☺

AMALFI, *Salerno*   18

Caleidoscopio (HCR)
☎ 089 871220
🖃 84011

5 *a* -/- 30 *a* -/-
🛇 🅿 ⚴ ⴸ 🄳 🄿 🆆🅲 🐾

★ ★ ★ ★ ★ **Lidomare** (HP)
Largo Piccolomin 19
☎ 089 871332 fax 089 857972
🖃 84011

2 *a* -/53000 excl. breakfast 11 *a* -/63000 excl.
breakfast
⚴ 🄳 🄿 🆆🅲

ANACAPRI, *Napoli*   17

★ ★ ★ ★ **Europa Palace Capri** (HCR)
Via Capodimonte 2
☎ 081 8370955 telex 710397 fax 081 8373191
🖃 80071

open 25.03 - 15.11
* 15 *a* 230000/300000 78 *a* 360000/470000
🄰🄴 ⓪ 🄴 ⚒ �"" ☉ 🅿 🅿 ⚴ ⴸ 🄳 🄿 🆆🅲 🆃🆅 🍽 ⬥ ☺ 🐾

★ ★ ★ **San Michele** (HCR)
Via G. Orland 3
☎ 081 8371442 fax 081 8372733
🖃 80071

10 *a* -/- 48 *a* -/-
🄰🄴 ⓪ 🄴 ⚒ ◈ 🅿 🅿 ⚴ ⴸ ⵌ ⴵ 🄳 🄿 🆆🅲 🆃🆅 🍽 🐾

DIANA GRAND HOTEL★★★★

Rivièra
I-17021 ALASSIO

By the sea and open throughout the year.
Air conditioning. Parking space, private
beach. Outdoor grill-restaurant and piano
bar from June to September. Banquets can
be organised (classic or creative cuisine).
American bar, garden, solarium, conference
room for 90 persons. Heated indoor swimming pool with hydromassage, sauna,
equipped gymnasium. Special weekly prices
for 'relaxing in the winter'.

Tel.: 0182-642701. Fax: 0182-640304.

ANCONA, Ancona   11

★ ★ ★ ★ **Grandhotel Passetto** (HG)
Via Thaon De Revel 1
☎ 071 31307 fax 071 32856
✉ 60124

15 🛏 -/140000 excl. breakfast 30 🛏 -/235000 excl.
breakfast
⅃ 🅿 ☂ ♨ ⑪ 🔲 🄵 🆆🅲 📺 🐾

★ ★ ★ ★ **Jolly** (HCR)
Rupi Di Via 29 Septembre
☎ 071 201171 telex 560343 fax 071 206823
✉ 60122

* 40 🛏 160000/- 49 🛏 220000/-
🆎 ⑩ 🄴 ⚒ ⅃ 🅿 ☂ ⑪ 🔲 🄵 🆆🅲 📺 🍽 ☺

★ ★ ★ ★ **Palace** (HCR)
Lungomare Vanvitelli 24
☎ 071 201813 fax 071 2074832
✉ 60121

* 14 🛏 130000/- excl. breakfast 27 🛏 230000/-
excl. breakfast
🆎 ⑩ 🄴 ⚒ ⅃ ⊙ ☂ ☂ ⑪ 🔲 🄵 🆆🅲 📺 ☺

ARMA DI TÁGGIA, Imperia   07

★ ★ ★ **Vittoria** (HCR)
Lungomare
☎ 0184 43495 telex 28345
✉ 18011

- 🛏 -/ 77 🛏 -/-
🚶 🅿 ☂ ⚓ 🛁 🔲 🄵 🆆🅲 🐾

ARONA, Novara   03

★ ★ **La Coccia Del Lago** (HCR)
Viale Boracca 18
☎ 0321 44227
✉ 28041

- 🛏 -/ 9 🛏 -/-
🚶 ⊙ ◈ 🅿 ☂ 🔲 🍽

ASSISI, Perugia   14

★ ★ ★ ★ **Fontebella** (HCR)
Via Fontebella 25
☎ 075 812883 telex 660122 fax 075 812944
✉ 06081

10 🛏 -/110000 excl. breakfast 36 🛏 -/180000 excl.
breakfast
🆎 ⑩ 🄴 ⚒ ⅃ ⊙ 🅿 ⑪ 🔲 📺 🍽 🏠

★ ★ ★ ★ **Giotto** (HCR)   🅰🅰 ANWB

Via Fontebella 41
☎ 075 812209 telex
660122 fax 075 816479
✉ 06082

The Hotel Giotto is
beautifully situated high
up in the old heart of
the town of Assisi. The
rooms are tastefully
furnished and equipped
with modern amenities.
From the rooms and from the terrace, where
vines provide the shade, the guests get a breathtaking view over the hills and fields of Umbria.
The rustically furnished restaurant has a relaxed
atmosphere, and parking facilities are available.

16 🛏 85000/- excl. breakfast 54 🛏 -/140000 excl.
breakfast
⅃ ⊙ 🅿 ☂ ⑪ 🛏 🔲 🄵 🆆🅲 📺 🐾

ITALY

★ ★ ★ **San Francesco** (HCR)   AA ANWB
Via San Francesco 48
☎ 075 812281 telex
660122 fax 075 816237
✉ 06081

Hotel Assisi is situated
in the beautiful medie-
val centre of Assisi right
opposite the basilica of
the same name. This
historic hotel features
44 rooms equipped with
a toilet and shower/bath - a number of the rooms
have their own TV. Weather permitting, it is
pleasant to sit on the terrace, which has a view of
the church. Parking space is available in the
secure garage which can be locked.

* 9 ♨ -/98000 excl. breakfast 35 ♨ -/137000 excl.
breakfast
🈸 ⓪ 🄴 ⥂ 🔔 ⊙ 🅿 👕 🐕 ⇅ 🛏 🖥 🖨 🆆🅲 📺 🍽

AVELLINO, *Avellino*   **18**

★ ★ ★ ★ **Jolly** (HCR)
Via Tuoro Capucinni 97a
☎ 0825 25922 telex 722584 fax 0825 780029
✉ 83100

- ♨ -/130000 74 ♨ -/185000
🈸 ⓪ 🄴 ⥂ 🅿 🖨 🐾

BÁIA SARDÍNIA, *Sassari*   **12**

★ ★ ★ ★ **La Bisaccia** (HCR)
Baja Sardinia
☎ 0789 99002 telex 630541 fax 0789 99162
✉ 07020

4 ♨ -/275000 96 ♨ -/500000
⥂ 🔔 ⊙ 🅿 👕 🐕 ⇅ 🛏 🖥 🖨 🆆🅲 🍽 ⊙

★ ★ ★ **Ringo** (HCR)
Cala Bitta
☎ 0789 99024 telex 790073
✉ 07021

15 ♨ -/- 100 ♨ -/-
⥂ 🔔 🕯 🅿 🐕 🛏 🖨 🆆🅲 🍽 ⊙

★ ★ ★ ★ **Smeraldo Beach** (HCR)
☎ 0789 99046 telex 791123 fax 0789 99500
✉ 07021

- ♨ -/- 175 ♨ -/-
⥂ 🔔 🕯 🅿 👕 🐕 🐾 ⇅ 🛏 🖥 🖨 🆆🅲 📺 🍽 🐕 🐾

BARDOLINO, *Verona*   **04**

★ ★ ★ **Cristina** (HP)   AA ANWB
Via Del Alpino 2
☎ 045 7210339
fax 045 7212697
✉ 37011

The Hotel Christina can
be found on the boule-
vard of the lively little
tourist town of Bardo-
lino which is situated on
the eastern side of Lake
Garda. It is a comfort-
able holiday hotel with a big swimming pool,
sunbathing terrace with bar, private tennis court
and a pleasant restaurant. All the rooms have a
bathroom en suite, and most feature a balcony
with a view over the swimming pool or the lake.
Guests can also make the most of the leisure
facilities of hotel Maria Pia, which is situated next
door.

open 04.04 - 20.10
* 6 ♨ 69000/89000 42 ♨ 98000/116000
⥂ 🔔 🍷 ⊙ ◈ 🅿 👕 🐕 ⇅ 🖥 🖨 🆆🅲 ⊙

★ ★ **Maria Pia** (HR)
Via S. Cristina 5
☎ 045 7210233 fax 045 7212697
✉ 37011

open 04.04 - 20.10
* 6 ♨ 52000/63000 22 ♨ 88000/110000
🍷 🅿 👕 🐕 🖨 🆆🅲 ⊙

BARI, *Bari*   **19**

★ ★ ★ **Agip** (MT)
Torre A Mare
☎ 080 300266 telex 812288 fax 080 300739
✉ 70045

- ♨ -/- 95 ♨ -/-
🈸 ⓪ 🄴 ⥂ 🅿 ⇅ 🖨 🆆🅲 📺 🍽

★ ★ ★ **Jolly** (HCR)
Via Guilio Petroni 15
☎ 080 364366 telex 810274
✉ 70100

- ♨ -/210000 164 ♨ -/275000
🅿 🖨 🐾

★ ★ ★ ★ **Palace Hotel Bari** (HCR)
Via Lombardi 13
☏ 080 5216551 telex 810111 fax 080 5211499
✉ 70122

* 73 ♨ 190000/225000 127 ♨ 300000/360000
AE ⓘ 🄴 🎿 ⊙ 🄿 🅿 🛎 🍴 📶 🖥 🄿 TV 🕪 🐾

★ ★ ★ **Victor** (HP)
Via Nicolai 69
☏ 080 216600
✉ 70122

5 ♨ -/- 70 ♨ -/-
🎿 ⊙ 🄿 🍴 🖥 🄿 WC TV 🐾

BAVENO, *Novara*   **03**

★ ★ ★ ★ **Grandhotel Dino** (HCR)
Corso Garibaldi 20
☏ 0323 922201 telex 200217 fax 0323 924515
✉ 28042

* 40 ♨ 130000/230000 360 ♨ 160000/300000
AE ⓘ 🄴 🎿 🛁 ⊙ ◆ 🄿 🅿 🛎 🍴 📶 🖥 🄿 WC TV
🕪 ☺

★ ★ ★ **Simplon** (HCR)
Corso Garibaldi 52
☏ 0323 924112 telex 200217 fax 0323 924515
✉ 28042

open 20.03 - 03.11
* 8 ♨ 50000/90000 excl. breakfast 82 ♨ 65000/130000 excl. breakfast
AE ⓘ 🄴 🎿 🛁 ⊙ ◆ 🄿 🅿 🛎 🍴 📶 🖥 WC 🕪 ☺

★ ★ ★ ★ **Splendid** (HR)
Via Sempione 12
☏ 0323 924583 telex 200217 fax 0323 924515
✉ 28042

open 20.03 - 10.11
* 20 ♨ 80000/130000 80 ♨ 100000/180000
AE ⓘ 🄴 🎿 🛁 🛁 ⊙ ◆ 🄿 🅿 🛎 🍴 📶 🖥 🄿 WC TV 🕪

BELGIRATE, Novara   03

★ ★ ★ ★ Best Western Hotel Milano (HCR)
Via Sempione 4
☎ 0322 76525 telex 200490 fax 0322 76295
res nr 1678 20080
✉ 28040

* 4 🛏 86000/120000 44 🛏 128000/168000
🆎 ⓪ 🅴 ⊒ 👤 🐾 ☉ 🅿 👕 🍽 🍸 ⚓ 🚤 †⬦ 🔲 🏠 📺 🚾 📺 🍴 ⊗
⊗

★ ★ ★ ★ Best Western Hotel Villa Carlotta (HCR)   🔤 ANWB
Via Sempione 119
☎ 0322 76461 telex
200490 fax 0322 76705
res nr 1678 20080
✉ 28040

The Best Western Hotel
Villa Carlotta is situated
on the road leading
along the west shore of
the Lake Maggiore. The
hotel is, as the name suggests, a beautiful villa. It
features an attractive park which contains a
swimming pool and a tennis court. The rooms are
spacious and have a bathroom and TV. Meals can
be enjoyed on the covered restaurant terrace. On
the other side, the hotel has its own small private
beach with mooring.

* 5 🛏 98000/138000 135 🛏 165000/195000
🆎 ⓪ 🅴 ⊒ 👤 🐾 ☉ ⬦ 🅿 🍽 ⚓ 🚤 †⬦ 🔲 🏠 🚾 📺 🍴 ⊗

BELLÁGIO, Como   03

★ Roma (HCR)
Via Grandi 6
☎ 031 950424
✉ 22021

open 20.03 - 20.10
* 5 🛏 25000/38000 excl. breakfast 21 🛏 38000/
69000 excl. breakfast
🆎 ⓪ 🅴 ⊒ 👤 ☉ 🍽 †⬦ 🔲 🏠 🚾 🍴 ⊗

BELLANO, Como   03

★ ★ ★ Meridiana (HCR)
Carlo Alberto 19
☎ 0341 821126 fax 0341 821261
✉ 22051

open 10.01 - 21.12
4 🛏 45000/70000 excl. breakfast 31 🛏 65000/
75000 excl. breakfast
🆎 ⓪ 🅴 ⊒ 👤 🐾 ⬦ 🅿 🍽 †⬦🔲 🏠 🚾 🍴 ⊗

BELLÁRIA IGEA MARINA, Forli   10

★ ★ ★ Miramare (HCR)
Viale Colombo 37
☎ 0541 344131 telex 550531 fax 0541 347316
✉ 47041

open 15.05 - 30.09
7 🛏 45000/50000 45 🛏 60000/90000
⓪ ⊒ 👤 🐾 ☉ 🅿 🍽 ⚓ †⬦ 🔲 📺 🍴 ⊗

BELLUNO, Belluno   05

★ ★ ★ Astor (HG)
Piazza Dei Martiri 26/e
☎ 0437 942094 fax 0437 942493
✉ 32100

* 5 🛏 60000/90000 excl. breakfast 27 🛏 90000/
120000 excl. breakfast
🆎 ⓪ 🅴 ⊒ 🐾 ☉ ⬦ †⬦ 🔲 🏠 🚾 📺 ⊗

BIBIONE, Venezia   06

★ ★ Bellevue (HCR)
Via Croce Del Sud 42
☎ 0431 43168 telex 450417
✉ 30020

- 🛏 -/- 51 🛏 46000/66000 excl. breakfast
👤 🐾 ☉ 🅿 🍽 ⚓ †⬦ 🔲 🏠 🚾 🍴 ⊗

★ ★ ★ Bembo (HCR)
Corso Europa 35
☎ 0431 43418 fax 0431 720420
✉ 30020

8 🛏 -/- 52 🛏 -/-
👤 🐾 ☉ 🅿 🍽 ⚓ †⬦ 🏠 🚾 🍴 ⊗

★ ★ ★ Excelsior (HCR)
Via Croce Del Sud 2
☎ 0431 43377 fax 0431 720420
✉ 30020

12 🛏 -/- 80 🛏 63000/95000 excl. breakfast
👤 🐾 ☉ 🅿 🍽 †⬦ 🔲 🏠 🚾 🍴 ⊗

★ ★ ★ Principe (HCR)
Via Ariete 41
☎ 0431 43256 telex 461075 fax 0431 433294
✉ 30020

- 🛏 -/- 80 🛏 -/-
👤 🐾 ☉ 🅿 🍽 †⬦ 🔲 🏠 🚾 🍴 ⊗

BOGLIASCO, *Genova* 08

★ ★ Villa Flora (HCR)
Via Aurelia 5
☎ 010 3470013
✉ 16031

11 🛏 -/- 18 🛏 -/-
🖿 ⌖ ◆ 🅿 📼 📺 ⛲

BOLOGNA, *Bologna* 10

Bologna is the capital of Emilia-Romagna, a region bordered by the River Po, the Adriatic and the Apennine mountains. Its distinctive old centre is built of brick; its leaning towers - two out of several hundred that were erected in the city as a medieval status symbol by the great ruling families - are of special interest. From the top of the Asinelli Tower (320ft) there is a magnificent bird's-eye view over the terracotta rooftops and slender church spires . The old city revolves around the two adjacent squares, Piazza del Nettunoa and Piazza Maggiore. In the first is Giovanni Bologna's splendid bronze statue of Neptune and the opulent *Palazzo di Re Enzo*, in the second, the vast Basilica of San Petronio and the Renaissance-style *Palazzo del Podesta*. The university, the oldest in Europe, is a notable seat of learning, and the *Pinacoteca Nazionale* beyond it, offers a comprehensive view of Bolognese art. Definitely not to be missed is the sanctuary of the Madonna di San Luca, linked to the city gate by a portico of arches over 2 miles long and commanding views across Bologna to the Apennines beyond. Bologna is noted for its pasta sauces, *mortadella* sausages, *tortellini*, and *tagliatelli*, reputedly invented for the wedding of Lucrezia Borgia. Regional wines are sparkling Lambrusco, red Sangiovese, and the whites, Albana and Trebbiano.

★ ★ ★ Agip (HCR)
Via Lepido 203
☎ 051 401130 telex 583187
✉ 40132

- 🛏 -/- 64 🛏 -/230000
🆎 ⓘ 🖿 ⌖ ⚡ ◆ 🅿 ⇅ 🄿 📼 📺 🍴 🐾

★ ★ ★ Jolly (HCR)
Piazza X X Settembre 2
☎ 051 248921 telex 510076 fax 051 249764
✉ 40121

- 🛏 -/222000 168 🛏 -/330000
🆎 ⓘ 🖿 ⌖ ⊙ ⇅ 🄿 📼 📺 🍴

★ ★ ★ La Pioppa (HCR)
Via Marco Em. Lepido 217
☎ 051 402324 fax 051 402079
✉ 40132

8 🛏 102000/110000 34 🛏 156000/170000
🆎 ⓘ 🖿 ⌖ ⚡ ◆ 🅿 🄿 ⇅ 🄿 📼 📺 ⛲

★ ★ ★ ★ Pullman (HCR)
Viale Pietramellara 59
☎ 051 248248 telex 520643 fax 051 2492421
✉ 40121

48 🛏 -/232000 196 🛏 -/334000
🆎 ⓘ 🖿 ⌖ ⊙ 🄿 ⇅ 🄿 📼 📺 🐾 🍴

BOLZANO, *Bolzano* 05

★ ★ Herzog (HG)
Piazza Del Grano 2
☎ 0471 976267
✉ 39100

3 🛏 -/- 22 🛏 -/-
🆎 🖿 ⌖ ⚡ ⊙ 🅿 ⇅ 🄿 📼 📺

BORDIGHERA, *Imperia* 07

★ ★ ★ Albergo la Sirena (HP)
Via Regina Margherita 26
☎ 0184 262528
✉ 18012

3 🛏 -/50000 17 🛏 -/78000
🅿 ⇅ 🄿 📼 🐾

★ ★ ★ Aurora (HP)
Via Pelloux 42/b
☎ 0184 261311 fax 0184 261312
✉ 18012

open 01.01 - 10.10
* 4 🛏 55000/90000 26 🛏 75000/120000
🆎 ⓘ 🖿 ⌖ ⚡ ⊙ 🅿 ⇅ 🄿 📼 🐾

Belvédere Lombardi (HP)
Via Romana 56
☎ 0184 261408

8 🛏 -/- 70 🛏 -/-
⚡ 🅿 ⇅ 🄿 📼 🐾

★ ★ ★ ★ Cap Ampelio (HR)
Via Virgilio 5
☎ 0184 264333 telex 282553 fax 0184 264244

* 44 🛏 139000/141000 60 🛏 242000/247000
🆎 ⓘ 🖿 ⌖ ⚡ ⚘ ⊙ 🅿 🄿 ⇅ ⇅ 🄿 📼 📺 🍴 ⛲

ITALY

Jolanda (HR)
Corso Italia 85
☎ 0184 261325
✉ 18012

8 🛏 -/- 38 🛏 -/-
🅿 💺 🖭 🏇

★ ★ ★ **Del Mare** (HCR)
Via Portico Della Punta
☎ 0184 266762 telex 270535 fax 0184 262394

open 24.12 - 18.10
* 5 🛏 150000/200000 106 🛏 234000/344000
🆎 🅴 ⚡ ≈ ⚓ 🔆 🅿 🍴 💺 ≈ ⇅ 🔔 💺 🖭 🅿 🆆🅲 📺 🍽 ☺
See advertisement on page 41

★ ★ ★ **Villa Elisa** (HP)
Romana 70
☎ 0184 261313 telex 272540 fax 0184 261942

open 20.12 - 30.11
2 🛏 75000/85000 32 🛏 115000/135000
🆎 🅴 ⚡ 🔥 ⚓ 🔆 🅿 🍴 ≈ ⇅ 💺 🖭 🅿 📺 🍽 ☺

★ ★ **Nike** (HP)
Marniga 69
☎ 045 7420149 telex 480448 fax 045 7420149
✉ 37010

open 27.03 - 30.10
* 8 🛏 70000/82000 36 🛏 96000/111000
⚓ 🔆 🅿 🍴 ≈ ⇅ 🔔 💺 🖭 🆆🅲 ⬆ ☺

★ ★ **Rabay** (HCR)
☎ 045 7430273 fax 045 7430273
✉ 37010

* 3 🛏 41500/56300 34 🛏 68000/97600
⚓ 🔆 🅿 🍴 ⇅ 💺 🆆🅲 🏇

★ ★ ★ **Santa Maria** (HP)
Benaco 12
☎ 045 7420045 telex 480448 fax 045 7420149
✉ 37010

open 27.03 - 30.10
* - 🛏 90000/97000 23 🛏 108000/132000
≈ ⚓ ◆ 🅿 🍴 ≈ 🔔 💺 🆆🅲 🍽 ⬆ ☺

★ ★ ★ **Löwenhof** (HCR)
Brennerstrasse 13
☎ 0472 36216 fax 0472 801337
✉ 39042

* - 🛏 60000/73000 27 🛏 80000/96000
🅴 ⚡ 🔥 🔆 ◆ 🅿 🍴 ≈ ≈ ≈ ⇅ 💺 🖭 🅿 🆆🅲 📺 🍽 ☺

★ ★ **Mediterraneo** (HR)
Viale Aldo Moro 70
☎ 0831 82811 telex 813291
✉ 72100

26 🛏 -/- 43 🛏 -/-
🔆 ☉ 🅿 🍴 ⇅ ⚓ 💺 🖭 🅿 🆆🅲 📺 🍽 ⬆ 🏇

★ ★ **Post** (HCR)   **AA** **ANWB**
Graben 9
☎ 0474 85127
telex 400350
✉ 39031

The Hotel-Restaurant
Post is an old-fashioned
hotel, full of character,
which has been owned
by the same family
since 1850. It is situated
in the small tourist and
winter-sports town of Bruneck. It features 60
rooms, of which half have a private toilet and
bath, and some have a TV. A pleasant terrace can
be found on the front of the hotel. The surrounding area is ideally suited for walking and winter-
sports holidays.

19 🛏 -/- 41 🛏 43000/74000
≈ ☉ ◆ 🅿 ≈ 💺 🖭 🅿 🆆🅲 📺 🍽

★ ★ ★ **Britannia Excelsior** (HCR)
Via Regina
☎ 0344 40413 telex 312136
✉ 22011

13 🛏 -/- 120 🛏 -/-
🆎 ◑ 🅴 ⚡ ◆ 🅿 🍴 ≈ ≈ ⇅ 💺 🅿 🆆🅲 🍽

★ ★ ★ **Agip** (MT)
Circonvalla. Nuova
☎ 070 521373 telex 792104 fax 070 502222
res nr 06 4821651
✉ 09124

3 🛏 -/95000 129 🛏 -/140000
☽ ◆ 🅿 ⇅ 💺 🅿 🆆🅲 📺 🏇

CALCERÁNICA AL LAGO, Trento   05

★ ★ **Bellavista** (HG)
Viale Venezia 10
☎ 0461 723214
✉ 38050

open 01.04 - 30.09
* 2 🛏 32000/38000 excl. breakfast 18 🛏 58000/70000 excl. breakfast
🦌 🍴 🚲 🅾 🅿 🎿 🎿 🅿 🆆🅲 ☺

CALDARO, Bolzano   05

★ ★ ★ ★ **Kartheinerhof** (HCR)
Weinstrasse 22
☎ 0471 963240 telex 400333 fax 0471 963145
✉ 39052

- 🛏 -/- 33 🛏 -/-
🆎 🅾 🅴 🎿 🍴 🚲 🅾 🅿 🎿 🎿 🎿 🍴 🆋 🆆🅲 📺 ☺

CAMOGLI, Genova   08

★ ★ ★ ★ **Cenobio Dei Dogi** (HCR)
Via Cuneo 34
☎ 0185 770041 telex 281116 fax 0185 772796
✉ 16032

open 15.03 - 10.01
* 16 🛏 160000/200000 73 🛏 290000/370000
🆎 🅴 🎿 🦌 🚲 🅾 🅿 🎿 🍴 🍴 🆋 🆆🅲 📺 ☺

CAMPOROSSO, Imperia   07

Résidence Monterosso (HR)
Via Della Olandaise 211
☎ 0184 293642
✉ 18033

- 🛏 -/- 16 🛏 -/-
🦌 🚲 🅿 🎿 🍴 🍴 🅾 🐕 🐴

CANAZEI, Trento   05

★ ★ **Chalet Pineta** (HCR)
☎ 0462 61162
✉ 38032

1 🛏 -/46000 excl. breakfast 15 🛏 -/73000 excl. breakfast
🦌 🅿 🍴 🆋 🆆🅲 🐴

CÁNNERO RIVIERA, Novara   03

★ ★ ★ **Cannero** (HCR)   🆎 ANWB
Piazza Umberto I, N. 2
☎ 0323 788046 telex 200285 fax 0323 788048
✉ 28051

The inviting frontage of the Hotel Cannero is one of the most attractive and eye-catching façades on the boulevard at Cannero, situated on the Lago Maggiore. This pleasant peaceful hotel offers 36 tastefully furnished rooms, all with private toilet and bath/shower, and most of them with a balcony. There is a stylishly decorated restaurant and a pleasant terrace right by the lake. The hotel also features an attractive swimming pool and a tennis court.

open 15.03 - 05.11
* 6 🛏 60000/70000 30 🛏 110000/120000
🆎 🅾 🅴 🎿 🦌 🚲 🅾 🅿 🎿 🎿 🍴 🍴 🆋 🆆🅲 📺 🍴 🐕 ☺

★ ★ ★ **Park Italia** (HR)
Via Magnolie 19
☎ 0323 788488 fax 0323 788498
✉ 28051

open 06.04 - 02.11
1 🛌 63000/85000 24 🛏 102000/130000
🅰🅴 ⓞ 🅴 ⚒ 🕴 🍽 ♨ ⊙ 🅿 🛎 🍴 🛗 🔲 🄲 🆆🄲 🍽 🛗

CANNÓBIO, Novara   03

★ **Cannobio** (HCR)
Piazza Lago 6
☎ 0323 7390
✉ 28052

5 🛌 -/- 17 🛏 -/-
🅰🅴 🅴 🍽 ♨ ⊙ ◆ 🛎 🍴 🔲 🄲 🆆🄲 🍽

CÁORLE, Venezia   06

★ ★ ★ ★ **Airone** (HCR)
Via Pola 1
☎ 0421 81570 telex 1410482 fax 0421 82074
✉ 30021

open 20.05 - 20.09
5 🛌 74000/95000 73 🛏 116000/148000
ⓞ 🅴 ⚒ 🕴 ♨ 🛎 🍴 🔲 🄲 🆆🄲 🍽 🛗 🐎

★ ★ ★ **Garden** (HCR)
Piazza Belvedere 2
☎ 0421 210036 telex 410482 fax 0421 210037
✉ 30021

open 11.04 - 10.10
5 🛌 35000/45000 excl. breakfast 45 🛏 55000/
80000 excl. breakfast
🕴 ♨ 🅿 🛎 🍴 🔲 🄲 🆆🄲 🍽 🛗

·★ ★ ★ **Splendid** (HCR)
Viale S. Margherita 31
☎ 0421 81316 fax 0421 83379
✉ 30021

open 10.05 - 20.09
6 🛌 39000/54000 36 🛏 60000/94000
♨ ⊙ ◆ 🅿 🛎 🍴 🔲 🄲 🆆🄲 🍽 🛗

CAPOLÍVERI, Livorno   12

★ ★ ★ **Antares** (HR)
☎ 0565 940131 telex 400082 fax 0565 940084
✉ 57031

open 25.04 - 17.10
* 2 🛌 -/- 40 🛏 98000/130000
🕴 🍴 ♨ 🅿 🛎 🔲 🄲 🆆🄲 🛗

CAPRI, Napoli   17

★ ★ **Canasta** (HP)
Via Compo Di Teste 6
☎ 081 8370561
✉ 80073

6 🛌 -/- 10 🛏 -/-
🔲 🄲 🆆🄲 🐎

★ ★ **Club Villa Pina** (HP)
Via Tuoro 11
☎ 081 8377517 telex 710482
✉ 80073

2 🛌 -/- 43 🛏 -/-
🕴 🍴 🛎 ♨ 🔲 🄲 🆆🄲

★ ★ ★ **La Pineta** (HCR)
Via Tragara 6
☎ 081 8370644 telex 710011 fax 081 8376445
✉ 80073

* 6 🛌 80000/180000 40 🛏 120000/300000
🅰🅴 ⓞ 🅴 ⚒ 🕴 🍴 ♨ 🛎 ♨ 🔲 🆆🄲 📺 🛗

★ ★ ★ **Syrene** (HR)
Via Camerelle 51
☎ 081 8370102 fax 081 8370857
✉ 80073

3 🛌 -/- 31 🛏 -/-
🕴 ⊙ 🛎 ♨ 🍴 🔲 🔲 📺

★ ★ ★ **Villa Igea** (HP)
Via Fuorlovado 36
☎ 081 8376055
✉ 80073

3 🛌 -/- 20 🛏 -/-
♨ 🛎 🔲 🄲 🆆🄲 🐎

CASTELLETTO DI BRENZONE, Verona

★ ★ ★ **Residence Hotel Castelli**
☎ 045 7430174 fax 045 7430020
✉ 37010

4 🛌 -/- 42 🛏 -/-
🍽 ♨ 🅿 🛎 🍴 🔲 🄲 🆆🄲 📺 🛗 🛗

CASTELROTTO, *Bolzano* 05

★ ★ **Belvedere Schoenblick** (HG) *AA ANWB*
Oswald V. Wolkenstein 47
☎ 0471 706336
✉ 39040

Hotel Schönblick is peacefully situated amid alpine meadows just outside the centre of the elevated town of Kastelruth. The tops of the Dolomites in the near surroundings give a beautiful panoramic view. All the rooms have a balcony, most of them also feature a private toilet, bath or shower, and some have a TV. There is a sauna and various leisure facilities. This hotel is in an area popular for walking and winter sports.

13 ⌇ 46000/80000 21 ⌇ -/-
🌣 🐾 ◆ P ⅔ 🖃 🏠 wc tv iⓞi ☺

RESIDENCE HOTEL Castelli

I-37010 CASTELLETO DI BRENZONE
- Lake Garda -

Hotel rooms with shower/wc, balcony, half-board from ITL 45,000 per person. Generous buffet breakfast. Apartments with terraces overlooking the sea for 2-4 persons from ITL 67,000 per day. PRIVATE BEACH and boat quay, anchoring buoys, snack bar close to beautiful heated swimming pool, wind surfing. Locked parking area, garden, beautifully located on the lake.
Ask for our prices and folder.

Tel.: 045-7430174, private: 7420104, fax 7430020, German speaking.

CASTIGLIONE DELLA PESCÁIA, *Grosseto* 13

★ ★ ★ **Lucerna** (HCR)
Via 4 Novembre 27
☎ 0564 933620 fax 0564 935771
✉ 58043

5 ⌇ -/- 48 ⌇ -/-
⊙ P ⅔ ↕ 🖃 🏠 wc

CATÀNIA, *Catania* 17

★ ★ **Agip** (MT)
Via Messina 626
☎ 095 494003 telex 912379
res nr 06 4821651
✉ 95100

- ⌇ -/- 45 ⌇ -/142000
P 🖃 🏠

★ ★ ★ ★ **Jolly** (HCR)
Piazza Trento 13
☎ 095 494003 telex 912379

- ⌇ -/158000 excl. breakfast 45 ⌇ -/200000 excl. breakfast
P 🖃 🏠 🐾

★ ★ ★ **Moderno** (HP)
Via Alessi 9
☎ 095 325309
✉ 95100

7 ⌇ -/- 40 ⌇ -/-
↕ 🖃 🏠 wc 🐾

★ ★ ★ **Nettuno** (HR)
Via Ruggero Di Lauria 121
☎ 095 7125252 telex 971451 fax 095 498066
✉ 95126

- ⌇ -/100000 80 ⌇ -/160000
AE ⓞ E 🍽 P ⅔ ↕ 🖃 🏠 wc tv 🐾

CATANZARO, *Catanzaro* 21

★ ★ ★ **Motel Agip** (HCR)
Via G. Da Fiore 2
☎ 0961 771791 telex 912543 fax 0961 773366
✉ 88100

- ⌇ 93000/- 76 ⌇ 146000/-
AE ⓞ E 🍽 🌣 P ⅔ 🥢 ↕ 🏠 wc tv iⓞi ☺

CATTÓLICA, *Forli*　　　　　11

★ ★ ★ Des Bains (HP)

AA *ANWB*

Viale Carducci 129
☎ 0541 961490
telex 551084
fax 0541 961011
✉ 47033

Hotel des Bains is right opposite the beach and within walking distance of the centre of Cattolica. It features some striking architecture, modern and light, with an amusing façade. The rooms have a toilet, bath/shower and a balcony. The attractive exterior design extends inside into the public rooms, restaurant and bar. A pleasant terrace can be found by the side of the street, and there is a roof terrace with deck chairs for sunbathing.

open 15.05 - 30.09
* 12 ♨ -/45000 44 ♨ -/82000
🏧 🔷 🅴 ⚍ ⅄ 🚲 ☉ 🅿 ⼁ 🐕 🐾 ↿ ⊟ 🅲 🆆🅲 🍽 ☺

★ ★ ★ ★ ★ Caravella (HCR)
Via Padova 6
☎ 0541 962416

1 ♨ -/100000 44 ♨ -/190000
🚲 ⼁ ⚔ ↿ 🅲 🆆🅲

★ ★ ★ ★ Madison (HR)
Via Don Minzoni 80
☎ 0541 968306 telex 551084 fax 0541 961470
✉ 47033

9 ♨ 60000/90000 72 ♨ 150000/-
🔷 🅴 ⚍ ⅄ 🚲 ☉ 🅿 ⼁ 🐕 ⚔ ↿ ⊟ 🅲 🆆🅲 📺

★ ★ ★ Mediterraneo (HP)
Viale Carducci 141 B
☎ 0541 963468 telex 551084 fax 0541 953670

open 15.05 - 15.09
* 13 ♨ 55000/85000 42 ♨ 70000/95000
🚲 ☉ 🅿 ⼁ 🐕 ↿ ⊟ 🅲 🆆🅲 📺 🍽 ☺

★ ★ ★ ★ Royal Sands (HCR)
Viale Carducci 30
☎ 0541 954133 fax 0541 954670
✉ 47033

open 26.05 - 15.09
15 ♨ 41000/91400 50 ♨ 84000/108500
⅄ 🚲 ☉ 🅿 ⼁ 🐕 🐾 ⚔ ↿ ⊟ 🅲 🆆🅲 🍽 ☺

★ ★ Sirenella (HR)
Via Pisacano 24
☎ 0541 962131

4 ♨ -/- 20 ♨ -/-
⅄ 🚲 🅿 ⼁ 🅲 🆆🅲

★ ★ ★ Universal San Marco (HP)
Viale Carducci 108
☎ 0541 963461
✉ 47033

5 ♨ -/- 60 ♨ -/-
🚲 ☉ 🅿 ⼁ ↿ 🅲 🆆🅲 ↿ ☺

CAVALESE, *Trento*　　　　　05

★ ★ ★ Eurotel Cermis (HP)
☎ 0462 30572 telex 400096
✉ 38033

9 ♨ -/- 43 ♨ -/-
⅄ 🚲 🐾 ⚐ ⊟ 🅲 🆆🅲 🏂

CAVALLINA, *Firenze*　　　　　10

★ ★ ★ Barberino (HCR)
Viale Don Minzoni 55
☎ 055 8420051 fax 055 8420432
✉ 50030

27 ♨ 65000/85000 51 ♨ 95000/125000
🏧 🔷 🅴 ⚍ ⅄ 🔷 🅿 🐾 ↿ ⊟ 🅲 🆆🅲 📺 ☺

CAVALLINO, *Venezia*　　　　　05

★ ★ ★ Fenix (HCR)
Via F. Baracca 45
☎ 041 968040 telex 4104331 fax 041 968831
✉ 30013

open 15.05 - 26.09
* 14 ♨ 55000/72000 56 ♨ 88000/122000
🏧 ⅄ 🚲 🔷 🅿 🐾 ⚔ ↿ ⊟ 🅲 🆆🅲 🍽 ☺

CELLE LÍGURE, *Savona*　　　　　08

★ ★ Riviera (HCR)
Via Colla 55
☎ 019 990541
✉ 17015

2 ♨ -/- 50 ♨ -/110000 excl. breakfast
↿ ⊟ 🅲 🆆🅲 🏂

CERIALE, *Savona* 08

★ **Miramare** (HCR)
Lungomare Diaz 57
☎ 0182 90006
✉ 17023

1 🛏 -/- 17 🛏 -/-
🛌 📠 ⊙ 🅿 🅟 ⛄ ⬛ 🐕

CERNÓBBIO, *Como* 03

★ ★ ★ ★ **Asnigo** (HCR)
Piazza Santo Stefano
☎ 031 510062 fax 031 510249
✉ 22012

2 🛏 90000/125000 excl. breakfast 28 🛏 130000/170000 excl. breakfast
🆎 ⊙ 🅴 ⛽ 🛎 ⊙ 🅿 🅟 ⛄ 🍴 ⬛ 🅟 🆆🅲 📺 🍽

★ ★ ★ ★ **Regina Olga Reine du Lac** (HCR)
Via Regina 18
☎ 031 510171 telex 380821 fax 031 340604
✉ 22012
open 31.01 - 30.11
* 11 🛏 160000/175000 72 🛏 225000/270000
🆎 ⊙ 🅴 ⛽ ⊙ ◆ 🅿 🅟 ⛄ 🛌 🍴 ⬛ 🅟 🆆🅲 📺 🍽

CÉRVIA, *Ravenna* 10

★ ★ **Nettuno** (HR)
Lungomare D' Annunzio 34
☎ 0544 971156 telex 550232
✉ 48015

6 🛏 -/50000 excl. breakfast 38 🛏 -/90000 excl. breakfast
🅿 🍴 🛌 🍽 ⬛ 🅟 🆆🅲 🐕

★ ★ **Strand** (HCR)
Lungomare G. Deledda 102
☎ 0544 72325
✉ 48015

3 🛏 -/- 30 🛏 -/70000 excl. breakfast
🛌 🅿 🍴 🍽 ⬛ 🅟 🆆🅲 🐕

CESENÁTICO, *Forli* 10

★ ★ ★ **Domus Mea** (HG)
Via Del Fortino 7
☎ 0547 82119 fax 0547 82441
✉ 47042

open 01.05 - 15.09
* 13 🛏 36000/53500 22 🛏 51000/86000
🆎 ⊙ 🅴 ⛽ 🛎 ⊙ 🅿 🅟 ⛄ 🍴 🍽 ⬛ 🅟 🆆🅲 📺 ☺

★ ★ ★ **Grandhotel** (HR)
Plazza Costa 1
☎ 0547 80012
✉ 47042

20 🛏 -/- 76 🛏 -/-
🚗 ⊙ 🅿 ☂ 👯 ↑↓ 🔲 🔁 🅾️

★ ★ ★ **Internazionale** (HR)
Via Ferrara 7
☎ 0547 80231
✉ 47042

1 🛏 -/55000 excl. breakfast 50 🛏 -/85000 excl.
breakfast
👯 🚗 🅿 🔲 🔁 WC 🐎

★ **New Bristol** (HR)
Viale Del Fortino 9
☎ 0547 80047
✉ 47042

4 🛏 -/- 48 🛏 -/-
👯 ↑↓ 🔁 WC 🐎

★ ★ **San Pietro** (HR)
Viale Carducci 194
☎ 0547 82496
✉ 47042

15 🛏 -/60000 excl. breakfast 80 🛏 -/90000 excl.
breakfast
👯 🚗 🅿 ☂ ⬅ ↑↓ 🔲 🔁 WC 🐎

CETRARO, *Cosenza*   **19**

★ ★ ★ ★ ★ **Grand San Michele** (HR)
Contraba Bosco 8/9
☎ 0982 91012 fax 0982 91430
✉ 87022

open 01.12 - 31.10
* 6 🛏 110000/160000 65 🛏 180000/300000
🆎 🅾 🇪 ⚖ 👯 🚗 🌑 ◆ 🅿 ☂ 👯 ⬅ ↑↓ 🔲 🔁 WC 📺 🅾️ 🌐

CHIÁVARI, *Genova*   **08**

★ ★ ★ **Monterosa**
Via Monsign. Marinetti 6
☎ 0185 300321
✉ 16043

30 🛏 -/50000 38 🛏 -/75000
👯 ⊙ ☂ ↑↓ 🔲 🔁 WC 🐎

CHIETI, *Chieti*   **15**

★ ★ ★ **Grande Albergo Abruzzo** (HCR)
Via Asinio Herio 20
☎ 0871 42041 telex 601054 fax 0871 42042
✉ 66100

open 01.12 - 30.11
* 31 🛏 87500/91800 excl. breakfast 30 🛏 124500/
130700 excl. breakfast
🆎 🅾 🇪 ⚖ 👯 ⊙ 🅿 ☂ 👯 ↑↓ 🔲 🔁 WC 📺 🌐

COLLE ISARCO, *Bolzano*   **05**

★ ★ **Schuster** (HCR)   🅰🅰 ANW🅱
Pfarrgasse 1
☎ 0472 62322
fax 0472 62580
✉ 39040

The Hotel Schuster can
be found in the centre
of Gossensass, a
winter-sport and tourist
resort at 1100m. Des-
pite the fact that it is in
the main street, it offers
a peaceful and comfortable stay; 26 tastefully
furnished rooms all have toilet and bath or shower, and a relaxed and rustic atmosphere in the
restaurant. The sunny terrace overlooks the tops
of the Alps in the surrounding area. The hotel also
features a sauna.

open 15.05 - 30.10 + 30.11 - 30.04
2 🛏 44500/50000 24 🛏 70000/80000
🇪 ⚖ 👯 ⊙ ◆ 👯 ↑↓ 🔥 🔲 🔁 WC 🅾️ 🌐

COMO, *Como*   **03**

★ ★ ★ ★ **Barchetta Excelsior** (HCR)
Piazza Cavour 1
☎ 031 3221 telex 380435 fax 031 302622
✉ 22100

1 🛏 -/209000 84 🛏 -/225000
🆎 🅾 🇪 ⚖ 👯 ⊙ ↑↓ 🔲 🔁 WC 📺 🅾️

★ ★ **Moderno** (HCR)
Via G. Majocchi 2
☎ 031 281028
✉ 22100

- 🛏 -/- 23 🛏 -/-
👯 🕯 ↑↓ 🔲 🔁 🅾️

★ ★ ★ **Park** (HG)
Viale Rosselli 20
☎ 031 572615 telex 573360 fax 031 574302
✉ 22100

open 01.03 - 30.11
7 🛏 86000/- excl. breakfast 33 🛏 132000/- excl. breakfast
🄰🄴 ⓞ 🄴 ⚏ ⊙ ↕ ⬛ 🄿 ⟨wc⟩ ⟨tv⟩

CORTINA D'AMPEZZO, Belluno   05

★ ★ ★ **Columbia** (HG)
Via Ronco 75
☎ 0436 3607 telex 440066 fax 0436 3607
✉ 32043

open 05.12 - 18.04 + 10.06 - 11.10
* 4 🛏 48000/115000 excl. breakfast 16 🛏 70000/140000 excl. breakfast
🄴 ⚏ ↕ ♨ ⓞ 🄿 ⚲ ⬛ 🄿 ⟨wc⟩ ⟨tv⟩ ⤪

★ ★ ★ ★ ★ **Cristallo** (HCR)
Via Menardi 42
☎ 0436 4281 telex 440090 fax 0436 868058

22 🛏 381000/- excl. breakfast 59 🛏 -/714000 excl. breakfast
↕ 🄿 ⌓ ⚓ ↕ ⬛ ⟨wc⟩

★ ★ ★ **Menardi** (HCR)
Via Majon 112
☎ 0436 2400 telex 440066 fax 0436 862183
✉ 32043

open 18.06 - 19.09 + 22.12 - 07.04
* 18 🛏 70000/130000 33 🛏 110000/200000
🄴 ⚏ ↕ ⓞ 🄿 🄿 ⬛ 🄿 ⟨wc⟩ ⟨tv⟩ ⤪

★ ★ ★ ★ ★ **Miramonti Majestic** (HCR)
Via Pezzie 103
☎ 0436 4201 telex 440069 fax 0436 867019
✉ 32043

open 21.12 - 13.04 + 01.07 - 10.09
27 🛏 200000/450000 excl. breakfast 79 🛏 300000/700000 excl. breakfast
🄰🄴 ⓞ 🄴 ⚏ ⓞ 🄿 🄿 ⚲ ↕ ⬛ 🄿 ⟨tv⟩ ⊙

★ ★ **Montana** (HG)
Corso Italia 94
☎ 0436 862126 fax 0436 868211

open 01.01 - 15.10 + 15.12 - 15.05
* 12 🛏 56000/70000 11 🛏 88000/120000
🄰🄴 ⓞ ⚏ ⊙ 🄿 ↕ ⬛ ⟨wc⟩ ⟨tv⟩ ⊙

COSENZA, Cosenza   21

Agip (MT)
Bivio Strade Statale 107
☎ 0984 839101 telex 912553
res nr 06 4821651
✉ 87100

- 🛏 -/95000 65 🛏 -/144000
🄿 ⬛ 🄿 ⤪

CREMONA, Cremona   09

★ ★ ★ ★ **Motel Agip** (HCR)
Autostr. Brescia-piachza
☎ 0372 434045 telex 340620 fax 0372 451097
✉ 26100

7 🛏 160000/118000 70 🛏 -/-
🄰🄴 ⓞ 🄴 ⚏ ◈ 🄿 ⚲ ↕ ⬛ 🄿 ⟨wc⟩ ⟨tv⟩ ⟨iⓞi⟩

DESENZANO DEL GARDA, Brescia   04

★ ★ ★ **Miralago** (HG)
Viale Dal Molin 27
☎ 030 9141185
✉ 25015

12 🛏 -/- 16 🛏 -/-
🄰🄴 🄴 ⚏ ↕ ⏪ ⚓ ⓞ ◈ 🄿 ⚲ ↕ ⬛ 🄿 ⟨wc⟩ ⟨tv⟩ ⊙

★ ★ ★ **Piccola Vela** (HCR)
Viale Dal Molin 20
☎ 030 9141134 fax 030 9142733
✉ 25015

* 4 🛏 80000/- 39 🛏 130000/-
🄰🄴 ⓞ 🄴 ⚏ ⚓ ⓞ ◈ 🄿 🄿 ⚲ ↕ ⬛ 🄿 ⟨wc⟩ ⟨tv⟩ ⟨iⓞi⟩ �🏠 ⊙ ⤪

★ ★ ★ **Villa Rosa** (HG)
Cesare Battisti 89
☎ 030 9141974

* 1 🛏 -/75000 excl. breakfast 37 🛏 -/100000 excl. breakfast
🄿 🄿 ↕ ⬛ 🄿 ⟨wc⟩ ⤪

DIANO MARINA, Imperia   08

★ ★ ★ **Internazionale** (HA)
☎ 0183 48396
✉ 18013

5 🛏 -/69000 5 🛏 -/120000
↕ ⏪ 🄿 🄿

Motel Panorama (MT)
Viale Torino 64
☎ 0183 45216
✉ 18013

- ✎ -/- 46 ☎ -/-
👤 🚗 P ⛽ ⛄ 🍽 📶 wc

★ ★ Torino (HP)
Via Milano 42
☎ 0183 495106 fax 0183 404602
✉ 18013

open 11.01 - 05.11
* 10 ✎ 60000/75000 excl. breakfast 80 ☎ 70000/
110000 excl. breakfast
👤 ⊙ P ⛽ ⛄ 🍽 📶 wc 🐕 ✈

DOBBIACO, *Bolzano*   04

★ ★ ★ Nocker (HCR)
Dolomiti, 21
☎ 0474 72242 fax 0474 72773
✉ 39034

1 ✎ 35000/45000 23 ☎ 70000/90000
🖥 ⚞ ⊙ ◈ P ⛽ ⛄ 🍽 📶 wc tv ☺

ÉBOLI, *Salerno*   18

★ ★ ★ Grazia (HCR)
☎ 0828 38038
✉ 84025

20 ✎ -/44000 excl. breakfast 62 ☎ -/62000 excl.
breakfast
👤 P ⛽ ⛄ 🍽 📶 wc tv 🍴

FABRIANO, *Ancona*   11

★ ★ ★ ★ Janus (HCR)
Piazza Matteotti 45
☎ 0732 4191
✉ 60044

7 ✎ -/- 75 ☎ -/-
👤 ⊙ P ⛽ ⛄ 🍽 📶 wc 🐕 ✈

FANO, *Pesaro e Urbino*   11

★ ★ ★ Corallo (HR)
Via Leonardo Da Vinci 3
☎ 0721 804200 fax 0721 803637
✉ 61032

open 07.01 - 22.12
* 8 ✎ 55000/60000 excl. breakfast 18 ☎ 75000/
80000 excl. breakfast
AE ⓞ 🖥 ⚞ 👤 🚗 ⊙ P ⛽ 🍽 📶 wc tv 🍴 🏠 ☺

FIANO, *Torino*   02

★ ★ ★ ★ Eurohotel (HG)
Autostrade Firenze- Roma
☎ 0765 255511 fax 0765 255333
✉ 00065

- ✎ 140000/- 100 ☎ -/180000
AE ⓞ ⚞ 👤 ◈ P ⛽ ⛄ 🍽 📶 wc tv ✈

FINALE LÍGURE, *Savona*   08

★ ★ ★ Colibri (HCR)
Cristoforo Colombo 57
☎ 019 692681 telex 211065 fax 019 694206
✉ 17024

* 5 ✎ 55000/92000 36 ☎ 99000/144000
AE ⓞ 🖥 ⚞ 🚗 ⊙ P ⛽ ⛄ 🍽 📶 wc tv 🍴 ☺

★ ★ ★ Orizzonte (HG)
Via Caviglia 67
☎ 019 690624
✉ 17024

4 ✎ -/- 40 ☎ -/-
👤 P ⛽ ⛄ 🍽 📶 wc

FIRENZE, *Firenze*   10

Florence, spread along both banks of the River Arno, is an exquisite treasure chest of paintings, sculptures and Renaissance buildings, a tribute to artists such as Da Vinci, Botticelli and Michelangelo from a golden age which lasted three centuries. Places of interest are all within walking distance of each other, and now that more of the historic centre has been closed to coaches and visiting vehicles, sightseeing is a much pleasanter occupation.
If any one bulding could be said to epitomise the entire city, then it must surely be the *Duomo* (Cathedral), created by the architect Brunelleschi, whose marvellous dome is proof of Renaissance ingenuity. In front of it stands Giotto's handsome campanile, and the Baptistry with Ghiberti's famous bronze doors, often called 'the Gateway to Paradise'. Other architectural gems include the pretty churches of San Miniato (across the river); Santa Maria Novella (near the station) with its many famous works of art; and Santa Croce, containing the tombs of Michelangelo, Machiavelli and Galileo.
Renowned galleries include the world-famous Uffizi; the grand Palazzo Vecchio, the Pitti Palace, with paintings by Titian, Rubens and Raphael, the Accademia, which houses some of Michelangelo's most powerful statues, including the impressive *David*, originally on the Piazza della Signoria; and other museums like the *Bargello* and *San Marco*.
Shoppers will delight in the Via Tornabuoni, one of the most elegant streets in the world, and the Ponte Vecchio, the famous bridge lined with goldsmiths' and jewellers' shops. The biggest market is in the Piazza San Lorenzo (Tue-Sun). The remarkable Straw Market, the *Logge Mercato Nuovo*, near Piazza della Signoria,

sells everything from baskets to men's ties made from straw.
Florentine specialities include *bistecca all fiorentina*, a huge steak usually charcoal-grilled; *fegatelli*, sliced liver rolled in chopped fennel flowers; *Bruschetta*, a type of garlic bread with olive oil; or *baccala*, a robust cod stew. For starters, look out for delicious *prosciutto crudo con fichi*, raw ham with fresh figs. Moderately priced restaurants are to be found near Piazza Santa Croce, Borgo San Lorenzo or San Jacopo.

See cityplan on page 32

★ ★ ★ ★ Agip (MT)
Autostrada Del Sole
☎ 055 4211881 telex 570263 fax 055 4219015
res nr 06 4821651
✉ 50013

20 ♨ 149800/165000 152 ♨ 200000/240000
Ⓐ Ⓞ Ⓔ ⚏ ☙ ◈ Ⓟ ⚒ ↑↓ ▢ Ⓟ Ⓦ Ⓒ Ⓣ ⚡

★ ★ ★ ★ Vivahotel Alexander (HCR)
Viale Giudoni 101
☎ 055 4378951 telex 574026 fax 055 416818
res nr 1678 20080
✉ 50127

* 8 ♨ 155000/206000 80 ♨ 210000/278000
Ⓐ Ⓞ Ⓔ ⚏ ☙ ◈ Ⓟ ⚑ ↑↓ ▢ Ⓟ Ⓦ Ⓒ Ⓣ ⒪ ⚡

★ ★ ★ Astor (HR)
Viale Milton 41
☎ 055 483391 telex 573155
✉ 50129

8 ♨ -/- - ♨ -/-
Ⓐ Ⓞ Ⓔ ⚏ ⚘ ☉ ◈ ⚒ ↑↓ ⚭ ▢ Ⓟ Ⓦ Ⓣ

★ ★ ★ ★ Augustus (HG)
Vicolo Dell' Oro, 5
☎ 055 283054 telex 570110 fax 055 268557
✉ 50123

* 5 ♨ 140000/250000 excl. breakfast
62 ♨ 180000/310000 excl. breakfast
Ⓐ Ⓞ Ⓔ ⚏ ☉ Ⓟ ↑↓ ▢ Ⓟ Ⓦ Ⓒ Ⓣ ⚡

★ ★ ★ ★ Autostrada (HCR)
Viale Luigi Gori 31
☎ 055 316925 telex 574532 fax 055 375277
✉ 50127

12 ♨ 60000/72000 37 ♨ 104000/107000
Ⓞ Ⓔ ⚏ Ⓟ Ⓟ ⚒ ⚔ ↑↓ ▢ Ⓟ Ⓦ ⒪ ⚡

★ ★ ★ ★ Berchielli (HG)
Lungarno Acciaiuoli 14
☎ 055 264061 telex 575582 fax 055 218636
✉ 50123

* 5 ♨ 220000/245000 69 ♨ 300000/350000
Ⓐ Ⓞ Ⓔ ⚏ ⚓ ☉ ⚒ ↑↓ ▢ Ⓟ Ⓣ ⚡

★ ★ ★ Vivahotel Capitol (HCR)
Viale G.amendola 34
☎ 055 2343201 telex 575853 fax 055 2345925
res nr 1678 20080
✉ 50121

* 39 ♨ 100000/125000 53 ♨ 155000/195000
Ⓐ Ⓞ Ⓔ ⚏ ☉ ◈ ↑↓ ▢ Ⓟ Ⓦ Ⓒ Ⓣ ⚡

★ ★ ★ Best Western Hotel Croce Di Malta (HCR)
Via Della Scala 7
☎ 055 218351 telex 570540 fax 055 287121
res nr 1678 20080
✉ 50123

13 ♨ 140000/220000 85 ♨ 190000/330000
Ⓐ Ⓞ Ⓔ ⚏ ☉ ⚒ ⚔ ↑↓ ▢ Ⓟ Ⓦ Ⓒ Ⓣ ⒪ ⚡

See advertisement on page 51

★ ★ ★ Della Signoria (HG)
Via Delle Terme 1
☎ 055 296598 telex
571561 fax 055 216101
✉ 50123

The hotel is situated in
the heart of Florence,
above a row of shops
around the corner from
the Piazza Signoria and
close to the famous
Ponte Vecchio. It is a
comfortable hotel which was recently completely
renovated and which has 27 rooms with air
conditioning, en suite bathroom and TV. There is
a pleasant covered terrace at the front of the third
floor, overlooking the lively bustle in the street.

10 🛏 -/180000 17 🛏 -/230000
🅰🄴 ⓘ 🄴 ⚏ ⓢ ☉ 🛎 †↑ 🖦 🄿 🆆🄲 🆃🆅

★ ★ ★ Vivahotel Fleming (HG)
Viale Guidoni 87
☎ 055 4376773 telex 574027 fax 055 435894
res nr 1678 20080
✉ 50127

* 29 🛏 100000/114000 88 🛏 145000/180000
🅰🄴 ⓘ 🄴 ⚏ 🕔 ◆ 🄿 ⛱ †↑ 🖦 🄿 🆆🄲 🆃🆅 ☻

★ ★ ★ Grand Hotel Majestic
☎ 055 264021 fax 055 268428
✉ 50123

23 🛏 -/- 80 🛏 -/-
🅰🄴 ⓘ 🄴 ⚏ ☉ 🄿 †↑ 🖦 🄿 🆆🄲 🆃🆅 🍽 ☻

★ ★ ★ Grand Hotel Minerva (HCR)
Pza. S. Maria Novella16
☎ 055 284555 telex 570414 fax 055 268281
✉ 50123

* 19 🛏 168000/270000 80 🛏 250000/350000
🅰🄴 ⓘ 🄴 ⚏ ⓢ ☉ ⛱ 🌤 ⚓ †↑ 🖦 🄿 🆆🄲 🆃🆅 🍽

★ ★ ★ Holiday Inn Garden Court (HCR)
Viale Europa 205
☎ 055 6531841 telex 570376 fax 055 6531806
✉ 50126

* - 🛏 -/257000 92 🛏 -/279000
🅰🄴 ⓘ 🄴 ⚏ 🕔 🄿 🌤 ⚓ †↑ 🖦 🄿 🆆🄲 🆃🆅 🍽 ☻

★ ★ ★ Jolly Carlton (HCR)
Piazza Vitt Veneto 4 A
☎ 055 2770 telex 570191 fax 055 294794
✉ 50123

* 41 🛏 -/240000 126 🛏 -/350000
🅰🄴 ⓘ 🄴 ⚏ 🕔 ◆ 🄿 🌤 ⚓ †↑ 🖦 🄿 🆆🄲 🆃🆅 🍽 ☻

★ ★ ★ ★ Best Western Hotel Kraft (HR)
Via Solferino 2
☎ 055 284273 telex 571523 fax 055 2398267
res nr 1678 20080
✉ 50123

* 13 🛏 170000/265000 60 🛏 220000/365000
🅰🄴 ⓘ 🄴 ⚏ ⓢ ☉ 🛎 ⚓ †↑ 🖦 🄿 🆆🄲 🆃🆅 ☻

★ ★ ★ ★ Londra (HCR)
Via J. Da Diacceto 18
☎ 055 2382791 telex 571152 fax 055 210682
✉ 50123

* 30 🛏 -/250000 128 🛏 -/350000
🅰🄴 ⓘ 🄴 ⚏ ☉ 🄿 ⛱ †↑ 🖦 🄿 🆆🄲 🆃🆅 ☻

★ ★ ★ ★ Lungarno (HG)
Borgo San Jacopo 14
☎ 055 264211 telex 570129 fax 055 268437
✉ 50125

* 7 🛏 170000/210000 excl. breakfast
59 🛏 235000/295000 excl. breakfast
🅰🄴 ⓘ 🄴 ⚏ ☉ ◆ 🄿 ⛱ 🌤 †↑ 🖦 🄿 🆃🆅 ☻

★ ★ ★ ★ Martelli (HG)
Via Panzani 8
☎ 055 217151 telex 573137 fax 055 268504
✉ 50123

4 🛏 90000/140000 excl. breakfast 47 🛏 140000/
190000 excl. breakfast
🅰🄴 ⓘ 🄴 ⚏ ⓢ ☉ 🌤 †↑ 🛎 🖦 🄿 🆆🄲 🆃🆅

★ Mia Cara (HG)
Via Faenza 58
☎ 055 216053
✉ 50123

6 🛏 38000/42000 14 🛏 56000/66000
🅰🄴 ⓘ 🄴 ⚏ ☉ 🖦 🄿

★ ★ ★ ★ Mirage (HCR)
Via F. Baracca 231/18
☎ 055 352011 telex 571469
✉ 50127

20 🛏 -/- 68 🛏 -/-
🅰🄴 ⓘ 🄴 ⚏ ◆ 🄿 †↑ 🖦 🆃🆅 🍽 ✖

★ ★ ★ ★ Pullman Astoria (HCR)
Via Del Giglio 9
☎ 055 2398095 telex 571070 fax 055 214632
✉ 50123

* 24 🛏 190000/240000 63 🛏 270000/320000
🅰🄴 ⓘ 🄴 ⚏ ☉ 🌤 †↑ 🖦 🄿 🆆🄲 🆃🆅 🍽 ☻

12 🝙 -/210000 53 🝙 -/280000
AE E ☰ ⅃ ☉ ☂ ↑↓ ▬ 🄿 WC TV ✈

★ ★ ★ Sanremo (HG)
Lungarno Serristori 13
☎ 055 2342823 fax 055 2342269
✉ 50125

* 5 🝙 -/100000 15 🝙 -/150000
☞ ☉ P ↑↓ ▬ 🄿 WC TV ☺

★ ★ ★ ★ Villa Carlotta (HCR)
Via Michele Di Lando 3
☎ 055 2336134 telex 573485 fax 055 2336147
✉ 50125

* 7 🝙 180000/240000 20 🝙 260000/340000
AE ⓪ E ☰ ⅃ ☉ ◈ P 🄿 ⚇ ↑↓ ⌂ ▬ 🄿 WC TV ☺

★ ★ ★ ★ Relais Certosa
Via Di Colle Ramole 2
☎ 055 2047171 telex 574332 fax 055 268575
✉ 50124

* 5 🝙 220000/- 64 🝙 220000/295000
AE ⓪ E ☰ ☉ ◈ P ⚇ ↑↓ ▬ 🄿 WC TV 🍴 ☺

★ ★ ★ Best Western Hotel Rivoli AA ANWB
(HG)
Via Della Scala 33
☎ 055 282853 telex
571004 fax 055 294041
res nr 1678 20080
✉ 50123
The Best Western Hotel
Rivoli is situated near
the central station in the
centre of Florence and
within walking distance

of the town's tourist attractions. It is a pleasant
hotel that was completely renovated and mod-
ernised in 1990. The rooms feature air conditioning and have bath, TV and a minibar. After a long,
tiring day spent sightseeing in the city, the guests
can relax in the swimming pool, sauna and on the
terrace behind the hotel.

★ ★ ★ **Villa le Rondini** (HR)

AA ANWB

Via Bolognese Vecchia224
℡ 055 400081 telex 575679 fax 055 268212
✉ 50139

Hotel Villa le Rondini consists of three elegant villas. At 6km from Florence, they are peacefully situated on the Monterinaldi which is covered with cypresses and olive trees and overlooks the city. Good taste and refinement are the characteristics of the restaurant, public rooms and the comfortable bedrooms. The big private park spans 22ha and contains a swimming pool, tennis court and riding stables. To get to the hotel, follow the road leading from Florence in the direction of Bologna. A public service bus stops there every 20 minutes.

* 4 126500/159500 39 203500/253000

FORTE DEI MARMI, *Lucca* 09

★ ★ ★ ★ **Best Western Hotel Park Raffaeli** (HCR)
Via Mazzini 37
℡ 0584 81494 telex 590239 fax 0584 81498
res nr 1678 20080
✉ 55042

5 116000/178000 29 172000/296000

★ ★ ★ **Piccolo** (HR)
Via Morin Zu 24
℡ 0584 80332 fax 0584 86203
✉ 55042

7 -/120000 excl. breakfast 28 -/180000 excl. breakfast

FROSINONE, *Frosinone* 14

★ ★ ★ ★ **Astor Hotel Bracaglia** (HCR)
Via Casillina Nord 83
℡ 0775 270131 fax 0775 270135
✉ 03100

- 78780/106050 excl. breakfast 52 111100/191900 excl. breakfast

GABICCE MARE, *Pesaro e Urbino* 11

De Bona (HR)
Via Panoramica 27
℡ 0541 962622
✉ 61011

10 -/- 40 -/-

★ ★ ★ **Marinella** (HCR)
Via Veneto 127
℡ 0541 954371 fax 0541 950426
✉ 61011

open 01.04 - 30.09
* - -/60000 51 -/100000

★ ★ **Panoramic** (HP)
Via Redipuqlia 29
℡ 0541 954722 telex 550535
✉ 61011

1 -/- 20 -/-

GABICCE MONTE, *Pesaro e Urbino* 11

★ ★ ★ ★ **Capo Est** (HCR)
Via Panoramica 123
℡ 0541 953333 telex 550637 fax 0541 952735
✉ 61011

18 -/160000 excl. breakfast 66 -/260000 excl. breakfast

GARDA, *Verona* 04

★ ★ ★ **Bisesti** (HCR)

AA ANWB

Corso Italia 44
℡ 045 7255766 telex 480154 fax 045 7255927
✉ 37016

Hotel Bisesti is situated in the centre of Garda, only 100m from the beach on the east side of the lake. It is a tastefully designed holiday hotel where most of the rooms have a private bathroom and most have a balcony. Tables with parasols and chairs are scattered around the garden which contains the spacious swimming pool with sunbathing terrace.

open 01.03 - 31.10
4 45000/90000 excl. breakfast 86 56000/112000 excl. breakfast

Forte dei Marmi

Tuscany coast

Piccolo Hotel

◆

Marvellous green location,
30 metres from the beach. Garden
and parking area. All rooms with
bath/shower, balcony and
telephone, television. Lift available.
Full board from ITL 120.000 to
ITL 200.000.

Ask for the folder.
Tel.: 0584-80332.
Fax: 0584-86203.

★ ★ **Capinera** (HG)
Via Delle Viole
☎ 045 7255409
✉ 37016

 AA ANWB

The Hotel Pension
Capinera is situated in
the centre of Garda, on
the sunny eastern bank
of the lake. It is an
average sized family
hotel with a personal
atmosphere. Most of
the rooms have a toilet, shower and balcony. If
the beach is occasionally too busy, the Capinera
roof terrace offers a sunny alternative.

open 26.04 - 11.10
5 ⊞ 50000/65000 24 ⊞ 67000/88000
⊙ P ⛺ ⇅ ⊡ WC ⤫

★ ★ **San Marco** (HCR)
Largo Pisanello
☎ 045 7255008
fax 045 7256749
✉ 37016

AA ANWB

Hotel San Marco is in a
wonderful position,
close to Lake Garda and
the centre. It has 15
well kept rooms, fully
equipped with modern
comforts. Drinks can be
enjoyed in the pleasant bar, and there is a range
of good food on the restaurant menu. The hotel
also has its own parking. Lake Garda offers a
variety of water sports; sailing and surfing les-
sons can be booked in the hotel, which provides
lock-up storage facilities for surfboards.

open 01.03 - 30.10
- ⊞ -/- 15 ⊞ -/180000 excl. breakfast
⚓ ⊛ ⇔ ⊙ P ⛺ ⇅ ⊡ WC |⊙| ⬆ ⤫

GARDONE RIVIERA, *Brescia*   04

Astoria (HP)
Via Spiaggia D' Oro
☎ 0365 20761 telex 301088
✉ 25083

5 ⊞ -/- 81 ⊞ -/-
⚓ ⇔ P ⛺ ⇅ ⇆ ⇅ ⊟ ⊡ WC |⊙| ⤫

★ ★ ★ **Montefiori** (HCR)
Via Dei Lauri 12
☎ 0365 21118 fax 0365 21488
✉ 25083

5 ⊞ -/80000 45 ⊞ -/130000
AE ⓪ ⊟ ⚓ ⑤ P ⛺ ⇅ ⇆ ⊟ ⊡ WC TV ⬆ ⊙

★ ★ ★ **Best Western Hotel Spiaggia d'Oro**
(HCR)
Via Spiaggia D' Oro 1
☎ 0365 290034 telex 301088 fax 0365 290092
res nr 1678 20080
✉ 25083

open 05.04 - 30.10
* 6 ⊞ 140000/155000 36 ⊞ 240000/270000
AE ⓪ ⊟ ⊟ ⇔ ⇔ ⑤ P ⛺ ⇅ ⇆ ⇅ ⊟ TV |⊙| ⊙

GATTÉO A MARE, Forli 10

★ ★ Flamingo (HR)
Viale Giulio Cesare 31
☎ 0547 87171
✉ 47043

1 🛏 -/60000 excl. breakfast 45 🛏 -/90000 excl. breakfast
🏊 ⛱ ♨ ⁑ 🅿 WC 🐕

★ ★ ★ Simon (HR)
Via Matteoi 41
☎ 0547 85224 telex 583449 fax 0547 85885
✉ 47043

open 01.03 - 23.09
3 🛏 30000/55000 42 🛏 60000/100000
🏊 🚗 ⊙ 🅿 ⁑ ♨ ⁑ 🍴 🅿 WC TV 🍽 🛗 ☺

★ ★ ★ Welt (HCR)
Via Milano
☎ 0547 86468

- 🛏 -/- 34 🛏 -/-
🏊 🚗 🅿 ⁑ 🖥 WC

GÈNOVA, Genova 08

★ ★ ★ ★ Best Western Hotel City   [AA] ANWB
(HR)
Via San Sebastiano 6
☎ 010 5545 telex
271686 fax 010 586301
res nr 1678 20080
✉ 16123
Situated in the centre of
Genoa, the Hotel City is
found in a side street off
the Via Roma and yet is
pleasantly peaceful. It
has 7 floors and 75 well kept rooms equipped
with all modern amenities: air conditioning,
bathroom, radio, TV and also a minibar. The hotel
has its own secure locked garage where guests
can park their cars.

* 7 🛏 130000/230000 44 🛏 190000/350000
[AE] ⓪ [E] 🚌 🏊 ⊙ ⛱ ⁑ 🖥 🅿 WC TV

★ ★ ★ ★ Jolly Hotel Plaza (HCR)
Via Martin Piaggio 11
☎ 010 893641 telex 283142 fax 010 891850
✉ 16122

17 🛏 -/21000 80 🛏 -/33000
[AE] ⓪ [E] 🚌 ⊙ 🅿 ⁑ 🖥 🅿 WC TV 🍽 ☺

★ ★ ★ ★ Savoia Majestic (HCR)
Piazza Stazione Principe
☎ 010 261641 telex 270426 fax 010 261883
✉ 16126

40 🛏 -/- 80 🛏 -/-
[AE] ⓪ [E] 🚌 ⊙ 🅿 ⁑ ⁑ 🖥 🅿 WC TV 🍽 ☺

GÈNOVA/NERVI, Genova 08

★ ★ ★ ★ Astor (HCR)
Viale Delle Palme 16
NERVI
☎ 010 3728325 telex 286577 fax 010 3728486
✉ 16167

* 26 🛏 117000/163500 excl. breakfast
29 🛏 163500/216500 excl. breakfast
[AE] ⓪ [E] 🚌 🏊 🚗 🅿 ⛱ ⁑ ♨ ⁑ 🖥 🅿 WC TV 🍽 🐕

GIULIANOVA, Teramo 15

★ ★ ★ ★ Don Juan (HR)
Lungomare Zara 97
☎ 085 8002341 telex 600061 fax 085 8004805
✉ 64022

open 20.05 - 27.09
* 10 🛏 70000/95000 138 🛏 120000/150000
[AE] ⓪ [E] 🚌 🏊 🚗 ⊙ 🅿 ⁑ ♨ ⁑ 🍴 🖥 🅿 WC TV 🍽 ☺

GOLFO ARANCI, Sassari 12

★ ★ ★ Gabbiano Azzurro (HCR)
Via Dei Gabbiani
☎ 0789 46929 fax 0789 615056
✉ 07020

open 01.06 - 30.09
6 🛏 70000/105000 excl. breakfast 50 🛏 90000/
120000 excl. breakfast
[AE] 🏊 🚗 🅿 🅿 ⛱ ♨ ⁑ 🖥 🅿 WC TV 🛗 ☺

GOZZANO, Novara 03

★ ★ ★ Nuova Italia (HCR)
Beltrami F 19
☎ 0322 94393 telex 223329 fax 0322 93774
✉ 28024

open 01.02 - 05.01
4 🛏 70000/80000 excl. breakfast 32 🛏 106000/
112000 excl. breakfast
[E] 🚌 🏊 ⊙ ◈ 🅿 ⛱ ♨ ⁑ 🖥 WC TV 🍽 🛗 ☺

★ ★ ★ **Il Guscio** (HG)
Via Venezia 5
☎ 0431 82200
✉ 34073

open 20.04 - 10.10
* 2 ♨ 45000/55000 10 ✍ 80000/85000
🚃 ⅄ 🚗 ⊙ 🅿 ⚐ ↟ ⊟ 🄴 🆆 🍽 ☺

GROSSETO, *Grosseto* 13

★ ★ ★ **Agip** (HCR)
Aurelia Sud Km 779
☎ 0564 24100 fax 0564 24123
res nr 06 4821651
✉ 58100

- ♨ 50000/- 32 ✍ 83000/-
◐ ◈ 🅿 ⚐ ⊟ 🄴 🆅 🍽 ☺

GRADO, *Gorizia* 06

★ ★ ★ ★ **Adria** (HCR)
Viale Europa Unita 18
☎ 0431 80037 telex 460594 fax 0431 83519
✉ 34073

8 ♨ 90000/- 63 ✍ 160000/-
🚗 ⊙ 🅿 ↟ ⚐ ↟ ⊟ 🄴 🆆 🍽 🐕 ☺

★ ★ ★ **Al Bosco** (HCR)
La Rotta
☎ 0431 80485
✉ 34073

9 ♨ -/46000 excl. breakfast 25 ✍ -/80000 excl. breakfast
⅄ 🚗 ◐ 🅿 ⚐ ↟ 🄴 🆆 🍽 🐾

★ ★ **Cristina** (HCR)
Viale Mart. D Liberta 11
☎ 0431 80989
✉ 34073

open 01.04 - 30.09
5 ♨ 31000/35000 excl. breakfast 21 ✍ 54000/64000 excl. breakfast
⅄ 🚗 ◐ 🅿 ⚐ ⊟ 🄴 🆆 🍽 ↟ ☺

ISCHIA, *Napoli*   **17**

★ ★ ★ ★ **Jolly** (HCR)
Via De Luca 42
☎ 081 991744 telex 710267 fax 081 993156
✉ 80077

- *a* -/175000 208 *æ* -/320000
[AE] ⓪ [E] ⚒ ⊙ [P] ⚓ ⚔ ⚙ ↕ 🔌 🔲 ⊡ [TV] ❘◎❘ ⋔ ❌

★ ★ ★ **Miramare e Castello** (HCR)
Via Pontano 5
☎ 081 991333
✉ 80077

5 *a* -/- 40 *æ* -/-
⚓ [P] ⚙ ↕ 🔲 ⊡ [WC] ⋔

ISOLA DI STRÓMBOLI, *Messina*   **17**

★ ★ **Villaggio Stromboli** (HCR)
Via Regina Elena
☎ 090 986018 telex 980120 fax 090 986298
✉ 98050

open 01.04 - 30.10
* 2 *a* 60000/- excl. breakfast 28 *æ* -/100000 excl.
breakfast
[AE] ⋋ ⚓ ◎ ⚙ ⊡ [WC] ❘◎❘ ⊛

LA CALETTA, *Nuoro*   **12**

★ ★ ★ **La Caletta** (HCR)
Via Cagliari 26
☎ 0784 810077 fax 0784 810505
✉ 08029

12 *a* -/- 100 *æ* -/-
⋋ ⚓ ◎ [P] ⚙ ⚔ ↕ 🔌 🔲 ⊡ [WC] ❘◎❘ ⋔ ❌

LACCO AMENO, *Napoli*   **17**

★ ★ ★ ★ ★ **Regina Isabella Sporting** (HR)
Piazza Santa Restituta
☎ 081 994322 telex 710120
✉ 80076

46 *a* -/267000 87 *æ* -/480000
⋋ ⚓ ◎ [P] ⚓ ⚔ ↕ [WC] ⋔

LAIGUÉGLIA, *Savona*   **08**

★ ★ ★ ★ **Résidence Laiguéglia** (HR)
Plazza Liberte 14
☎ 0182 690001 fax 0182 690003
✉ 17020

open 01.04 - 31.10
* - *a* 65000/110000 excl. breakfast 38 *æ* 65000/
135000 excl. breakfast
[AE] ⓪ ⚒ ⋋ ◎ ⚓ ⚙ ↕ 🔲 [WC] [TV] ❘◎❘

LA SPÈZIA, *La Spezia*   **09**

★ ★ **Diana** (HG)
Via Colombo 30
☎ 0187 25120
✉ 19100

4 *a* -/40000 15 *æ* -/65000
⊙ ⊡ [WC]

★ ★ ★ ★ **Jolly** (HCR)
Via 20 Settembre 2
☎ 0187 27200 telex 281047 fax 0187 22129
✉ 19100

* 33 *a* 125000/195000 80 *æ* 185000/270000
[AE] ⓪ [E] ⚒ ⚓ ⊙ ⚙ ↕ 🔲 ⊡ [WC] [TV] ❘◎❘ ⊛

LAVENO-MOMBELLO, *Varese*   **03**

★ ★ ★ **Moderno** (HG)
Via Garibaldi 15
☎ 0332 668373
✉ 21014

open 01.03 - 31.10
* - *a* 52000/70000 excl. breakfast 14 *æ* 71500/
90000 excl. breakfast
⚒ ⊙ ⚓ ↕ 🔲 ⊡ [WC] ⊛

LECCO, *Como*   **03**

★ ★ ★ **Moderno** (HG)
Piazza Diaz 5
☎ 0341 286519
✉ 22053

6 *a* 40000/50000 excl. breakfast 17 *æ* 70000/
80000 excl. breakfast
[AE] ⓪ [E] ⚒ ⊙ [P] ⚓ 🔲 ⊡ [WC] [TV] ⊛

LENNO, *Como*   **03**

★ ★ **Roma** (HCR)
Via Lomazzi 25
☎ 0344 55137
✉ 22016

6 *a* -/- 21 *æ* -/-
⋋ ⊕ ⚓ [P] ⚓ ⚙ ↕ 🔲 ⊡ [WC] ❘◎❘

LESA, *Novara*   **03**

★ ★ **Isoletta** (HCR)
Sempione 37
☎ 0322 7326 fax 0322 76646
✉ 28040

2 *a* -/- 26 *æ* -/-
[AE] ⓪ [E] ⚒ ⚓ ⊙ ◈ [P] ⚓ ⚙ 🔲 ⊡ ❘◎❘ ⋔ ⊛

LÉVANTO, *La Spezia*　08

★ ★ ★ Dora (HCR)
Via Martiri Della Lib.27
☎ 0187 808168
✉ 19015

4 ⌂ 35000/- 34 ⌸ 58000/-
🅴 ⌷ ⚡ 🅿 🅟 🍴 ⌷ 📺 WC ⦿

LÉVICO TERME, *Trento*　05

★ ★ Levico (HCR)
Viale Vittorio Emanuelle
☎ 0461 706335
✉ 38056

15 ⌂ 50000/- 27 ⌸ -/80000
🅿 🍴 ⌷ WC ⦿ ⚞

LIDO DEGLI ESTENSI, *Ferrara*　10

★ ★ ★ Conca Del Lido (HP)
V. Le G. Pascoli 42
☎ 0533 327459 telex 522151 fax 0533 327934
✉ 44024

4 ⌂ -/53000 excl. breakfast 55 ⌸ -/69000 excl.
breakfast
🅿 ⦿ 🅿 🅟 🍴 ⌷ 📺 WC 📺 ⦿

★ ★ ★ Tropicana (HCR)
Via Ugo Foscolo 2
☎ 0533 327301 fax 0533 327673
✉ 44024

open 01.04 - 30.09
21 ⌂ 50000/70000 40 ⌸ 80000/100000
🆎 ⓪ 🅴 ⌷ ⚡ ⦿ 🅿 🅟 🍴 ⌷ WC ⦿

LIDO DI CAMAIORE, *Lucca*　09

★ ★ ★ ★ Grandhotel e Riviera (HR)
Lungomare Pistelli 59
☎ 0584 617571 telex 502180 fax 0584 619533
res nr 1678 20080
✉ 55043
open 01.04 - 31.10
* 13 ⌂ 150000/180000 51 ⌸ 200000/240000
🆎 ⓪ 🅴 ⌷ ⚡ ⦿ 🅿 🍴 ⌷ WC 📺 ⦿

LIDO DI JÉSOLO, *Venezia*　06

★ ★ Ancora (HCR)
Via Baf. 14 Ac Al Mare 4
☎ 0421 370507
✉ 30017

12 ⌂ -/- 55 ⌸ -/-
⌷ ⦿ ⚡ 🍴 ⌷ WC ⦿

★ ★ ★ Anthony (HCR)
Via Padova 25
☎ 0421 971711 telex 420124 fax 0421 370979
✉ 30017

12 ⌂ -/- 47 ⌸ -/-
⌷ ⦿ ◆ 🅿 🅟 ⚡ 🍴 ⌷ WC 📺 ⦿ ⚞ ⚞

★ ★ ★ Aurora (HCR)
Piazza Aurora 8
☎ 0421 972027 fax 0421 370971
✉ 30017

19 ⌂ -/- 58 ⌸ -/-
⦿ ◆ 🅿 🅟 ⚡ 🍴 ⌷ WC 📺 ⦿

★ ★ ★ Byron Bellavista (HCR)
Via Padova 85
☎ 0421 371023 fax 0421 371073
✉ 30017

12 ⌂ -/100000 excl. breakfast 36 ⌸ -/115000 excl.
breakfast
🆎 ⓪ 🅴 ⌷ ⚡ ⦿ 🅿 🅟 ⚡ 🍴 ⌷ WC ⦿ ⦿

★ ★ ★ Cambridge (HCR)
Via Bafile 431
☎ 0421 972751 telex 410687 fax 0421 971638
✉ 30017

- ⌂ -/- 80 ⌸ -/-
⦿ 🅿 🅟 ⚡ 🍴 ⌷ WC ⦿ ⚞ ⦿

★ ★ ★ Danmark (HCR)
Via Airone 1
☎ 0421 961013 telex 410433 fax 0421 362389
✉ 30017

open 01.05 - 30.09
* 11 ⌂ 45000/80000 47 ⌸ 80000/120000
🅴 ⌷ ⚡ ⦿ 🅿 🅟 ⚡ 🍴 ⌷ WC ⚞
See advertisement on page 59

★ ★ ★ **Lilia** (HCR)
Viale Venezia
☎ 0421 380257
fax 0421 380670
✉ 30017

Hotel Lilia is a peacefully situated holiday hotel
in the centre of Lido di
Jesolo, only 30m from
the beach. All the
rooms have a balcony
and a private bathroom.
The restaurant's speciality is the Venetian cuisine.
The guests can enjoy a drink in the relaxed bar or
on the pleasant covered terrace. The Hotel Lilia
shares the use of leisure facilities, such as a
tennis court and fitness room, with some of the
other hotels nearby.

5 ♪ 26000/42000 30 ☞ 50000/82000
🏊 � ⊙ 🅿 ♊ 🎾 †↕ 🖵 🚾 🔊 🐕

★ ★ ★ ★ **Majestic Toscanelli** (HCR)
Via Canova 2
☎ 0421 371331 telex 420366 fax 0421 371054
✉ 30017

open 15.05 - 20.09
* 6 ♪ 62000/77000 49 ☞ 110000/140000
🚶⊙🅿♊🏊†↕🖵🚾📺🐕

★ ★ ★ ★ **Park Brasilia** (HCR)
V Levantina 2 Acc Al
Mar
☎ 0421 380851 telex
410433 fax 0421 92244
✉ 30017

The Park Hotel Brasilia
is a mature beach hotel;
due to recent reno-
vation, it now has a very
modern appearance.
The interior has also
benefited from this modernisation, taking in the
fashionable public rooms, restaurant and bar. The
luxurious bedooms (all with balcony) are
equipped with all the modern amenities. On one
side of the hotel is a spacious garden, and in the
front there is a swimming pool with terrace and
deck chairs.

* 6 ♪ 80000/110000 34 ☞ 128000/190000
AE ⓪ E ⚡ 👤 🚶 ⊙ 🅿 🎾 ♊ 🏊 †↕ 🖵 🚾 📺 🔊 🐕

★ ★ ★ **Regina** (HCR)
Via Bafile 115
☎ 0421 380383 telex 410433 fax 0421 93522
✉ 30017

6 ♪ -/- 49 ☞ -/-
🚶 ⊙ ◆ 🅿 ♊ †↕ 🖵 🚾 🔊 🐕

★ ★ ★ **Tahiti** (HCR)
Via Dante Alighieri 44
☎ 0421 380465 telex 433031 fax 0421 362060
✉ 30017

10 ♪ -/- 79 ☞ -/-
👤 🚶 ⊙ 🅿 ♊ †↕ 🖵 🚾 🔊 🏠 🐕

LIDO DI VENÉZIA, *Venezia*   05

★ ★ ★ ★ **Biasutti** (HCR)
V. Dandolo 29
☎ 041 5260120 telex 410666 fax 041 5261259
✉ 30126

open 15.01 - 15.12
* 10 ♪ 100000/250000 60 ☞ 180000/380000
AE ⓪ E ⚡ 👤 🚶 ⊙ 🅿 ♊ †↕ 🖵 🚾 📺 🔊 🐕

★ ★ **Villa Pannonia** (HCR)
Via Doge Michiel 48
☎ 041 5260162 fax 041 5265277
✉ 30126

open 27.12 - 22.12
* 6 ♪ 44000/94000 24 ☞ 84000/131000
AE ⓪ E ⚡ 👤 🚶 ⊙ 🅿 📞 🖵 🚾 🐕

LIGNANO RIVIERA, *Udine*   06

★ ★ ★ ★ **Arizona** (HCR)
Calle Prassitele 2
☎ 0431 428529 fax 0431 427373
✉ 33054

open 15.05 - 20.09
* 5 ♪ 62000/72000 36 ☞ 110000/196000
E ⚡ 👤 ⊙ ◆ 🅿 ♊ †↕ 🖵 🚾 🔊 🐕

★ ★ ★ ★ **Eurotel** (HCR)
Calle Mendelssohn 13
☎ 0431 428992 telex 450211
✉ 33054

5 ♪ -/90000 55 ☞ -/150000
AE ⓪ E ⚡ 👤 🏊 🚶 🅿 ♊ 🏊 †↕ 🖵 🚾 🏠 🐕

HOTEL DANMARK

I-30017 LIDO DI JESOLO (Venice)

**Via Airone 1/3 - tel.:0421-961013
(from 1.10 to 30.4 inclusive tel:92389)
Fax 362389**

The ideal hotel for a stay by the sea between the greenery of pine woods and a large peaceful beach. The hotel has a private beach, swimming pool, parking area, garden and park. Excellent cuisine and à la carte menu. English, French and German spoken.

LIGNANO SABBIADORO, *Udine*   **06**
See advertisement on page 61

★ ★ Ambra (HCR)
Lungomare Trieste 126
☏ 0431 71027 fax 0431 71600
✉ 33050

open 01.05 - 25.09
15 ▯ -/- 33 ▯ 40000/44000
🚗⊙◈🅿🏊↑▮🖥🚽WC⏺☺

★ ★ ★ Bella Venezia Mare (HCR)
Arco Del Grecale 18a
☏ 0431 422184 fax 0431 422352
✉ 33054

open 15.05 - 15.09
* 1 ▯ 53000/73000 39 ▯ 94000/134000
AE⊙E▰🚗⊙◈🅿🏊↑▮🖥🚽WC⏺☺

★ ★ ★ Columbus (HP)
Lungomare Trieste 22
☏ 0431 71516

12 ▯ -/- 48 ▯ -/-
▮🚗🅿🖥▮🚽WC

★ ★ ★ Medusa Splendid (HCR)
Raggio Dello Scirocco 13
☏ 0431 422211 fax 0431 422251
✉ 33054

8 ▯ -/76000 excl. breakfast 48 ▯ -/106000 excl. breakfast
🚗⊙◈🅿🏊↑▮🖥🚽WCTV⏺↑☺

★ ★ ★ Vittoria (HCR)
Lungomare Trieste 14
☏ 0431 71241 fax 0431 73292

open 10.05 - 30.09
* 1 ▯ 52000/67000 47 ▯ 78000/104000
▰▮🚗⊙🅿🏊↑▮🖥🚽WC🐎

LIMONE SUL GARDA, *Brescia*   **04**

★ Lido (HCR)
☏ 0365 954100
✉ 25010

1 ▯ -/- 25 ▯ -/90000 excl. breakfast
▮🚗🅿🖥🚽WC

LIVORNO/STAGNO, *Livorno*   08

★ ★ ★ ★ **Motel Agip** (MT)
Aurelia 25
LIVORNO
☎ 0586 943067 telex 502049 fax 0586 943483
✉ 57017

10 *ð* -/- 40 *æ* -/-
AE ⓪ E ☎ ◈ P ↟ 🖪 🖵 WC TV 🍽 ☺

LOANO, *Savona*   08

★ ★ ★ **Garden Lido** (HP)
Lungomare N.sauro 9
☎ 019 669666 telex 213178
✉ 17025

12 *ð* -/75000 excl. breakfast 77 *æ* -/103000 excl.
breakfast
🐎 🐾 ⊙ P 👆 ↟ 🖪 🖵 WC 🍽 🏇

★ ★ **Perelli** (HCR)
Corso Roma 13
☎ 019 668002

11 *ð* -/68000 excl. breakfast 30 *æ* -/100000 excl.
breakfast   .
🐾 ⊙ P ↟ 🖪 🖵 WC 🏇

LUÍNO, *Varese*   03

★ ★ ★ **Ancora** (HCR)
Piazza Liberta 7
☎ 0332 530451 fax 0332 530451
✉ 21016

open 01.03 - 30.11
* 4 *ð* 54000/60000 10 *æ* 78000/88000
E ☎ 🐾 ⊙ 👆 👆 🖵 WC TV 🍽 ☺

★ ★ **Internazionale** (HG)
Piazza Marconi
☎ 0332 530193
✉ 21016

12 *ð* -/49000 excl. breakfast 28 *æ* -/60000 excl.
breakfast
🐎 ⊙ P ↟ 🖪 🖵 WC

MACERATA, *Macerata*   11

★ ★ ★ ★ **Agip** (HCR)
Via Roma 149
☎ 0733 34248 fax 0733 32722
✉ 62100

- *ð* -/- 51 *æ* -/153000
🐎 🐾 ⓪ P ↟ 🖪 🖵 WC TV 🏇

MACOMER, *Nuoro*   12

★ ★ ★ **Agip** (MT)
Corso Umberto 1
☎ 0785 71066 fax 0785 72631
res nr 06 4821651
✉ 08015

- *ð* -/- 96 *æ* -/99000
🐎 ⓪ P 👆 🖪 🖵 WC TV 🍽 ☺

MADERNO, *Brescia*   04

Benaco (HCR)
☎ 0365 641110
✉ 25080

1 *ð* -/- 25 *æ* -/-
P 👆 🖪 🖵

MADONNA DI CAMPIGLIO, *Trento*   04

★ ★ ★ ★ **Cristallo** (HCR)
Via Dolomiti
☎ 0465 41132 telex 401148 fax 0465 40687
✉ 38084

open 01.12 - 20.04 + 20.06 - 10.09
* 5 *ð* 150000/295000 38 *æ* 250000/480000
AE ⓪ ☎ 🐎 🐾 ⊙ P 👆 🤾 ↟ 🖪 🖵 WC TV 🍽 🛗 ☺

MALCÉSINE, *Verona*   04

★ ★ **Sirena** (HCR)
Viale Roma 4
☎ 045 7400019
✉ 37018

open 01.04 - 18.10
2 *ð* 32000/40000 22 *æ* 56000/76000
🐎 🐾 P 🤾 ↟ 🖵 WC 🛗

★ ★ **Vega** (HCR)
Viale Roma 10
☎ 045 7400151 telex 480448 fax 045 7400151
✉ 37018

3 *ð* -/- 16 *æ* -/-
AE ⓪ E ☎ 🐎 🐾 🐾 ⊙ P 👆 🤾 ↟ 🖪 🖵 WC TV 🏇

The peninsula of Lignano joined up to the international road network is located between Venice and Trieste and offers one of the most beautiful bathing beaches of Italy. This shallow beach, 8 km long and 100 metres wide, is especially suitable for children. Bathing facilities, good hotels and guest houses. Villas and furnished dwellings for rent, camp sites and other tourist amenities. 8 marinas with moorings for more than 5500 boats. Sailing, mini golf, tennis, roller-skating rink, riding school, bowling, target shooting. Entertainment. Packages. Dance-hall. Thermal facilities. Zoological garden. Park with water sports facilities. 18 hole golf course.

Information:
Tourist Office I-33054
LIGNANO SABBIADORO - Via Latisana, 42
Tel.: 0431-71821 - Telefax: 0431-70449
Telex: 450 193 LIGNI

Lignano Sabbiadoro: see also page 59

MÁLLES VENOSTA/RESCHEN, *Bolzano*   04

★ ★ ★ **Garberhof** (HCR)   🅰🅰 *ANWB*
Staatsstr 25
MÁLLES VENOSTA
☎ 0473 81399
fax 0473 81950
✉ 39024

The Hotel Garberhof is a fairly new hotel peacefully situated one km from Malles and surrounded by the meadows and mountains of Obervinschgau. The tone is set by the design of the hotel, which incorporates various types of wood, both on the outside, and inside in the dining rooms and bedrooms. The bedrooms are fitted out with a range of modern comforts and feature a balcony or terrace. There is a sauna in the basement of the hotel and a swimming pool with a superb view.

1 ⌑ 65000/70000 28 ⌗ 110000/120000
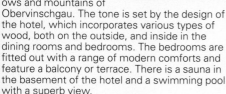

MARCIANA MARINA, *Livorno*   12

★ ★ ★ **Gabbiano Azzurro** (HCR)
☎ 0565 997035 fax 0565 99497
✉ 57033

* 9 ⌑ 50000/100000 51 ⌗ 90000/300000
🅰🅴 ⌗ ⊙ 🅿 ⍟ ⌗ ⌗ ⌗ ⌗ 🅿 🆆🅲 🆃🆅 🍽 ✈
See advertisement on page 63

★ ★ **Imperia** (HP)
☎ 0565 99082

1 ⌑ -/- 20 ⌗ -/-
⌗ 🅿 🆆🅲

MARGHERA, *Venezia*   05

★ ★ ★ ★ **Agip** (MT)
Rotonda Romea 1
☎ 041 936900 telex 223446 fax 041 936960
res nr 06 4821651
✉ 30175

- ⌑ -/- 188 ⌗ -/240000
🅰🅴 ⓪ 🅴 ⌗ ◐ ◆ 🅿 ⌗ 🅿 🆆🅲 🆃🆅 🍽 ⊙

ITALY

62 ITALY

MARGHERA/VENEZIA, *Venezia*   05

★ ★ ★ **Vienna** (HCR)
Via Rizzardi 54
MARGHERA
☎ 041 936600 fax 041 936856
✉ 30175

10 🛏 -/89000 excl. breakfast 62 🛏 -/126000 excl.
breakfast
🆎 💿 📧 ≡ ♨ ⊙ 🅿 🛎 †↓ ⊷ 🔲 🄿 📶 📺 🍴 ☺

MARINA DI CAMPO, *Livorno*   12

★ ★ ★ ★ **Montecristo** (HCR)
☎ 0565 976861 telex 590220 fax 0565 976597
✉ 57034

open Easter - 31.10
9 🛏 70000/180000 34 🛏 120000/300000
🆎 💿 📧 ≡ ⊷ 🅿 ⚓ †↓ 🔲 🄿 📶 📺 🦮

★ ★ ★ **Thomas** (HP)
Via Giannutri
☎ 0565 97286
fax 0565 976870
✉ 57034

AA ANWB

The Hotel Thomas is
situated on the island of
Elba, opposite the west
coast of Italy, in the
small town of Marina di
Campo, 150m from the
sea. It is a small hotel
with 25 rooms, most of which have a private
toilet and shower. The rustically furnished restaurant offers guests a choice of Italian culinary
delights. There is a cosy terrace, and shaded
parking for the car.

- 🛏 -/- 25 🛏 -/60000 excl. breakfast
⚓ 🅿 🛎 ⊷ 🄿 📶 🦮

Villa Edy (HP)
Via Lungomare 315
☎ 0565 680808
✉ 57034

- 🛏 -/- 21 🛏 -/-
⚓ ⊷ 🅿 🛎 ⊷ 🄿 📶 📺 🍴

MARINA DI RAVENNA, *Ravenna*   10

★ ★ ★ ★ **Parkhotel Ravenna** (HCR)
Viale Delle Nazioni 181
☎ 0544 531743 telex 550185 fax 0544 530430
✉ 48023

open 24.03 - 30.11
* 3 🛏 130000/160000 141 🛏 205000/240000
🆎 💿 📧 ≡ ♨ ⊷ 🅿 🛎 †↓ 🔲 📶 📺 🍴

MARSALA, *Trapani*   17

★ ★ ★ **Agip** (MT)
Via Mazara 14
☎ 0923 953003
res nr 06 4821651
✉ 91025

- 🛏 -/60000 41 🛏 -/97000
🆎 💿 📧 ≡ 🅿 †↓ 🔲 🄿 📺 🦮

MATÉLICA, *Macerata*   11

★ ★ ★ **Motel Agip** (HCR)
☎ 0737 85981
res nr 06 4821651
✉ 62024

- 🛏 -/41000 16 🛏 -/72000
🅿 🔲 🄿 🦮

MAZARA DEL VALLO, *Trapani*   17

★ ★ ★ **Hopps** (HCR)
☎ 0923 946133 telex 911261
✉ 91026

- 🛏 -/- 235 🛏 -/-
♨ ⊙ 🅿 ⚓ †↓ 🔲 🦮 🦮

MÉINA, *Novara*   03

★ ★ **Verbano** (HCR)
Via Sempione 60
☎ 0322 6229
✉ 28046

2 🛏 -/- 20 🛏 -/-
🆎 💿 📧 ≡ 🍴 ⊷ ◆ 🅿 🔲 🄿 📶 🍴 ☺

★ ★ ★ **Villa Paradiso** (HCR)
Via Sempione 125
☎ 0322 6488 telex 200481
✉ 28046

2 🛏 -/85000 excl. breakfast 58 🛏 -/100000 excl.
breakfast
🆎 💿 📧 ≡ 🍴 ⊷ ◐ ◆ 🅿 🛎 †↓ 🔲 🄿 📶 🍴 ☺

*Elegance and comfort
on the island of Elba!*

HOTEL GABBIANO AZZURRO ****
I-57033 MARCIANA MARINA (LI)
Tel.: 0565-997035
Fax: 0565-997034

*New apartment hotel by the sea.
20 elegant suites with air conditioning, heating, colour television,
minibar, hydromassage, telephone,
panoramic view from terrace.
Indoor and outdoor pool, solarium,
fitness club, sauna. Large parking
area, garage with repair shop.
Buffet breakfast and American bar.
The hotel is affiliated to a restaurant
close by serving regional cuisine.*

MENÁGGIO, *Como* 03

★ ★ ★ **Bellavista** (HCR) AA ANWB
Via 4 Novembre 9
☎ 0344 32136
fax 0344 31793
✉ 22017

The Hotel Bellavista can
be found in the centre
of Menaggio which is
situated on the west
bank of Lake Como.
Right on the edge of the
water, the hotel has
rooms with toilet, bath or shower. Half of the
rooms have a wonderful view over the lake and
the point of Bellagio opposite the hotel. The
restaurant is mostly contained inside a glass
conservatory but also extends outside onto a
beautiful terrace built over the water.
open 15.03 - 31.12
* 7 ♫ -/75000 excl. breakfast 39 ♫ -/110000 excl.
breakfast
AE ⓪ E ⚍ ➘ ⬭ ◆ P ⛴ ⚓ ⇂ ⬛ ☐ WC �🍴 ☻

★ ★ ★ ★ **Grandhotel Menaggio** (HCR)
Via 4 Novembre 69
☎ 0344 32640 telex 328471 fax 0344 32350
✉ 22017

1 ♫ 131000/- 48 ♫ 216000/-
E ⚍ ➘ ⬭ ◉ ◆ P ⛴ ⚓ ⇂ ⬛ ☐ WC TV 🍴

MENTANA, *Roma* 14

★ ★ ★ **Barba** (HCR)
Via Nomentana Km. 23
☎ 06 9090134 telex 614543
✉ 00013

2 ♫ -/- 80 ♫ -/-
⚓ ◆ P ⛴ ⚓ ⇂ ⬛ 🐴

MERANO, *Bolzano* 04

★ ★ ★ ★ **Best Western Hotel Irma** AA ANWB
(HP)
Belvedere Strasse 17
☎ 0473 212000 telex
401089 fax 0473 31355
res nr 1678 20080
✉ 39012

The Best Western Hotel
Irma is situated just
outside Merano, sur-
rounded by parks. It is a
well maintained hotel
where rooms are equipped with modern amenities and a balcony. Guests can either relax, or
keep themselves busy with the range of activities
and leisure facilities - organised walks, 2 appeal-
ing swimming pools, a tennis court and extensive
fitness facilities. There is a pleasant air of luxury
in the various restaurants and public rooms.

open 20.03 - 04.11
* 19 ♫ 55000/109000 33 ♫ 145000/225000
⚓ ⬭ P ⛴ ⚓ ⚓ ⇂ ⬛ ☐ WC TV 🍴 ☻

★ ★ ★ **Minerva** (HP)
Via Cavour 95
☎ 0473 36712 fax 0473 30460
✉ 39012

open 03.04 - 31.10
* 8 ♫ 70000/90000 37 ♫ 130000/160000
AE ⓪ E ⚍ ⚓ ◉ P ⛴ ⚓ ⇂ ⬛ ☐ WC 🍴 ☻

★ ★ ★ ★ **Mirabella** (HP)
Via Garibaldi 35
☎ 0473 36512 telex 400196
✉ 39012

5 ⌂ -/84000 excl. breakfast 25 ⇄ -/150000 excl. breakfast
⚘ ⊙ P ⛾ ⚓ ⩰ ¶ ⊟ ⊡ WC TV |◎|

★ ★ ★ ★ **Palace** (HR)
Cavourstr 2-4
☎ 0473 211300 telex 400256 fax 0473 34181
✉ 39012

open 20.03 - 10.01 + 20.12 - 10.01
43 ⌂ 130000/195000 58 ⇄ 220000/340000
AE ◐ E ⇄ ⚘ ⊙ ◆ P ⛾ ⬧ ⚓ ⩰ ¶ ⊟ ⊡ WC TV |◎|

★ ★ ★ **Steiner** (HP)
Laurin 60
☎ 0473 48800 fax 0473 48105
✉ 39012

open 28.03 - 11.11
9 ⌂ 40000/56000 26 ⇄ 61000/89000
⚘ ⊙ P ⛾ ⚓ ¶ ⬧ ⊟ ⊡ WC TV ☺

MESSINA, *Messina*   **17**

★ ★ ★ ★ **Jolly Hotel Dello Stretto** (HCR)
Corso Garibaldi 126
☎ 090 43401 telex 980074
✉ 98100

- ⌂ -/155000 99 ⇄ -/200000
P ⊟ ⊡ ⋈

★ ★ **Moderno Terminus** (HP)
Via 1 Settembre 15
☎ 090 710853
✉ 98100

4 ⌂ -/- 40 ⇄ -/-
¶ ⊟ ⊡ WC

MESTRE, *Venezia*   **05**

★ ★ ★ **Venezia** (HCR)   AA ANWB
Piazza 27 Ottobre
☎ 041 985533 telex 410693 fax 041 985490
✉ 30170

This hotel - which is situated near Venice - has
100 rooms, all equipped with air conditioning, a
toilet and bath/shower. Guests can have apéritifs
in the bar and enjoy good Italian food in the
restaurant. Parking facilities are available.

30 ⌂ -/80000 70 ⇄ -/140000
AE ◐ E ⇄ ⚘ ⊙ P ⛾ ¶ ⊟ ⊡ WC TV |◎| ⋈

MILANO, *Milano*   **03**

Rapidly rivalling Paris as a fashion capital, Milan
beckons life's connoisseurs. Elegant shops along the
Corso Venezia and Corso Vitorio Emanuele rarely fail to
inspire a spending spree, while enjoying an aperitif in
one of the many cafés of the elaborate Galleria can be
just as memorable. Tourist activity revolves round the
Piazza del Duomo and the white marble cathedral,
third largest in the world, where only the voices of the
opera singers at La Scala rise higher. In the church of
Santa Maria della Grazia you can gaze in awe at the
painting of the 'Last Supper' by Leonardo da Vinci. In
Milan's many and varied restaurants, delicious starters
to look out for include *antipasto misto*, which usually
comprises salami, olives, radishes, fennel and pickled
mushrooms; and minestrone soup, made from mixed
vegetables and tomatoes and served with a sprinkling
of grated Parmesan cheese. Other specialities are lake
perch and trout and seafood fried in batter. Milan is
famous for its ice creams, which make delicious
desserts. Regional cheeses include gorgonzola,
mascarpone and Bel Paese.

★ ★ ★ **Ambasciatori** (HG)
Galleria Del Corso 3
☎ 02 790241 telex 315489 fax 02 782700
✉ 20122

20 ⌂ -/- 63 ⇄ -/-
AE ◐ E ⇄ ⚘ ⊙ ¶ ⊟ ⊡ WC TV ☺

★ ★ ★ **Anderson** (HCR)
Pzza Luigi Di Savoia 20
☎ 02 6690141 telex 321018
✉ 20124

17 ⌂ -/210000 excl. breakfast 85 ⇄ -/226000 excl.
breakfast
P ¶ ⊟ TV

★ ★ ★ ★ **Best Western Hotel Antares
Acamemia** (HG)
Viale Certosa 68
☎ 02 39211122 telex 315550 fax 02 33103878
res nr 1678 20080
✉ 20155

16 ⌂ 125000/235000 51 ⇄ 170000/340000
AE ◐ E ⇄ ⊙ P ⛾ ¶ ⊟ ⊡ WC TV ⋈

★ ★ ★ ★ **Best Western Hotel Antares Rubens**
(HG)
Via Rubens 21
☎ 02 40302 telex 353617 fax 02 48193114
res nr 1678 20080
✉ 20148
open 31.08 - 31.07
28 ⌂ 220000/- 59 ⇄ 340000/-
AE ◐ E ⇄ ⊙ ⛾ ¶ ⊟ ⊡ WC TV ⋈

ITALY

★ ★ ★ ★ Atlantic (HG)
Via Napo Torriani 24
☎ 02 6691941 telex 321451 fax 02 6706533
✉ 20124

open 01.09 - 31.07
* - ▱ -/200000 62 ▰ -/300000
[AE][E][✆][⊙][P][↑][↥][⊟][☐][WC][TV]

★ ★ ★ Augustus (HG)
Via Napo Torriani 29
☎ 02 66988271 telex 333112 fax 02 6703096
✉ 20124

5 ▱ -/130000 51 ▰ -/195000
[AE][①][E][✆][⊙][↑][↥][⊟][☐][WC][TV][☺]

★ ★ ★ Auriga (HG)
Via Pirelli 7
☎ 02 66985851 telex 350146 fax 02 66980698
✉ 20124

- ▱ -/190000 excl. breakfast 65 ▰ -/235000 excl.
breakfast
[AE][①][E][✆][⊙][↥][⊟][☐][WC][TV][⚹]

★ ★ ★ Best Western Hotel Berlino (HG)
Via Plana 33
☎ 02 324141 telex 312609 fax 02 324145
res nr 1678 20080
✉ 20155

* 17 ▱ -/135000 30 ▰ -/205000
[AE][①][E][✆][◈][P][↥][⊟][☐][WC][TV][☺]

★ ★ ★ ★ Bristol (HG)
Via Scarlatti 32
☎ 02 6694141 telex 321162 fax 02 6702942
✉ 20124

31 ▱ -/223000 40 ▰ -/297000
[AE][①][E][✆][⊙][↥][⊟][☐][WC][TV]

★ ★ ★ ★ Cavour Milano (HR)
Via Fatebenefratelli 21
☎ 02 6572051 telex 320498 fax 02 6592263
✉ 20121

33 ▱ 225000/- 80 ▰ 270000/-
[AE][①][E][✆][⊙][↥][⊟][☐][WC][TV][❙◐❙]

★ ★ ★ Centro (HG)
Via Broletto 46
☎ 02 8692821 telex 332632 fax 02 875578
✉ 20121

10 ▱ -/112000 44 ▰ -/171500
[AE][①][E][✆][⊙][↥][⊟][☐][WC][TV]

★ ★ ★ ★ Best Western Hotel Concorde (HG)
Viale Monza 132
☎ 02 2895853 telex 315805 fax 02 656802
res nr 1678 20080
✉ 20125

45 ▱ -/210000 excl. breakfast 45 ▰ -/290000 excl.
breakfast
[AE][①][E][✆][⚹][◈][P][↥][⊟][☐][WC][TV][⚹]

★ ★ ★ ★ ★ Excelsior Gallia (HR)
Piazza Duca D'aosta 9
☎ 02 6785 telex 311160 fax 02 66713239
✉ 20124

90 ▱ 260000/370000 excl. breakfast 170 ▰
370000/495000 excl. breakfast
[AE][①][E][✆][⚹][⊙][P][↑][↥][⊟][☐][WC][TV][☺]

★ ★ ★ Flora (HG)
Via Napo Torriani 23
☎ 02 66988242 telex 312547 fax 02 66983594
✉ 20124

* 12 ▱ -/132000 37 ▰ -/195000
[AE][①][E][✆][⊙][↥][⊟][☐][WC][TV][⚹]

★ ★ ★ Best Western Hotel Florida (HG)
Via Lepetit 33
☎ 02 6705921 telex 314102 fax 02 6692867
res nr 1678 20080
✉ 20124

14 ▱ 110000/125000 39 ▰ 160000/190000
[AE][①][E][✆][⊙][↥][⊟][☐][WC][TV][☺]

★ ★ ★ Gala (HG)
Viale Zara 89
☎ 02 66800891 fax 02 66800463
✉ 20159

open 31.08 - 31.07
* 10 ▱ -/110000 excl. breakfast 19 ▰ -/150000
excl. breakfast
[AE][①][E][✆][⚹][⊙][P][↥][⊟][☐][WC][TV][☺]

★ ★ ★ ★ Jolly Hotel President (HCR)
Largo Augusto 10
☎ 02 7746 telex 312054 fax 02 783449
✉ 20122

* 20 ▱ 370000/- 200 ▰ 450000/-
[AE][①][E][✆][⚹][⊙][P][↥][⊟][☐][WC][TV][❙◐❙][☺]

★ ★ ★ ★ Jolly Hotel Touring (HCR)
Via U. Tarchetti 2
☎ 02 6335 telex 320118 fax 02 6592209
✉ 20121

40 ▱ 280000/330000 280 ▰ 340000/410000
[AE][①][E][✆][⚹][P][↑][↥][⊟][☐][WC][TV][❙◐❙][☺]

ITALY

★ ★ ★ **Lancaster** (HG)
Via Abb.sangiorgio 16
☎ 02 313472 fax 02 344649
✉ 20145

1 🛏 -/150000 28 🛏 -/240000
🄰🄴 🄴 ⇆ ⚲ ⇅ 🖳 🄲 🆆🄲 🆃🆅 🐾

★ ★ ★ **Mennini** (HG)
Via Napo Torriani 14
☎ 02 6690951 telex 334628 fax 02 6693437
✉ 20124

12 🛏 -/- 50 🛏 -/-
🄰🄴 ⓘ 🄴 ⇆ ⊙ ⇅ 🖳 🄲 🆆🄲 🆃🆅

★ ★ ★ **Nuovo Albergo Monopole** (HG)
Via Fabio Filizi 43
☎ 02 69984972 telex 335846 fax 02 66984972
✉ 20124

open 01.09 - 31.07
29 🛏 -/107000 50 🛏 -/165000
🄰🄴 ⓘ 🄴 ⇆ ⊙ 🄿 ⇅ 🖳 🄲 🆆🄲 🆃🆅

★ ★ ★ ★ **Motel Agip** (MT)
Assago
☎ 02 4880441 telex 325191 fax 02 4880441
✉ 20100

- 🛏 -/- 222 🛏 -/-
🄰🄴 ⓘ 🄴 ⇆ ⚲ 🄿 ⚲ ⇅ 🖳 🄲 🆆🄲 🆃🆅 🍽

Motel Agip (MT)
San Donato Milanese
☎ 02 512941 telex 320132 fax 02 512941
✉ 20097

20 🛏 -/- 255 🛏 -/-
🄰🄴 ⓘ 🄴 ⇆ ⚲ ⚲ 🄿 🖳 🄲 🆆🄲 🆃🆅 🍽

★ ★ ★ ★ **Mozart** (HG)
Pzza Gerusalemme 6
☎ 02 33104215 telex 353012 fax 02 33103231
✉ 20154

24 🛏 -/- 60 🛏 -/-
🄰🄴 🄴 ⇆ ⚲ ⚲ 🄿 🄿 ⇅ 🖳 🄲 🆆🄲 🆃🆅 🐾

★ ★ ★ ★ ★ **Principe Di Savoia** (HCR)
Pzza Della Republica 17
☎ 02 6230 telex 310052 fax 02 6595838
✉ 20124

81 🛏 333000/428000 excl. breakfast
235 🛏 476000/630000 excl. breakfast
🄰🄴 ⓘ 🄴 ⇆ ⊙ 🄿 🄿 ⇅ 🖳 🄲 🆃🆅 🍽 🐾

★ ★ ★ ★ **Royal** (HG)
Via Cardano 1
☎ 02 6709151 telex 333167 fax 02 6703024
✉ 20124

15 🛏 -/228000 excl. breakfast 200 🛏 -/292000
excl. breakfast
ⓘ 🄴 ⇆ ⚲ ⊙ 🄿 🄿 ⇅ 🖳 🄲 🆆🄲 🆃🆅 🐾

★ ★ ★ **San Guido** (HG)
Via Carlo Farini 1a
☎ 02 6552238 fax 02 6572890
✉ 20154

15 🛏 97000/- excl. breakfast 16 🛏 -/131000 excl.
breakfast
🄰🄴 🄴 ⇆ ⚲ ⇅ 🖳 🄲 🆆🄲 🆃🆅 🐾

★ ★ ★ **Sempione** (HCR)
Via Finocchiaro Aprile11
☎ 02 6570323 telex 340498 fax 02 6575379
✉ 20124

* 10 🛏 -/140000 30 🛏 -/200000
🄰🄴 🄴 ⇆ ⚲ ⊙ ⇅ 🖳 🄲 🆆🄲 🆃🆅 🍽 🐾

★ ★ ★ ★ **Starhotel Splendido** (HCR)
Via Andrea Doria 4
☎ 02 6789 telex 321413 fax 02 66713369
✉ 20124

* 72 🛏 220000/295000 94 🛏 260000/370000
🄰🄴 ⓘ 🄴 ⇆ ⊙ 🄿 ⇅ 🖳 🄲 🆆🄲 🆃🆅 🍽 🐾

MILANO MARITTIMA, *Ravenna*   **10**

★ ★ ★ **Ceasar** (HCR)
Viale Cadorna 16
☎ 0544 991203
✉ 48016

6 🛏 -/- 30 🛏 -/-
⇅ 🄲 🆆🄲 🐾

★ ★ ★ **Le Palme** (HCR)
Via Traversa 12
☎ 0544 994562
✉ 48015

4 🛏 -/100000 excl. breakfast 80 🛏 -/150000 excl.
breakfast
🄿 🛋 🖳 🄲 🐾

★ ★ ★ **Paradiso** (HCR)
Viale 2 Giugno 70
☎ 0544 991417

4 🛏 -/- 18 🛏 -/-
🄿 🛋 ⇅ 🖳 🄲 🆆🄲 🐾

MINORI, *Salerno*   18

★ ★ **Caporal** (HCR)
☎ 089 877408
✉ 84010

3 🛏 -/- 22 🍴 -/-
⚜ ⊙ P 🐕 🖃 ⋔ ✶

MÒDENA, *Modena*   09

★ ★ ★ **Agip** (MT)
Via Tre Olmi 19
☎ 059 518221 telex 522185 fax 059 518522
res nr 06 4821651
✉ 41010

- 🛏 -/135000 184 🍴 -/150000
AE ⑩ E ☎ ⋗ ☙ ❖ P ⋔ ⌐ 🖃 WC TV |⊙|

★ ★ ★ ★ **Real Fini** (HG)
Via Emilia Est 441
☎ 059 238091 telex 510286 fax 059 364804
✉ 41100

open 02.01 - 23.07 + 23.08 - 21.12
* 40 🛏 224500/244500 60 🍴 330000/370000
AE ⑩ E ☎ ☙ P ☂ ⋔ 🖃 🖃 WC TV ☺

MOLVENO, *Trento*   04

★ ★ ★ **Bellariva** (HP)
Lungolago 23
☎ 0461 586952
✉ 38018

- 🛏 -/- 27 🍴 -/-
⚜ 🚌 P ⋔ WC |⊙| ⋔

MONCALIERI, *Torino*   02

★ ★ ★ **La Darsena** (HCR)
Strada Torino 29
☎ 011 642448
✉ 10024

- 🛏 -/- 25 🍴 -/-
P ⋔ 🖃 🖃

MONTAGNA, *Bolzano*   05

★ ★ **Al Ponte Bruckenwirt** (HP)   AA ANWB
Kalditsch 16a
☎ 0471 819841
✉ 39040

Hotel Brückenwirt is situated 5km outside the centre of Montagna and is surrounded by meadows and densely forested mountains. This pleasantly peaceful country hotel has 27 well kept rooms with private toilet and shower; most also feature a balcony. It also has a restaurant which serves hearty dishes, and a pleasant terrace on the sunny side of the building. Montagna can be reached from the Brenner - Verona autostrada: leave the motorway at the Ehna-Ora exit, then follow the winding road heading in the direction of Cavalese.
open 01.12 - 31.10
1 🛏 25000/42000 26 🍴 50000/84000
E ☎ ⋗ ♨ ❖ P ☂ 🐕 ⤵ 🖃 WC |⊙| ⋔ ☺

MONTALTO DI CASTRO, *Viterbo*   13

★ ★ ★ **Agip** (MT)
Via Aurelia Km 108
☎ 0766 89090 fax 0766 898603
res nr 06 4821651
✉ 01014

- 🛏 -/- 32 🍴 -/-
☙ ❖ P ☂ 🖃 WC ✶

MONTECATINI TERME, *Pistoia*   09

★ ★ ★ **Cappelli Croce Di Savoie** (HP)
Viale Bicchierai 139
☎ 0572 71151 telex 580458 fax 0572 770545
✉ 51016

open 01.04 - 15.11
36 🛏 -/630000 excl. breakfast 36 🍴 -/100000 excl. breakfast
AE ⑩ E ☎ ⋗ ⊙ P ☂ 🐕 ⤵ ⋔ 🖃 🖃 WC TV |⊙|

★ ★ ★ Imperial Garden (HP) 🄰🄰 ANWB
Viale G. Puccini 20
☎ 0572 910862
fax 0572 910863
✉ 51016

The Hotel Imperial Garden is an attractive, 6-floor hotel-villa, situated in the green heart of the luxurious Montecatini Terme. The furnishings are stylish and refined, from the reception to the restaurant and the beautiful garden. The rooms have a bathroom en suite, and some have air conditioning or feature either a balcony or a minibar. The sunny roof terrace provides the guests with a wonderful view over the hills of Tuscany.

open 15.02 - 31.12
25 ♫ 72000/110000 61 ♬ -/122000 excl. breakfast
⚒ ⊙ ♒ ⚏ ↿↾ ▭ 🄿 🆆🅲 🅝 ☺

MONTEGROTTO TERME, Padova   05

★ ★ ★ ★ Garden Terme (HCR)
Corso Terme 7
☎ 049 794033 telex 43022 fax 049 8910182
✉ 35036

open 28.02 - 29.11
49 ♫ 70000/84000 excl. breakfast 63 ♬ 111000/137000 excl. breakfast
🄰🄴 🄴 ⚒ ⚊ ♒ ⚏ 🄿 ⚏ ♒ ⚏ ↿↾ ▭ 🄿 🆆🅲 🅝 🍴 ☺

MONTEROSSO AL MARE, La Spezia   09

★ ★ La Spiagga (HCR)
Lungmare 100
☎ 0187 817567 fax 0187 817567
✉ 19016

* 1 ♫ 45000/- 14 ♬ 80000/84000
🄰🄴 🅞 🄴 ⚒ ⚊ ⊙ 🄿 ⚏ 🄿 🆆🅲 🍴 🔔

MONTESILVANO, Pescara   15

★ ★ ★ ★ Serena Majestic (HCR)
Viale Kennedy 12
☎ 085 83699 telex 600186 fax 085 8369859
✉ 65016

* - ♫ 80000/- 500 ♬ 110000/-
🄰🄴 🅞 🄴 ⚒ ⚊ ♒ ⚏ 🄿 ⚏ ⚊ ↿↾ ▭ 🄿 🆆🅲 🔔

MONTEVARCHI, Arezzo   10

★ ★ ★ Delta (HG)
Viale Diaz 137
☎ 055 901213 fax 055 901727
✉ 52025

8 ♫ -/- 32 ♬ -/-
⚒ ⊙ ♒ 🄿 ⚏ ♒ ↿↾ ▭ 🄿 🆆🅲 🅝 ☺

MÚCCIA, Macerata   14

★ ★ ★ Agip (MT)
☎ 0737 43138
res nr 06 4821651

- ♫ -/- 37 ♬ -/72000
🄿 ▭ 🄿 🅝 🐕

MÚLES, Bolzano   05

★ ★ ★ Romantik Hotel Stafler (HR)
Brennerstrasse 10
☎ 0472 771136 fax 0472 771094
✉ 39040

open 22.12 - 10.11
11 ♫ 50000/65000 excl. breakfast 27 ♬ 70000/90000 excl. breakfast
🄴 ⚒ ⚒ ⊙ ♒ 🄿 ⚏ ♒ ⚊ ↿↾ ▭ 🄿 🆆🅲 🅝 🔔

NÀPOLI, Napoli   17

★ ★ ★ Agip (MT)
☎ 081 7540560 telex 720165
✉ 80100

- ♫ -/100000 57 ♬ -/150000
🄿 ▭ 🄿 🐕

★ ★ ★ Cavour (HR)
Piazza Garibaldi 32
☎ 081 267044 telex 720262 fax 081 264306
✉ 80142

18 ♫ -/104000 85 ♬ -/148000
🄰🄴 🅞 🄴 ⚒ ⊙ ♒ 🄿 ⚏ ↿↾ ▭ 🄿 🆆🅲 🅝 ☺

★ ★ ★ ★ ★ Excelsior (HR)
Via Partenope 48
☎ 081 417111 telex 710043
✉ 80100

37 ♫ -/286000 excl. breakfast 101 ♬ -/429000 excl. breakfast
⊙ ⚏ ♒ ↿↾ 🅝 🍴

ITALY

★ ★ ★ ★ **Jolly** (HCR)
Via Medina 70
☎ 081 416000 telex 720335 fax 081 5518010
✉ 80100

* 32 ᗡ -/210000 219 ⚏ -/270000
🅰🄴⓪🄴🎫⊙🄿🄿⍐↯🔲🄲📺🍽

★ ★ ★ ★ **Miramare** (HG)
Via Nazario Sauro 24
☎ 081 427388 telex 710121 fax 081 416775
✉ 80132

* 4 ᗡ 185000/230000 27 ⚏ 230000/310000
🅰⓪🄴🎫⊙◆🄿🄿⍐↯🍽🔲🄲📺⊙

★ ★ ★ **Paradiso** (HCR)
Via Catullo 11
☎ 081 7614161 telex 722049 fax 081 7613449
✉ 80100

18 ᗡ 135000/158000 60 ⚏ 198000/258000
🅰⓪🄴🎫Ⅎ⍐↯🍽🔲🄲📺🏠🐎

★ ★ ★ **Prati**
Via Cesare Rosaroll, 4
☎ 081 5541802 telex 720179 fax 081 268898
✉ 80139

5 ᗡ -/- 38 ⚏ -/-
🄿⍐◢↯🔲🄲📺🏠

★ ★ ★ **Splendid** (HCR)
Via Mazoni 96
☎ 081 655630 fax 081 659991
✉ 80100

* 4 ᗡ -/100000 excl. breakfast 52 ⚏ -/150000 excl.
breakfast
🅰🎫Ⅎ⊙🄿⍐🍽🔲🄲📺🍽⊙

NÙORO, *Nuoro* 12

★ ★ ★ **Agip** (MT)
Via Trieste 44
☎ 0784 34071 fax 0784 33643
res nr 06 4821651
✉ 08100

3 ᗡ -/66000 48 ⚏ -/99000
⊙◆🄿⍐🍽🄲📺📺🍽⊙

ÓLBIA, *Sassari* 12

★ ★ ★ ★ **President** (HCR)
Via Principe Umberto 9
☎ 0789 27501 fax 0789 27504
✉ 07026

4 ᗡ -/- 40 ⚏ -/-
⊙◆🄿⍐🔲🄲📺🍽⊙

ORTE, *Viterbo* 14

★ ★ ★ **Lazio** (HCR)
Via Lazio 1
☎ 0761 402575 fax 0761 402211
✉ 01028

* 6 ᗡ -/80000 27 ⚏ -/110000
🄴🎫Ⅎ◊◆🄿🄿⍐↯🔲🄲📺🐎

ORTISEI, *Bolzano* 05

★ ★ ★ **Angelo** (HR)    🄰🄰 *ANWB*
Petlin 35
☎ 0471 796336
fax 0471 796323
✉ 39046

Though Hotel Angelo is
situated in the centre of
Ortisei/Sankt Ulrich, it is
surrounded by a lush
garden and large sun-
bathing lawns. A com-
fortable holiday and
winter-sports hotel where the rooms - partly
situated in the annexe - have a private bathroom
(some also a balcony). The furnishings in the
restaurant are elegant and stylish, while the
attractive sauna with solarium and whirlpool offer
a few hours of perfect relaxation.

open 20.12 - 31.10
* 5 ᗡ 50000/75000 30 ⚏ 100000/150000
🄴🎫Ⅎ◊◆🄿↯🔲🄲📺🍽⊙

★ ★ ★ ★ **Hell** (HG)
☎ 0471 76785
✉ 39046

1 ᗡ -/90000 26 ⚏ -/160000
Ⅎ🄿⍐🔲🄲🐎

★ ★ ★ **Villa Emilia** (HCR)    🄰🄰 *ANWB*
Muredastrasse 61
☎ 0471 796171
fax 0471 707728
✉ 39046

Hotel Villa Emilia is
delightfully peaceful,
situated on a sunny
slope within walking
distance from the
tourist and winter-
sports resort of Ortisei-
Sankt Ulrich. This holiday hotel (which was
originally built as a villa) has 28 rooms, all with a
toilet and bath or shower. The dining and breakfast rooms are furnished in a pleasant rustic
style. The nearest ski lift is only 300m away, and

→

ITALY

if necessary, ski equipment can be rented from the hotel.

8 ☎ -/- 24 🛏 -/-
🚊⤳🕭🅿🏊♨🛎🖥🖨🇼🇨🍴⛲

PADENGHE SUL GARDA, Brescia   04

★ ★ ★ ★ **West Garda** (HCR)
☎ 030 917261 telex 30434

1 ☎ -/- 64 🛏 -/-
⤳🅿⚓♨🖥🖨🇼🇨

PÀDOVA, Padova   05

★ ★ ★ **Best Western Hotel Grande Italia** (HCR)
Corso Del Popolo 81
☎ 049 650877 telex 432224 fax 049 8750850
res nr 1678 20080
✉ 35100

* 24 ☎ 105000/112000 40 🛏 141500/150000
🆎⓪🇪🚊⊙◈🍴🖥🖨🇼🇨📺⛲

PAESTUM, Salerno   18

★ ★ ★ **Calypso** (HCR)
☎ 0828 811031 telex 722489
✉ 84063

5 ☎ -/- 25 🛏 60000/75000 excl. breakfast
🆎🚊⤳⛱⤳🕭🅿🏊♨⚓🍴🖥🖨🇼🇨⛲🐾

★ ★ ★ **Villa Rita** (HP)
Zona Archeologica
☎ 0828 722555 fax 0828 811028
✉ 84063

open 15.03 - 30.10
3 ☎ 40000/42000 excl. breakfast 10 🛏 60000/
65000 excl. breakfast
🆎🇪🚊⤳🅿🖥🖨🇼🇨🐾

PALAU, Sassari   12

★ ★ ★ **Altura** (HCR)
Localit Monte Actura
☎ 0789 709655 fax 0789 709081
✉ 07020

1 ☎ -/- 54 🛏 -/-
⤳⤳🕭🅿♨🛎🖥🖨🇼🇨⛲⛲

PALERMO, Palermo   17

★ ★ ★ ★ **Jolly** (HCR)
Foro Italico 22
☎ 091 6165090 telex 910076

- ☎ -/- 290 🛏 -/-
🅿⚓🍴🖥🖨📺🐾

PALINURO, Salerno   18

★ ★ ★ **La Torre** (HR)
Via Porto
☎ 0974 931107 fax 0947 931264
✉ 84064

open 12.06 - 11.09
3 ☎ -/- 31 🛏 -/-
⤳⛱⤳🅿♨⚓🍴🖥🖨🇼🇨⛲

PALLANZA, Novara   03

★ ★ ★ **Majestic** (HCR)
Via Vitt. Veneto 32
☎ 0323 504305 telex 223339 fax 0323 556379
✉ 28048

open Easter - 20.10
26 ☎ 130000/160000 93 🛏 220000/250000
🆎⓪🇪🚊⤳⤳🅿🏊♨⚓🍴🖥🖨🇼🇨🐾

PARMA, Parma   09

★ ★ ★ **Best Western Park Hotel Stendhal**
(HCR)
Via Bodoni 3
☎ 0521 208057 telex 531216 fax 0521 285655
res nr 1678 20080
✉ 43100

* 31 ☎ -/165000 29 🛏 -/240000
🆎⓪🇪🚊⊙♨🍴🖥🖨🇼🇨📺🍴⛲

PASSIGNANO SUL TRASIMENO, Perugia   14

★ ★ **Kursaal**
Viale Europa 41
☎ 075 827182 fax 075 827182
✉ 06065

open 01.04 - 10.10
* - ☎ 55000/60000 excl. breakfast 16 🛏 70000/
75000 excl. breakfast
🇪🚊🕭🅿♨⚓🖥🖨🇼🇨⛲

PASSO DELLA CONSUMA, Firenze   10

Il Laghetto Nel Bosco (HCR)
☎ 055 8606401 telex 575160
✉ 50060

- ☎ -/- 29 🛏 -/-
⤳🅿⚓🖥🖨🐾

PÈRUGIA, *Perugia* **14**

Best Western Hotel Colle Della Trinit (HCR)
Cosella Postale 118
☎ 075 79540 telex 662112
res nr 1678 20080

- *a* -/- 50 *ə* -/-
P 🖃 🎨 🐾

★ ★ ★ ★ **Grifone** (HCR)
Via Silvio Pellico 1
☎ 075 5837616 telex 660245 fax 075 5837619
✉ 06100

20 *a* -/90000 excl. breakfast 30 *ə* -/140000 excl.
breakfast
AE ⓪ 🖃 ⌶ **P** 🍽 ⚑ ↿↾ 🖃 🎨 🆆🅲 🐾

★ ★ **Signa** (HR)
Via Del Grillo 9
☎ 075 61080
✉ 6100

3 *a* 48000/52000 excl. breakfast 20 *ə* 65000/
75000 excl. breakfast
⓪ ⚑ ↿↾ 🖃 🎨 🆆🅲 🐾

PÈSARO, *Pesaro e Urbino* **11**

★ ★ ★ **Embassy** (HCR)
Viale Trieste 64
☎ 0721 68158 telex 561258
✉ 61100

5 *a* 44000/- 50 *ə* 64000/-
🚗 ⓪ **P** 🍽 ⚑ ↿↾ 🖃 🎨 🆆🅲 🅸🅾🅸 ⊙

★ ★ ★ **Excelcior** (HCR)
Lungomare N.sauro
☎ 0721 32720 telex 561011 fax 0721 24456
✉ 61100

7 *a* 44800/- 53 *ə* 65000/-
🚗 ⓪ **P** ⚑ ↿↾ 🖃 🎨 🆆🅲 ⊙

★ ★ ★ **Lido** (HCR)
☎ 0721 34643 telex 56062

- *a* -/- 5 *ə* -/-
🚗 ↿↾ 🎨 🆆🅲

★ ★ ★ **Majestic** (HCR)
Viale Trieste 80
☎ 0721 33667 fax 0721 27241
✉ 61100

10 *a* 44000/- 70 *ə* 64000/-
🚗 ⓪ **P** ⚑ ↿↾ 🖃 🎨 🆆🅲 🅸🅾🅸 🛎

★ ★ ★ **Nautilus** (HR)
Viale Trieste 26
☎ 0721 67125

10 *a* -/55000 excl. breakfast 40 *ə* -/75000 excl.
breakfast
🍽 ↿↾ 🖃 🎨 🆆🅲

★ ★ ★ ★ **Savoy** (HR)
V.le Della Repubblica 22
☎ 0721 67449 telex 561624 fax 0721 64429
✉ 61100

- *a* 150000/240000 54 *ə* -/-
AE ⓪ 🖃 ⌶ 🍽 ⚑ ↿↾ 🆣

★ ★ ★ ★ ★ **Best Western Hotel Vittoria** (HCR)
Piazza Della Liberta 2
☎ 0721 34343 telex 561624 fax 0721 68874
res nr 1678 20080
✉ 61100

5 *a* 185000/- 22 *ə* 285000/-
AE ⓪ 🖃 ⌶ ⅄ 🚗 ⓪ **P** 🍽 ⚑ ↿↾ 🖃 🎨 🆆🅲 🆣 🅸🅾🅸 🐾

PIACENZA, *Pescara* **09**

★ ★ ★ **K 2** (MT)
Via E. Parmense 133
☎ 0523 65558
✉ 29100

7 *a* -/- 38 *ə* -/-
◆ **P** 🍽 ↿↾ 🎨 🆆🅲 🅸🅾🅸

PIETRA LIGURE, *Savona* **08**

★ ★ ★ **Geppi** (HR)
☎ 019 647730
✉ 17027

1 *a* -/- 10 *ə* -/-
⅄ **P** ⚑ ↿↾ 🎨 🆆🅲 🆣 🅸🅾🅸

PINARELLA, *Ravenna* **10**

★ ★ ★ **Bamar** (HP)
Viale Valsesia 6
☎ 0544 987441 telex 550498
✉ 48015

* 5 *a* -/44000 29 *ə* -/60000
🖃 ⌶ ⅄ 🛵 🚗 ⓪ **P** ↿↾ 🛏 🎨 🆆🅲 ⊙

ITALY

PINZOLO, *Trento* **04**

★ ★ ★ **Corona** (HCR)
☎ 0465 51030 fax 0465 52778
✉ 38086

open 01.06 - 30.09 + 01.12 - 30.04
* 8 ♪ 58000/73000 37 ♫ 110000/145000
🄰🄴 ⓘ 🄴 ⊃ ⊙ 🄿 ♨ ↾↿ 🔌 🄵 🄿 TV ☺

PISA, *Pisa* **09**

★ ★ ★ **Arno** (HR)
Piazza Della Republ. 7
☎ 050 542648 fax 050 543441
✉ 56127

3 ♪ -/74500 30 ♫ -/105000
🄰🄴 ⓘ 🄴 ⊃ ⊙ ↾↿ 🄵 WC ☺

★ ★ ★ **California** (HCR)
Via Aurelia Km 338
☎ 050 890726 telex 502161 fax 050 890727
✉ 56100

open 01.03 - 30.11
7 ♪ -/85000 67 ♫ -/130000
🄰🄴 ⓘ 🄴 ⊃ ♪ ♨ ♦ 🄿 ♨ ⊂ ⊞ 🔌 🄵 🄿 TV 🕪 ☺

★ ★ ★ ★ **Best Western Hotel D'Azeglio** (HG)
Piazza V Emanuele I I,18
☎ 050 500310 telex 590092
res nr 1678 20080
✉ 56125

6 ♪ 155000/- 23 ♫ 208000/-
🄰🄴 ⓘ 🄴 ⊃ ⊙ 🄿 ↾↿ 🔌 🄵 WC TV ☺

★ ★ ★ **Terminus e Plaza** (HG)
Via Colombo 45
☎ 050 500303 telex 501047 fax 050 618363
✉ 56125

7 ♪ -/80000 excl. breakfast 48 ♫ -/115000 excl. breakfast
🄰🄴 ⓘ 🄴 ⊃ ♪ ⊙ ↾↿ 🔌 🄵 WC ☺

PISTICCI, *Matera* **19**

★ ★ ★ **Agip** (HCR)
Pisticci Scalo
☎ 0835 462007
res nr 06 4821651

- ♪ -/- 64 ♫ -/-
🄿 🔌 🄵 🕪

PISTÒIA/PONTE NUOVO, *Pistoia* **09**

★ ★ ★ **Albergo Il Convento** (HR)
Via S. Quirico 33
PISTÒIA
☎ 0573 452651 fax 0573 453578
✉ 51100

4 ♪ -/70000 23 ♫ -/91000
🄴 ⊃ ♪ ♨ 🄿 ♨ ⊂ 🔌 🄵 WC 🕪 🕷

PISTÒIA/VAIONI, *Pistoia* **09**

★ **Burchietti** (HCR)
Via Bolognese 164-166
PISTO'IA
☎ 0573 48457

3 ♪ -/- 4 ♫ -/-
♪ ♦ 🄿 ♨ ⊂ 🄵 WC TV 🕪

PLAN, *Bolzano* **04**

Enzian (HR)
☎ 0473 85708
✉ 39013

2 ♪ -/- 15 ♫ -/-
♪ 🄿 ♨ 🄵 WC TV 🕷

POMPÉI, *Napoli* **17**

★ ★ ★ **Diomede** (HR)
Viale Mazzini 40
☎ 081 8631520
✉ 80045

* 6 ♪ 50000/- excl. breakfast 18 ♫ -/95000 excl. breakfast
⊙ ♦ 🄿 🄿 ↾↿ 🔌 🄵 WC ☺

PORLEZZA, *Como* **03**

★ ★ ★ **Europa** (HCR)
Lugo Lago Matteoti 19
☎ 0344 61142 fax 0344 72256
✉ 22018

4 ♪ 5200/6600 34 ♫ 7900/10600
🄰🄴 ⓘ 🄴 ⊃ ♪ ⋯ 🄿 🄿 ♨ ↾↿ 🔌 🄵 WC 🕪
See advertisement on page 75

ITALY

PORTO AZZURRO, Livorno 12

★ ★ ★ **Belmare** (HCR)
Via 4 Novembre 22
☎ 0565 95012
✉ 57036

2 🛏 -/- 25 🛏 -/-
▣ 🖻 WC |◎| ⬆ 🍴

PORTO CERVO, Sassari 12

★ ★ ★ ★ ★ **Cervo** (HCR)
☎ 0789 92003 telex 790037 fax 0789 92593
✉ 07020

- 🛏 -/- 90 🛏 -/-
🏊 🚗 ⊙ ♞ 🍴 ⚓ 🔌 ▣ 🖻 WC TV |◎| ⬆ 🐕 🍴

★ ★ ★ ★ **Le Ginestre** (HCR)
☎ 0789 92030 telex 792163 fax 0789 94087
✉ 07020

open 15.12 - 10.10
- 🛏 -/- 77 🛏 -/-
AE ⓪ E 🍴 🏊 🚗 ⓢ ▣ ♞ 🍴 ⚓ 🔌 ▣ 🖻 WC TV ⬆ 🐕 🍴

PORTOFERRÁIO, Livorno 12

★ ★ ★ **Adriana** (HCR)
Localita Padulella
☎ 0565 92057 telex 590220

3 🛏 -/- 20 🛏 -/-
▣ ♞ 🍴 🖻 WC

★ ★ ★ **Touring** (HP)
☎ 0565 93851

2 🛏 -/- 30 🛏 -/-
🍴 🖻 WC 🍴

PORTOFINO, Genova 08

★ ★ ★ **Piccolo** (HCR)
Via Provinciale 29
☎ 0185 69015
✉ 16034

5 🛏 -/- 27 🛏 -/-
🏊 🚗 ▣ 🍴 ♞ ▣ 🖻 WC

★ ★ ★ ★ ★ **Splendido** (HCR)
Viale Baratta 13
☎ 0185 269551 telex 281057 fax 0185 269614
✉ 16034

open 15.04 - 26.10
10 🛏 301000/331000 55 🛏 507000/574000
AE ⓪ E 🍴 🏊 ⓢ ▣ 🍴 ♞ ⚓ 🍴 ▣ 🖻 WC TV |◎| ⬆ ⓧ

PORTO ROTONDO, Sassari 12

★ ★ ★ ★ ★ **Sporting** (HCR)
☎ 0789 34005 telex 790113 fax 0789 34383
✉ 07026

- 🛏 -/- 27 🛏 -/-
🏊 🚗 ⊙ ▣ 🍴 🔌 ▣ 🖻 WC TV |◎| ⬆ 🐕

PORTOVÉNERE, La Spezia 09

★ ★ ★ **Royal Sporting** (HCR)
Via Olivo 345
☎ 0187 900326 fax 0187 529060
✉ 19025

20 🛏 -/160000 60 🛏 -/220000
🏊 🚗 ▣ ♞ 🍴 TV |◎|
See advertisement on page 77

POSITANO, Salerno 17

★ ★ ★ ★ **Miramare** (HCR)
Via Trara Gendino 25-27
☎ 089 875219 telex 770072 fax 089 875219
✉ 84017

open 15.03 - 15.11
* 3 🛏 115000/165000 10 🛏 180000/280000
AE E 🍴 🏊 ⊙ ▣ ♞ ▣ 🖻 WC |◎| ⊙

★ ★ ★ ★ **Poseidon** (HCR)
☎ 089 875014 telex 770058 fax 089 875014
✉ 84017

open 16.04 - 14.10
3 🛏 125000/195000 50 🛏 180000/290000
AE ⓪ E 🍴 🚗 ▣ ♞ 🍴 ▣ 🖻 WC 🍴

★ ★ ★ **Villa Franca** (HCR)
☎ 089 875035
✉ 84017

5 🛏 -/190000 20 🛏 -/200000
▣ 🍴 ▣ 🖻 WC 🍴

PREGNANA MILANESE/MILANO, Milano 03

★ ★ ★ **Monica Motor Hotel** (MT)
Via Olivetti 3
PREGNANA MILANESE
☎ 02 93290920 fax 02 93290608
✉ 20010

* - 🛏 -/90000 36 🛏 -/120000
AE ⓪ 🏊 ◈ ▣ ♞ 🔌 ▣ 🖻 WC TV |◎| ⬆ ⊙

PRÓCCHIO, *Livorno*   **12**

★ **Desiree** (HCR)
Loc. Spartaia
☎ 0565 907311 telex 590649 fax 0565 907884
✉ 57030

open 16.04 - 04.10
5 🛏 90000/140000 64 🛏 180000/300000
AE ⓞ 🄴 ⌷ 🏧 ⓞ 🅿 🄿 ☂ ⚓ 🗲 🖭 🖃 🄲 WC TV 🍴 🛎 ☺
See advertisement on page 77

PRÓCIDA, *Napoli*   **17**

★ ★ **Arcate** (HCR)
Via Scotti 16
☎ 081 8967120
✉ 80079

6 🛏 -/- 30 🛏 -/-
🏧 ⚓ 🅿 ☂ 🖃 🄲 WC 🍴

PUNTA ALA, *Grosseto*   **12**

★ ★ ★ ★ **Gallia Palace** (HR)
☎ 0564 922022 telex 590454 fax 0564 920229
✉ 58040

open 15.05 - 30.09
* 26 🛏 172000/260000 excl. breakfast
72 🛏 220000/440000 excl. breakfast
AE ⓞ 🄴 ⌷ 🏧 🎾 ⚓ 🅿 ☂ 🗲 🖭 🖃 🄲 TV 🛎 ☺

RAPALLO, *Genova*   **08**

★ ★ ★ ★ **Eurotel Rapallo** (HCR)
Via Aurelia Pon. 22
☎ 0185 60981 telex 283851 fax 0185 50635
✉ 16035

24 🛏 -/155000 40 🛏 -/235000
⌷ 🅿 🄿 ☂ 🗲 🖭 🖃 🄲 WC TV 🍴 🛎 ☺

★ ★ ★ **Miramare** (HCR)
Via Vittorio Veneto 27
☎ 0185 230261 fax 0185 273570
✉ 16035

5 🛏 80000/- 23 🛏 100000/150000
AE ⓞ 🄴 ⌷ 🏧 ⓞ ◆ 🅿 🄿 ☂ 🗲 🖭 🖃 🄲 WC TV 🍴 ☺

RAVENNA, *Ravenna*   **10**

★ ★ ★ **Bisanzio** (HG)
Via Salara, 30
☎ 0544 217111 telex 551070 fax 0544 32539
res nr 1678 20080
✉ 48100

open 01.01 - 08.01 + 08.02 - 20.12
* 12 🛏 110000/130000 26 🛏 150000/190000
AE ⓞ 🄴 ⌷ 🏧 ⓞ 🖭 🖃 🄲 WC TV ☺

★ ★ ★ **Centrale Byron** (HG)
Via 4 Novembre 14
☎ 0544 33479 telex 551070 fax 0544 32539
✉ 48100

open 11.01 - 31.12
* 21 🛏 74500/90500 36 🛏 108000/123000
AE ⓞ 🄴 ⌷ 🏧 ⓞ 🖭 🖃 🄲 WC TV 🍴

★ ★ ★ **Jolly** (HCR)
Piazza Memeli 1
☎ 0544 35762 telex 550575 fax 0544 39541

* 36 🛏 -/- 38 🛏 145000/210000
AE ⓞ 🄴 ⌷ 🏧 🖭 🖃 🄲 WC TV 🍴 ☺

RÈGGIO DI CÀLABRIA, *Reggio di Calabria*   **21**

★ ★ ★ **Excelsior** (HCR)
Via Vittorio Veneto Nr66
☎ 0965 25801 telex 912583
✉ 89100

5 🛏 -/- 87 🛏 -/-
⚓ ⓞ 🅿 🄿 🖭 🖃 🄲 WC TV 🍴

RÉSIA, *Bolzano*   **04**

★ ★ **Etschquelle** (HR)
☎ 0473 633071
✉ 39027

open 02.07 - 31.05
* 1 🛏 34000/48000 22 🛏 56000/84000
ⓞ 🄴 ⌷ 🏧 ⓞ 🅿 ☂ 🖃 WC 🍴 🎾

RICCIONE, *Forli*   **11**

★ ★ ★ ★ **Best Western Hotel Abner's** (HCR)
Lungomare Della Repub. 7
☎ 0541 600601 telex 550153 fax 0541 605400
res nr 1678 20080
✉ 47036

* 2 🛏 97000/135000 58 🛏 150000/220000
AE ⓞ 🄴 ⌷ 🏧 ⓞ 🅿 ☂ ☂ 🗲 🖭 🖃 🄲 WC TV 🍴 ☺
See advertisement on page 79

RESTAURANT HOTEL EUROPA

I-22018 PORLEZZA (Como) Lake Lugano

Telephone: 0344-61142   Telefax: 0344-72256

Hotel, restaurant, bar 300 m from the centre. Quiet location on the lake with panoramic view. Each room has a shower/WC en suite. Sun terrace, garden, private car park, and just 10 minutes from Lugano. Our prices for the 1993 season:

single room	L. 40.000-54.000	double room/breakfast	L. 79.000-106.000
single room/breakfast	L. 52.000-66.000	full board	L. 69.000- 86.000
double room	L. 55.000-82.000	half board	L. 62.000- 79.000

ITALY

★ ★ ★ ★ **Alexandra Plaza** (HCR)
Viale Torino 61
☎ 0541 610344 telex 550330 fax 0541 610483
✉ 47036

5 🛏 -/- 55 🛏 -/170000 excl. breakfast

★ ★ ★ **Augustus** (HCR)
Viale Oberdan 18
☎ 0541 43434

1 🛏 -/- 47 🛏 105000/170000 excl. breakfast

★ ★ ★ **Baltic** (HCR)
Piazzale Di Vittorio 1
☎ 0541 600966 fax 0541 601978
✉ 47036

12 🛏 60000/100000 60 🛏 90000/170000

★ ★ **Brig** (HCR)
Cima Rosa 2
☎ 0541 642014 fax 0541 642782
✉ 47036

9 🛏 -/- 21 🛏 -/-

★ ★ ★ **Corallo** (HCR)
Viale Gramsci 113
☎ 0541 600807 telex 550391 fax 0541 601276
✉ 47036

10 🛏 -/- 58 🛏 -/-

★ ★ ★ **Diamond** (HP)
Via Fratelli Bandiera 1
☎ 0541 602600 telex 550561

2 🛏 -/90000 25 🛏 -/160000

★ ★ ★ **Maestri** (HCR)
Viale Gorizia 4
☎ 0541 43201

1 🛏 -/60000 excl. breakfast 37 🛏 -/97000 excl.
breakfast

★ ★ ★ **Romagna** (HR)
Viale Gramsci 64
☎ 0541 600604
✉ 47036

open 01.06 - 18.09
10 🛏 45000/55000 excl. breakfast 40 🛏 65000/
90000 excl. breakfast

★ ★ ★ **Sole** (HCR)
Viale Dante 82
☎ 0541 41484

1 🛏 -/- 29 🛏 -/-

★ ★ ★ **Vienna Touring** (HCR)   *AA ANWB*
Viale Milano 78c
☎ 0541 601700 telex
550153 fax 0541
601762
✉ 47036

Hotel Vienna Touring
can be found just
behind the boulevard in
the centre of Riccione,
close to the sea. This
stylish seaside hotel
might appear somewhat old-fashioned, but it is
well maintained and offers all modern amenities.
The rooms have a bathroom, balcony and minibar. It features a restaurant with a spacious
conservatory, a big lounge, a pleasant covered
terrace, a sauna and fitness facilities.

open 01.05 - 30.09
35 🛏 -/- 58 🛏 -/-

RIMINI, *Forlì*   **11**

★ ★ ★ ★ **Ambasciatori** (HCR)
Viale Vespucci 22
☎ 0541 55561 telex 550132 fax 0541 23790

* 16 🛏 145000/250000 50 🛏 240000/380000

★ **Atlas** (HP)
Viale Regina Elena 74
☎ 0541 380561 fax 0541 380561
✉ 47037

open 01.05 - 30.09
12 🛏 35000/39000 64 🛏 56000/65000

★ ★ ★ **Columbia** (HCR)
Viale Regina Elena 4
☎ 0541 26926

1 🛏 -/- 54 🛏 -/-

★ ★ ★ ★ **Diplomat Palace** (HCR)
Viale Regina Elena 70
☎ 0541 380011 fax 0541 380414

15 🛏 100000/140000 25 🛏 130000/160000

★ ★ ★ **Sporting** (HCR)
Viale Vespucci 20
☎ 0541 55391

1 🛏 -/- 77 🛏 -/-
🏊 �͏ P 🚲 ⊪ ▬ P̄ WC

★ ★ ★ **Villa Rosa Riviera** (HCR)
Viale Vespucci 71
☎ 0541 22506

1 🛏 -/130000 50 🛏 -/180000
P̄ ⊪ ▬ P̄ WC

★ ★ ★ **Villa Verdi** (HCR)
Viale Vespucci 38
☎ 0541 24742
✉ 47037

1 🛏 -/- 34 🛏 -/-
🏊 P ⊪ ▬ P̄ WC 🐕

★ ★ ★ **Waldorf** (HCR)
Viale Vespucci 28
☎ 0541 54725 telex 551262
open 02.07 - 31.05
15 🛏 -/260000 50 🛏 -/300000
🏊 �͏ P ⊪ ▬ P̄ WC TV

★ ★ ★ **Best Western Hotel Astoria** (HCR)
Viale Trento 9
☎ 0464 552658 telex 401042 fax 0464 552659
res nr 1678 20080
✉ 38066

open 04.04 - 31.10
22 🛏 75000/95000 72 🛏 110000/150000
AE ⓓ E ≖ 🚲 ⓥ ◆ P 🚲 🚟 ⊪ ▬ P̄ WC Ⅵ ⊙

★ ★ ★ **Du Lac et du Parc** (HR)   AA ANWB
Viale Rovereto 44
☎ 0464 551500 telex
400258 fax 0464
555200
✉ 38066

Hotel du Lac et du Parc is a modern, elegant holiday and conference hotel situated - as the name suggests - by the side of a small lake in a lush green park. There is an aura of refinement inside the hotel, in the attractively furnished bedrooms (which offer all possible modern comforts and views over Lake Garda) and the fine restaurant and public lounges. The swim-

→

ITALY

ming pools are very well designed, and there is plenty of opportunity to practise other sports.

open 08.04 - 20.10
* 24 ♨ 130000/150000 148 ♨ 220000/320000
🏧 ⓞ 🅴 ⚞ 🛎 ☺ 🕭 ◆ 🅿 🇵 🐕 🌊 🏔 ↟ ⊞ ▣ 🄵 🆆🅲 📺 🍽 ⛺
☺

★ ★ ★ **Best Western Hotel Europa** 🄰🄰 ANWB (HCR)
Piazza Catena 9
☎ 0464 521777 telex 401350 fax 0464 552337
res nr 1678 20080
🖂 38066
The colourful frontage of the Best Western Hotel Europa is an attractive, eye-catching

feature of the boulevard at Riva. The hotel is right by Lake Garda, at the foot of a steep mountain. The rooms have air conditioning, a bathroom, TV and a minibar; most of them look out over the lake. The restaurant is tastefully furnished, and from the terrace, guests get a pleasant view of the bustle around the small harbour.

6 ♨ 90000/110000 57 ♨ 140000/180000
🏧 ⓞ 🅴 ⚞ 🛎 🐎 ☺ ☺ 🐕 🇵 🏔 ↟ ▣ 🄵 🆆🅲 🍽 ☺

★ ★ ★ **Gardesana** (HR)
Via Brione 1
☎ 0464 552793 fax 0464 555814
🖂 38066

open 01.04 - 20.10
* 10 ♨ 50000/70000 28 ♨ 90000/130000
🅿 🐕 🌊 🏔 ▣ 🄵 🆆🅲 🐎

★ ★ ★ **Luise** (HCR)
Viale Rovereto 9
☎ 0464 512796
🖂 38066

1 ♨ -/- 58 ♨ -/-
🅿 🇵 🌊 🏔 ▣ 🄵 🆆🅲

★ ★ ★ **Riviera** (HCR)
Viale Rovereto 95
☎ 0464 552279 fax 0464 554140
🖂 38066

open 04.04 - 25.10
6 ♨ 46000/56000 excl. breakfast 30 ♨ 74000/86000 excl. breakfast
ⓞ 🅴 ⚞ 🛎 ☺ 🕭 🅿 🇵 🐕 🌊 🏔 ▣ 🄵 🆆🅲 🍽

★ ★ ★ **Motel Agip** (HCR)
☎ 0864 62443 fax 0864 62443
🖂 67037

* - ♨ -/50000 excl. breakfast 57 ♨ -/77000 excl. breakfast
🏧 ⓞ 🅴 🛎 🕭 🅿 ▣ 🄵 🆆🅲 🐎

Population 3,000,000 *Local Tourist Office* Via Parigi 5
☎ (06) 461851
Rome is one of the world's greatest cultural centres, with evidence of its ancient glory to be found everywhere. The Forum contains the ruins of the centre of the Empire's administration, and the heart of its cultural and political life; close by are Trajan's Column, magnificent with its pictorial spiral illustrating the city's earliest history, and the awe-inspiring Colosseum, notorious for its gladiatorial combats.
A short drive away is the Vatican City, the world's smallest sovereign state. This contains not only the residence of the Pope but also the world's largest church and St Peter's Square, an immense masterpiece designed and completed in less than 12 years, and an incomparable achievement in symmetry. The 1st-century Egyptian obelisk in the centre was once the goal post of Nero's Circus.
The treasures of St Peter's Basilica include Michelangelo's *Pieta* and a 13th-century bronze statue of St Peter by Arnolfo do Cambio, its foot worn smooth by the kisses of countless pilgrims. Climb to the top of the Basilica for a magnificent view of Rome and the Vatican City.
In addition to its wide range of museums, art galleries and churches, the city offers delightful parks and gardens to stroll in, especially the beautiful Villa Borghese and Giardini degli Aranci. Markets abound - the best-known are the Sunday market at Porta Portese and daily market at Piazza Vittorio Emanuele, while Roma's best known stores are found close to the Spanish Steps and in Via del Corso, where designer labels include Valentino and Gucci.
You need not spend a fortune to eat in Rome. In traditional areas such as Trastevere you will find small, family-run *trattorie* serving Roman cooking at its best. No visit to Rome would be complete without having tried an appetising pizza or a dish of homemade pasta, such as *spaghetti carbonara*, made with a creamy sauce of beaten egg with smoked bacon. The meat dishes are delicious, too, especially the *saltimbocca*, veal with sage and ham in Marsala wine. You will find daily menus (*piatto del giorno*) in inexpensive *trattorie* where a carafe of house wine (*vino della casa*) provides an excellent accompaniment to your meal. For local flavour, try Frascati and Marion wines which are produced from the vineyards on the hills surrounding the city.
Try cafés in the elegant Via Condotti for *capuccino* or *espresso* coffee to go with pastries like *maritozze*, a kind of sweet brioche roll with a custard filling.

See cityplan on page 31

RICCIONE/Adria
ABNER'S HOTEL ★ ★ ★ ★

Open throughout the year. In a first-class location in a unique area by the sea. Tennis court and midget golf next to the hotel. All rooms equipped with bath, shower and WC, telephone and balcony with sea view, television and/or minibar, air conditioning. **APARTMENTS** also available. Garden, parking spaces, breakfast buffet, excellent cuisine with à la carte menu. Plenty of entertainment in the evening. Heated swimming pool. P.O.Box 219. Telephone 0541-600601, Fax 605400, Telex 550153 FAOTEL-I. Visa and American Express.

RICCIONE/Adria
HOTEL VIENNA TOURING ★ ★ ★ ★

By the sea. International hotel with modern comforts. Wonderfully quiet location on the beach. Private tennis court. Two large gardens, heated swimming pool, sauna, massage parlour, keep-fit area, swimming pool buffet in the afternoon. All rooms with bath, shower, WC, balcony, telephone and minibar, colour television on request. **COMFORTABLE APARTMENTS** Private parking area under surveillance. Buffet breakfast, in-house cuisine with à la carte menu. Weekly dance evening. P.O.Box 219. Telephone 0541-601700, Fax 601762, Telex 550153 FAOTEL-I. American Express and Visa.

★ ★ ★ Agip (HCR)
Via Aurelia Km 8,4
☎ 06 6379001 telex 613699 fax 06 6379001
res nr 06 4821651
✉ 00163

10 ⌿ -/165000 202 ⌿ -/240000
⚞ ⚟ ◆ 🅿 ⚙ ⚏ ↟↡ ⚍ 🄯 🆆🄲 🆃🅅 🍽

★ ★ ★ Atlante Garden (HG)
Via Crescenzio 78
☎ 06 6872361 telex 623172 fax 06 6872315
✉ 00193

5 ⌿ -/252000 55 ⌿ -/297000
🄰🄴 ⓪ 🄴 ⚎ ⊙ 🅿 ⚙ ↟↡ ⚍ 🄯 🆆🄲 🆃🅅

★ ★ ★ ★ ★ Atlante Star (HR)
Via G. Vitelleschi 34
☎ 06 6879558 telex 622355 fax 06 6872300
✉ 00193

Hotel Atlante Star is only 300m from St Peter's Square in the heart of historic Rome, and is an ideal base for visiting the city and the Vatican. The elegant 'Centro Commerciale di Via Cola di Rienzo' is within walking distance. The hotel has its own rooftop garden with restaurant where guests can dine while enjoying a splendid view across the city. There is also a sunbathing terrace, cocktail bar, conference facilities and private garage. All 70 rooms have modern facilities.

2 ⌿ -/- 68 ⌿ 400000/425000
🄰🄴 ⓪ 🄴 ⚎ ⊙ 🅿 ⚙ ⚏ ↟↡ ⚍ 🄯 🆆🄲 🆃🅅 🍽

★ ★ ★ Atlantico
Via Cavour 23
☎ 06 485951 telex 610556 fax 06 4744105
✉ 00184

- ⌿ -/- - ⌿ 183000/254000
🄰🄴 ⓪ 🄴 ⚎

★ ★ ★ Best Western Hotel Canada (HR)
Via Vicenza 58
☎ 06 4457770 telex 613037 fax 06 4450749
res nr 1678 20080
✉ 00185

* 6 ⌿ 108000/130000 64 ⌿ 156000/186000
🄰🄴 ⓪ 🄴 ⚎ ▥ ◆ 🅿 ⚙ ⚏ ↟↡ ⚍ 🄯 🆆🄲 🆃🅅 🍽 ↟ ⚶

★ ★ ★ Condotti (HG)
Via Mario De'fiori 37
☎ 06 6794661 fax 06 6790457
✉ 00187

* - ⌿ 180000/210000 15 ⌿ 210000/270000
🄰🄴 ⓪ 🄴 ⚎ ⊙ ⚍ 🄯 🆆🄲 🆃🅅 ⚶

★ ★ ★ Colonna Palace (HG)
Pzza Di Montecitorio 12
☎ 06 6781341 telex 621467 fax 06 6794496
✉ 00186

30 ⌿ 325000/- 80 ⌿ 441000/-
🄰🄴 ⓪ 🄴 ⚎ ⊙ ↟↡ ⚍ 🄯 🆆🄲 🆃🅅 ⚶

ITALY

★ ★ ★ **Delle Muse** (HP)
Via Tommaso Salvini 18
☎ 06 8088333 telex 612537 fax 06 8085749
✉ 00197

* 15 ♨ -/93000 45 ♨ -/147000
🅰🅴 ⓪ 🄴 ☴ ⅄ ⑤ ☂ ☂ ⑭ 🍴 ➖ 🄵 ⓦⓒ ⓣⓥ ⑩ ⊙

★ ★ ★ **Diana** (HCR)
Via Principe Amedeo 4
☎ 06 4827541 telex 611198 fax 06 486998
✉ 00185

61 ♨ -/- 126 ♨ -/-
🅿 ⑭ ➖ 🄵 ⓦⓒ ⓣⓥ

★ ★ ★ **Diplomatic** (HCR)
Via Vittoria Colonna 28
☎ 06 6542084 telex 610506
✉ 00193

3 ♨ -/180000 37 ♨ -/213000
⊙ ◈ ⑭ 🄵 ⓦⓒ ⓣⓥ

★ ★ ★ **Eliseo** (HCR)
Via Di Porta Pinciana 30
☎ 06 4870456 telex 610693 fax 06 4819629
✉ 00187

6 ♨ 150000/200000 50 ♨ 220000/310000
🅰🅴 ⓪ 🄴 ☴ ⅄ ⊙ ⑭ 🍴 ➖ 🄵 ⓦⓒ ⓣⓥ ⑩ ⊙

★ ★ **Flavio** (HG)
Via Frangipane 34
☎ 06 6797203
✉ 00184

7 ♨ -/- 16 ♨ -/-
⊙ ⑭ 🍴 🄵 ⓦⓒ 🐾

★ ★ ★ **Forum** (HCR)
Via Tor De' Conti 25
☎ 06 6792446 telex 622549 fax 06 6786479
✉ 00184

* 16 ♨ 230000/320000 60 ♨ 320000/475000
🅰🅴 ⓪ 🄴 ☴ ⊙ ☂ ⑭ 🍴 ➖ 🄵 ⓦⓒ ⓣⓥ ⊙

★ ★ ★ **Grand Hotel Flora** (HG)
Via V. Veneto 191
☎ 06 497821 telex 622256 fax 06 4820359
✉ 00187

* 68 ♨ 230000/270000 107 ♨ 290000/360000
🅰🅴 ⓪ 🄴 ☴ ⅄ ⊙ ⑭ 🍴 ➖ 🄵 ⓦⓒ ⓣⓥ 🐾

★ ★ ★ **Hiberia** (HG)
Via 24 Maggio 7
☎ 06 6782662 telex 624151 fax 06 6794600
✉ 00187

* 4 ♨ 100000/154000 18 ♨ 149000/205000
🅰🅴 ⓪ 🄴 ☴ ⊙ ⑭ 🍴 ➖ 🄵 ⓦⓒ ⓣⓥ 🐾

★ ★ ★ ★ **Jollyhotel L. da Vinci** (HCR)
Via Dei Gracchi 324
☎ 06 32499 telex 611182 fax 06 3610138
✉ 00192

12 ♨ 220000/250000 244 ♨ 300000/360000
🅰🅴 ⓪ 🄴 ☴ ⊙ ☂ ⑭ 🍴 ➖ 🄵 ⓦⓒ ⓣⓥ ⑩ ⊙

★ ★ ★ ★ **Jollyhotel Vittorio** (HCR)
Corso D' Italia
☎ 06 8495 telex 612293 fax 06 8841104
✉ 00198

50 ♨ 255000/275000 153 ♨ 365000/400000
⅄ ⊙ 🅿 ☂ ⑭ 🍴 ➖ 🄵 ⓦⓒ ⓣⓥ ⑩ 🐾

★ ★ ★ ★ ★ **Lord Byron** (HR)
Via G. De Notaris 5
☎ 06 3220404 telex 611217 fax 06 3220405
✉ 00197

* 1 ♨ 280000/350000 36 ♨ 400000/540000
🅰🅴 ⓪ 🄴 ☴ ⅄ ⊙ 🅿 ☂ ⑭ 🍴 ➖ 🄵 ⓦⓒ ⓣⓥ ⑩ 🐾

★ ★ ★ ★ **Majestic** (HCR)
Via Veneto 50
☎ 06 486841 telex 622262 fax 06 460984
✉ 00187

14 ♨ -/400000 55 ♨ -/540000
🅰🅴 ⅄ ⊙ ☂ ⑭ 🍴 ➖ 🄵 ⓦⓒ ⓣⓥ ⑩ 🐾

★ ★ ★ ★ **Massimo d'Azeglio** (HCR)
Via Cavour 18
☎ 06 4870270 telex 610556 fax 06 4827386
✉ 00184

10 ♨ -/215000 200 ♨ -/298000
🅰🅴 ⓪ 🄴 ☴ ⊙ ⑭ 🍴 ➖ 🄵 ⓦⓒ ⓣⓥ ⊙

★ ★ ★ ★ **Mediterraneo**
Via Cavour 15
☎ 06 4884051 telex 610556 fax 06 4744105
✉ 00184

86 ♨ -/- 184 ♨ 247000/343000
🅰🅴 ⓪ 🄴 ☴ ⑭ 🍴 ➖ 🄵 ⓣⓥ 🐾

★ ★ ★ **Milani** (HG)
Via Magenta 12
☎ 06 4457051 telex 614356 fax 06 4462317
✉ 00185

* 8 ♨ -/135000 70 ♨ -/190000
🅰🅴 ⓪ 🄴 ☴ ⊙ ⑭ 🍴 ➖ 🄵 ⓦⓒ ⓣⓥ 🐾

★ ★ ★ ★ **Best Western Hotel Mondial** (HG)
Via Torino 127
☎ 06 472861 telex 612219 fax 06 4824822
res nr 1678 20080
✉ 00184

17 🛏 125000/202000 61 🛏 180000/286000
🄰🄴 🜛 🄴 ⚍ ⊙ 🄿 🍴 🛏 ⚍ 🄲 🆆🄲 🆃🆅 ✈

★ ★ ★ ★ **Napoleon** (HCR)
Pza V Emanuele 105
☎ 06 4467264 telex 611069 fax 06 4467282
✉ 00185

16 🛏 -/170000 64 🛏 -/275000
🄰🄴 🜛 🄴 ⚍ ⊙ 🍴 ⚍ 🄲 🆆🄲 🆃🆅 🍽 ☺

★ ★ ★ **Nord Nuova Roma**
Via G Amendola 3
☎ 06 4885441 telex 610556 fax 06 4817163
✉ 00185

- 🛏 -/- - 🛏 151000/210000
🄰🄴 🜛 🄴 ⚍

★ ★ ★ **Oxford** (HCR)
Via Boncompagni 89
☎ 06 4828952 telex 630392 fax 06 4815349
✉ 00187

10 🛏 -/- 50 🛏 -/-
🛎 ⊙ 🍴 ⚍ 🄲 🆆🄲 🆃🆅 🍽

★ ★ ★ **Pace Elvezia** (HG)
Via 4 Novembre 104
☎ 06 6791044 telex 623651 fax 06 6791044
✉ 00187

19 🛏 -/- 57 🛏 -/-
🛎 ⊙ 🍴 🄲 🆆🄲 🆃🆅

★ ★ ★ **Pavia** (HG)
Via Gaeta 83
☎ 06 483801 telex 622176 fax 06 4819090
✉ 00185

* 8 🛏 110000/145000 20 🛏 150000/180000
🄰🄴 🜛 🄴 ⚍ ⊙ ◆ 🄿 🄿 🍴 🛏 🄲 🆆🄲 🆃🆅 ☺

★ ★ ★ **Best Western Hotel Picadilly** (HG)
Via Magna Grecia 122
☎ 06 777017 telex 621525 fax 06 576686
res nr 1678 20080
✉ 00183

12 🛏 95000/116000 43 🛏 135000/168000
⊙ 🍴 ⚍ 🄲 🆆🄲 🆃🆅 ✈

★ ★ **Prati** (HG)
Via Crescenzio 87
☎ 06 6875357
✉ 00193

10 🛏 -/- 13 🛏 -/-
⊙ ◆ ⚍ 🄲 🆆🄲

★ ★ ★ ★ **Best Western Hotel President** (HCR)
Via E. Filberto 173
☎ 06 770121 telex 611192 fax 06 7008740
res nr 1678 20080
✉ 00185

61 🛏 120000/140000 119 🛏 180000/265000
☽ 🄿 🍴 ⚍ 🄲 🆆🄲 🆃🆅 🍽

★ ★ ★ **Pullman Boston** (HCR)
Via Lombardia 47
☎ 06 473951 telex 622247 fax 06 4821019
✉ 00100

- 🛏 -/- 128 🛏 -/-
🄰🄴 🜛 🄴 ⚍ 🛎 ⊙ 🄿 🄿 🍴 ⚍ 🄲 🆆🄲 🆃🆅 ☺

★ ★ ★ **River** (HG)
Via Flaminia 39
☎ 06 3200841 telex 626833 fax 06 6793397
✉ 00176

1 🛏 -/- 40 🛏 -/-
⊙ 🍴 🄲 🆆🄲 🆃🆅 ☺

★ ★ ★ ★ **Best Western Hotel Rivoli** (HCR)
Via Torquato Taramelli 7
☎ 06 3224042 telex 614615 fax 06 3227373
res nr 1678 20080
✉ 00197

- 🛏 155000/188000 55 🛏 195000/260000
🄰🄴 🜛 🄴 ⚍ ☽ 🍴 🛏 ⚍ 🄲 🆆🄲 🆃🆅 🍽

★ ★ ★ **San Anselmo** (HG)
Piazza S. Anselmo 2
☎ 06 5745231 telex 622812 fax 06 5783604
✉ 00153

10 🛏 -/120000 145 🛏 -/170000
🛎 ⊙ 🍴 ⚍ 🄲 🐾 ✈

★ ★ ★ ★ **San Giorgio**
Via G Amendola 61
☎ 06 4827341 telex 610556 fax 06 4883191
✉ 00185

- 🛏 -/- - 🛏 183000/254000
🄰🄴 🜛 🄴 ⚍

★ ★ ★ **Sistina** (HG)
Via Sistina 136
☎ 06 4818804 telex 623651 fax 06 4818867
✉ 00187

* 2 🛏 -/150000 21 🛏 -/220000
AE ⓘ E 🔄 ⊙ 🎾 †⌐ ⌐ ⌐ WC TV 🐕

★ ★ ★ ★ **Best Western Hotel Universo** (HCR)
Via Principe Amedeo 5
☎ 06 476811 telex 610342 fax 06 4745125
res nr 1678 20080
✉ 00185

65 🛏 120000/203000 131 🛏 180000/300000
🔄 ⊙ 🎾 †⌐ ⌐ ⌐ WC TV 🍽 ☺

★ ★ ★ **Best Western Hotel Villafranca** (HG)
Via Villafranca 9
☎ 06 4440364 telex 611031 fax 06 4440364
res nr 1678 20080
✉ 00185

* 20 🛏 100000/130000 50 🛏 150000/180000
AE ⓘ E 🔄 ⊙ 🎾 †⌐ ⌐ ⌐ WC TV 🍽 ☺

★ ★ ★ **Villa Glori** (HG)
Viale Del Vignola 28
☎ 06 3227658 telex 621071 fax 06 3219495
✉ 00196

18 🛏 -/- 26 🛏 -/-
AE ⓘ E 🔄 🔄 ⊙ †⌐ ⌐ ⌐ WC TV 🐕

★ ★ ★ **Viminale** (HG)
Via Balbo 31
☎ 06 4881910 telex 623225 fax 06 4744728
✉ 00184

18 🛏 120000/140000 20 🛏 188000/215000
AE ⓘ E 🔄 🔄 ⊙ 🎾 †⌐ ⌐ ⌐ WC TV 🐕 🐕

SALERNO, Salerno   18

★ ★ ★ ★ **Jolly** (HCR)
Lungomare Trieste 1
☎ 089 225222 telex 770050 fax 089 237571
✉ 84100

12 🛏 -/160000 80 🛏 -/200000
🔄 ⊙ P †⌐ ⌐ ⌐ WC TV 🐕

★ ★ ★ **Montestella** (HP)
Corso V Emanuele 156
☎ 089 225122 fax 089 229167
✉ 84100

10 🛏 -/60000 excl. breakfast 41 🛏 -/91000 excl.
breakfast
AE E 🔄 P †⌐ ⌐ ⌐ WC TV 🐕

★ ★ ★ **Plaza** (HCR)
Piazza F O V Veneto 42
☎ 089 224477 fax 089 237311
✉ 84100

2 🛏 60500/- excl. breakfast 40 🛏 96800/- excl.
breakfast
AE ⓘ E 🔄 ⊙ †⌐ ⌐ ⌐ WC 🐕

SÁLO, Brescia   04

★ ★ ★ **Benaco** (HR)
Lungolago Zanardelli 44
☎ 0365 20308
✉ 25087

3 🛏 -/- 17 🛏 -/-
AE ⓘ E 🔄 🍽 ⊙ P 🎾 †⌐ ⌐ ⌐ WC TV 🐕

★ ★ ★ **Duomo** (HCR)
Lungo Lago Zanardelli 91
☎ 0365 21026 fax 0365 21028
✉ 25087

1 🛏 -/103000 21 🛏 -/162000
AE ⓘ E 🔄 🔄 🍽 ⊙ 🎾 🎾 🎾 †⌐ ⌐ ⌐ WC TV

SAN FELICE DEL BENACO, Brescia   04

★ ★ ★ ★ **Parkhotel Casimiro** (HCR)
Via Porto Pertese 22
☎ 0365 626262 fax 0365 62092
✉ 25010

9 🛏 -/- 109 🛏 -/-
AE ⓘ E 🔄 🔄 🍽 ⊙ P 🎾 🎾 🎾 ⚓ 🎾 †⌐ ⌐ ⌐ WC TV 🍽

SAN LEONARDO IN PASSIRIA, Bolzano   04

★ ★ ★ ★ **Stroblhof** (HCR)
Passeirerstr. 28/29
☎ 0473 86128 fax 0473 86468
✉ 39015

open 01.02 - 10.11
* 15 🛏 -/70000 55 🛏 -/90000
🔄 ⊙ P 🎾 🎾 ⚓ 🎾 †⌐ ⌐ ⌐ WC TV 🏠

SAN MAMETE/VALSOLDA, *Como*   03

★ ★ ★ **Stella d'Italia** (HR)   [AA] [ANWB]
Piazza Roma 1
SAN MAMETE
☎ 0344 68139 fax 0344 68729
✉ 22010

This small hotel, situated on Lake Lugano, has been in the hands of the Ortelli family for 3 generations. The large rooms are modestly furnished, offering good modern amenities. There is a pleasant, quiet lounge. There are good walks in the lovely hotel garden.

open 05.04 - 05.10
* 4 ♨ -/63000 31 ♨ 80000/120000
[AE] [E] ⚏ ⚘ ⛴ ⚉ ⊙ ◆ ⛛ ♨ ♯ ⛾ ⛶ [WC] [⬤] ☺

SAN MARCO, *Salerno*   18

Castelsandra (HP)
Piano Melaino
☎ 0974 966021 telex 721651
✉ 84071

- ♨ -/- 125 ♨ -/-
⚏ ⛻ [P] ♨ ⚉ ♯ ⛾ ⛶ [P] [WC] [TV] 🐾

SAN MARTINO DI CASTROZZA, *Trento*   05

★ ★ ★ **San Martino** (HP)
Via Passo Rolle 279
☎ 0439 68381 fax 0439 68841
✉ 38058

open 20.12 - 10.04 + 01.07 - 15.09
10 ♨ 65000/- excl. breakfast 38 ♨ -/-
⚏ [P] ⛛ ♨ ⚉ ⛶ [P] [WC]

★ ★ ★ ★ **Savoia** (HCR)
☎ 0439 68094
✉ 35058

1 ♨ -/135000 excl. breakfast 72 ♨ -/175000 excl. breakfast
[P] ⛛ ♯ ⛶ [P] [WC]

SAN NICOLÓ, *Catanzaro*   21

St.Nicolas (HCR)
Fraz. Fossaz 4
☎ 0165 98824
✉ 11010

4 ♨ -/- 18 ♨ -/-
⚏ ⛻ [P] ♨ [P] [WC]

SAN REMO, *Imperia*   07
See advertisement on page 87

★ ★ ★ **Beau Rivage** (HR)   [AA] [ANWB]
Lungomare Trieste 49
☎ 0184 85146 telex 270620
✉ 18038

The Hotel Beau Rivage is a small traditional hotel, situated on the promenade in the heart of San Remo by the little beach near the yachting harbour. The bedrooms all feature a private toilet and shower, and half of them have a TV; the rooms at the front of the building have a balcony with a beautiful view over the beach, the harbour and the sea. At the back of the hotel is a lush garden with a pleasant, peaceful terrace.

5 ♨ -/48500 25 ♨ -/82000
⚏ ⛻ ⊙ ⛛ ♨ ♯ ⛶ [P] [WC] [TV] ☺

★ ★ ★ **Miramare** (HP)
Corso Matuzia 9
☎ 0184 667601 fax 0184 667655
✉ 18038

open 20.12 - 30.09
* 12 ♨ 130000/150000 excl. breakfast
47 ♨ 200000/250000 excl. breakfast
[AE] [D] [E] ⚏ ⚘ ⊙ [P] ♨ ⚉ ♯ ⛶ [WC] [TV] [⬤] ☺

★ ★ ★ **Nazionale** (HCR)
Via Matteotti 5
☎ 0184 77577
✉ 18038

6 ♨ -/78000 excl. breakfast 80 ♨ -/125000 excl. breakfast
♯ ⛶ [P] [WC] 🐾

★ ★ ★ **Paradiso** (HR)   [AA] [ANWB]
Via Roccasterone 12
☎ 0184 532415 telex 272264 fax 0184 578176
✉ 18038

The Hotel Paradiso is within walking distance of the centre of San Remo, surrounded by parks and only 150m from the beach. It has a well maintained and fairly luxurious appearance. All the 41 tastefully furnished rooms are equipped with modern amenities, and some of them also feature a balcony. Drinks are served in the American-style bar; the restaurant offers a →

ITALY

choice of regional specialities, and when the weather is nice, guests can enjoy their meals on the covered terrace.

* 4 ⌂ 60000/85000 excl. breakfast 37 ⌂ 100000/130000 excl. breakfast
🆎 ⓪ 🄴 ⚏ ⅃ ⚲ ⊙ 🅿 🆃 🎅 ⑪ ▭ 🄫 ⤡ 🅆🄲 🄣 🍴 ☺

★ ★ ★ ★ Parigi (HG)
Corso Imperatrice 66
☎ 0184 505605 fax 0184 533020
✉ 18038

* 8 ⌂ -/130000 20 ⌂ -/240000
🆎 ⓪ 🄴 ⚏ ⊙ ◆ ⑪ ▭ 🄫 🅆🄲 🄣 ☺

★ ★ ★ ★ ★ Royal hotel (HCR)
Corso Imperatrice 80
☎ 0184 5391 telex 270511 fax 0184 61445
✉ 18038

open 20.12 - 08.10
* 19 ⌂ 170000/260000 130 ⌂ 290000/410000
🆎 ⓪ 🄴 ⚏ ⅃ ⊙ 🅿 🆃 🎅 ⚓ ⑪ ▭ 🄫 🅆🄲 🄣 🍴 ☺

★ ★ ★ Svizzera (HR)
Corso Raimondo 63
☎ 0184 84744
✉ 18038

3 ⌂ -/45000 20 ⌂ -/73000
⑪ ▭ 🄫 🅆🄲

★ ★ ★ Florio (MT)
☎ 0881 71936
✉ 71016

- ⌂ -/- 85 ⌂ -/-
🆎 ⓪ 🄴 ⚏ 🅿 ⚓ ⑪ ▭ 🅆🄲 🄣

★ ★ Ciamp (HP)
Via Chemun 55
☎ 0471 77203
✉ 39047

- ⌂ -/- 21 ⌂ -/-
⅃ ⚲ 🅿 ▭ 🄫 🅆🄲 ✿

★ ★ ★ Villa Pallua (HCR)
Palluastr. 16
☎ 0471 793366
✉ 39047

Hotel Villa Pallua is on a sunny slope about one km outside Santa Cristina, surrounded by the impressive country-side of Val Gardena. It is a quiet holiday hotel for the summer as well as the winter, featuring well kept rooms with private toilet, bath or shower; some also have a balcony. A rustic atmosphere characterises the restaurant and the bar, and after a day of walking or skiing in the countryside, the sauna offers relaxation.

2 ⌂ -/- 20 ⌂ -/-
⅃ ⚲ ◐ ◆ 🅿 🎅 ⑪ ▭ 🄫 🅆🄲 🍴 ✿

★ ★ ★ Fiorina (HCR)
Piazza Mazzini 26
☎ 0185 287517 fax 0185 281855
✉ 16038

open 23.12 - 31.10
8 ⌂ 65000/74000 47 ⌂ 104000/129000
🆎 ⓪ 🄴 ⚏ ⅃ ⊙ 🎅 ⑪ ▭ 🄫 🅆🄲 🄣 🍴 ✖

★ ★ ★ ★ Best Western Hotel Laurin (HG)
Lungomare Marconi 3
☎ 0185 289971 telex 275043 fax 0185 285709
res nr 1678 20080
✉ 16038

3 ⌂ 92000/127000 42 ⌂ 150000/198000
🆎 ⓪ 🄴 ⚏ ⚲ ⊙ 🎅 ⑪ ▭ 🄫 🅆🄲 🄣 ☺

★ ★ ★ Minerva (HCR)
Via Maragliano 34/d
☎ 0185 286073 telex 270630 fax 0185 281697
✉ 16038

* 9 ⌂ 78000/101000 21 ⌂ 128000/169000
🆎 ⓪ 🄴 ⚏ ⅃ ⊙ 🅿 🆃 🎅 ⑪ ▭ 🄫 🅆🄲 🄣 🍴 ✖

★ ★ ★ ★ Best Western Hotel Regina Elena (HCR)
Lungomare Mil. Ignoto 44
☎ 0185 287003 telex 271563 fax 0185 284473
res nr 1678 20080
✉ 16038

* 26 ⌂ -/151000 68 ⌂ -/261000
🆎 ⓪ 🄴 ⚏ ⚮ ⚲ ◆ 🅿 🎅 ⑪ ▭ 🄫 🅆🄲 🄣 🍴 ☺

HOTELPARADISO ***

SAN REMO

FLORAL RIVIERA

Quiet location near to centre and beach. Popular among motorists for its comfort.

All rooms with wc, direct dial telephone, minibar and balcony.

Restaurant with panoramic view.

Garden-garage-American bar. Entirely renovated in 1987.

Owner: Gaiani family

Tel. 0184-571211, Telex 272264 PARADII. Fax 578176

SANT' ANDRÉA, *Livorno*   **12**

★ ★ ★ **La Cernia** (HR)
☎ 0565 908194 fax 0565 908253
✉ 57030

open 01.04 - 20.10
* 4 ♫ 40000/80000 excl. breakfast 23 ♫ 50000/
120000 excl. breakfast
⚞⊙ℙ ☂ ♨ ◢ ◨ ☐ ⓦⒸ ☺

SAN VITO DI CADORE, *Belluno*   **05**

★ ★ ★ **Marcora** (HCR)
☎ 0436 9101 fax 0436 99156
✉ 32046

9 ♫ -/- 37 ♫ -/-
⚴ ⊙ ℙ ☂ ☎ ⇅ ◨ ☐ Ⓒ ⓦⒸ ⓉⓋ |◎| ☺

SARZANA, *La Spezia*   **09**

★ ★ ★ ★ **Agip** (MT)
Nuova Circonvalla 32
☎ 0187 621491 telex 272350 fax 0187 621494
res nr 06 4821651
✉ 19038

- ♫ -/- 51 ♫ -/-
ⒶⒺ ◑ Ⓔ ⚞ ◈ ℙ ⇅ ◨ ☐ Ⓒ ⓦⒸ ⓉⓋ |◎| ☺

SÀSSARI, *Sassari*   **12**

★ ★ ★ **Agip** (MT)
Localita Serra Secca
☎ 079 271440 telex 792095 fax 079 271440
res nr 06 4821651
✉ 07100

- ♫ -/- 57 ♫ -/-
⊜ ℙ ⇅ ◨ ☐ Ⓒ ⓦⒸ ⓉⓋ ☺

SATÚRNIA, *Grosseto*   13

★ ★ ★ ★ **Terme Di Saturnia** (HCR)
☎ 0564 601061 telex 500172 fax 0564 601266
✉ 58050

* 15 ⏁ 187000/- excl. breakfast 73 ⏁ 340000/-
excl. breakfast
🄰🄴 ⓄⒺ⚊⚊⚲🐎🅟⚓⚓⚓⇕⊟🄿Ⓦ🆃ⅣⅠ⓵🔔👁

SAVONA, *Savona*   08

★ ★ **Agip** (HCR)
Via Nizza 62
☎ 019 861961
res nr 06 4821651
✉ 17100

- ⏁ -/- 60 ⏁ -/132000
🅟⊟🄿👁

★ ★ **San Marco** (HCR)
Via Leoncavallo 32
☎ 019 803055
✉ 17100

5 ⏁ -/- 10 ⏁ -/-
⊟🄿Ⓦ👁

SCENA, *Bolzano*   04

★ ★ ★ **Sport st. Georgen** (HP)
St. Georgenstrasse 36 B
☎ 0473 95788
✉ 39017

- ⏁ -/- 18 ⏁ -/-
⚲🐎🆂🅟⚓⚓🄿ⓌⅣⅠ👁

SELVA DI VAL GARDENA, *Bolzano*   05

★ ★ ★ ★ **Aaritz** (HR)
☎ 0471 75011
✉ 39048

1 ⏁ -/- 41 ⏁ 85000/150000
🅟⚓⊟🄿👁

★ **Comploj** (HG)
Meisulesstr 50
☎ 0471 795383
✉ 39048

1 ⏁ -/- 9 ⏁ -/-
⚲🐎Ⓢ◈🅟⚓🄿Ⓦ

★ ★ ★ ★ **Tyrol** (HCR)
Puczstrasse 12
☎ 0471 795270 fax 0471 794022
✉ 39048

8 ⏁ 102000/190000 32 ⏁ -/-
⚲Ⓢ🅟⚓⚓⚓⇕⊟🄿ⓌⅣⅠ👁

SESTO, *Bolzano*   05

★ ★ ★ **Park** (HR)
☎ 0474 70305

6 ⏁ -/- 16 ⏁ -/-
⚲🐎🅟⊟🄿Ⅳ⑈👁

★ ★ ★ **San Vito** (HCR)
Europaweg 16
☎ 0474 70390 fax 0474 70072
✉ 39030

open 20.12 - 15.04 + 30.05 - 20.10
* 3 ⏁ 55000/- 22 ⏁ 90000/-
⚊⚲🐎Ⓢ🅟⚓⚓⚓⊟🄿Ⅳ🔔👁

SESTRI LEVANTE, *Genova*   08

★ ★ ★ **Mimosa** (HP)
☎ 0185 41449
✉ 16039

- ⏁ -/- 22 ⏁ -/-
⚲🐎⚓⚓⑈Ⅳ🔔

★ ★ ★ ★ **Vis a Vis**
Via Della Chiusa 28
☎ 0185 42661 telex 272443 fax 0185 480853
✉ 16039

open 20.12 - 20.11
* 8 ⏁ 100000/130000 42 ⏁ 140000/250000
🄰🄴ⓄⒺ⚊⚲🅟⚓⚓⚓⊟🄿Ⓦ Ⅳ⑈👁

See advertisement on page 89

SIENA, *Siena*   10

Sienna stands proudly 1,000ft up in the Tuscan hills at
the meeting point of three ridges. One of Italy's great
art centres, abounding with buildings of fascinating
historic and architectural merit, it also ranks among its
best preserved medieval towns and is a splendid
example of successful early town planning, with an
abundance of fascinating twisting lanes and alleys that
rise and dip as they follow the land's hilly contours.
Sienna's main square - the Campo - is a superb vista of
marble and red brick paving in the pattern of a gigantic
fan, dominated by the tower of the Gothic town hall
(1297 - 1310). The old Roman forum, surrounded by
ancient palaces, shops and restaurants is the focal
point of the city. A first glimpse quickly explains how
the colour known as burnt sienna obtained its name:
the pigment comes from this area, and its hue is
imprinted on many of the fine buildings.

San Remo: see also page 83 and 84

★ ★ **Chiusarelli** (HR)
Viale Curtona 9
☎ 0577 280562 telex 571044
✉ 53100

2 ♫ -/62000 excl. breakfast 50 ♫ -/98000 excl.
breakfast
⊙ 🅿 ⚘ 🍴 🖥 🎦 🆆🅲

★ ★ ★ ★ **Jolly** (HCR)
Plaza La Lizza
☎ 0577 288448 telex 573345 fax 0577 41272
✉ 53100

23 ♫ 260000/- 103 ♫ 375000/-
🆎 ⓪ 🅴 ⌘ ⚘ ⊙ 🅿 ↟ 🖥 🎦 🆃🆅 🍽

★ ★ ★ ★ **Villa Scacciapensieri** (HR)
Via Scacciapensiere 10
☎ 0577 41442 telex 573390 fax 0577 270854
✉ 53100

open 15.03 - 07.01
4 ♫ -/180000 24 ♫ -/290000
🆎 ⓪ 🅴 ⌘ ⚘ ⊙ 🅿 🎦 ⚘ ⌘ ↟ 🍴 🖥 🎦 🆆🅲 🆃🆅 🍽

SIRACUSA, *Siracusa*   **17**

★ ★ ★ **Agip** (MT)
Viale Terecati 30
☎ 0931 66944 telex 912480
res nr 06 4821651

- ♫ -/105000 76 ♫ -/160000
🅿 🖥 🎦 🍴

★ ★ ★ ★ **Jolly** (HCR)
Corso Gelone 43
☎ 0931 461111 telex 970108 fax 0931 461126
✉ 96100

52 ♫ 155000/170000 48 ♫ 200000/-
🆎 ⓪ 🅴 ⌘ 🅿 ↟ 🖥 🎦 🆆🅲 🆃🆅 🍽 ⊙

SIRMIONE, *Brescia*   **04**

★ ★ ★ **Brunello** (HCR)
Via Catullo 29
☎ 030 916115
✉ 25010

5 ♫ -/58000 excl. breakfast 19 ♫ -/90000 excl.
breakfast
⚘ 🅿 🎦 ⚘ 🖥 🎦 🆆🅲 ↟ 🍴

★ ★ ★ ★ **Continental** (HCR)
Punta Staffalo 7
☎ 030 916191 telex 305033 fax 030 916278
✉ 25010

12 🍴 -/95000 excl. breakfast 45 🛏 -/165000 excl. breakfast
🆎 ⓪ 🅴 ⚡ ⅄ ◉ ☕ ◉ 🅿 ⓟ 🍴 ⚓ ⅄ ↑↓ 🔲 📺 ⚓ ↑ ✕

★ ★ ★ ★ **Flaminia** (HG)
Piazza Flaminia 8
☎ 030 916078 telex 300395 fax 030 916193
✉ 25019

open 10.03 - 12.11
4 🍴 -/94000 44 🛏 130000/151000
🆎 ⓪ 🅴 ⚡ ⅄ ◉ ☕ ◉ 🅿 🍴 ↑↓ 🔲 📺 🆎 ☺

★ ★ ★ ★ ★ **Grandhotel Terme** (HCR)
Viale Marconi 7
☎ 030 916261 telex 305573 fax 030 916568
✉ 25019

open 16.04 - 27.10
3 🍴 210000/225000 55 🛏 300000/370000
🆎 ⓪ 🅴 ⚡ ◉ ☕ ◉ 🅿 🍴 ↑↓ 🔲 📺 🍽

SISTIANA, *Trieste* 06

★ ★ ★ **Posta** (HG)
Sistiana 51
☎ 040 299103 fax 040 291001
✉ 34019

2 🍴 -/68000 excl. breakfast 28 🛏 -/93000 excl. breakfast
☕ ◉ ◈ 🅿 🍴 ↑↓ 🆎 🔲 📺 ✕

SIUSI, *Bolzano* 05

★ ★ ★ **Aquila Nera** (HCR)
Via Laurino 7
☎ 0471 706146
✉ 39040

open 25.12 - 02.05
5 🍴 44000/60000 9 🛏 50000/71000
⅄ ◉ 🅿 🍴 ⚓ 🔲 🆎 🍽 ☺

★ ★ ★ ★ **Edelweiss** (HCR)
H. Ibsen-strasse 11
☎ 0471 706130 telex 400110 fax 0471 705439
✉ 39040

4 🍴 80000/160000 41 🛏 -/-
⅄ ☺ 🅿 🍴 ⚓ ↑↓ ↕ 🔲 🆎 🔲 🍽 ↑

★ ★ ★ **Genziana Enzian** (HG)
☎ 0471 71150
✉ 39040

1 🍴 56000/112000 31 🛏 -/-
⅄ 🅿 ☕ 🔲 🆎 🔲

Riposa Al Bosco (HR)
☎ 0471 71117
✉ 39040

1 🍴 -/- 29 🛏 -/-
⅄ 🅿 ⚓ 🔲 🆎 🔲

SIUSI ALLO SCILIAR, *Bolzano* 05

★ ★ ★ **Enzian** (HG)
Osw. V Wolkensteinpl. 2
SIUSI
☎ 0471 705050 fax 0471 707010
✉ 39040

9 🍴 -/- 24 🛏 -/-
🆎 ⅄ ◉ 🅿 🍴 ⚓ ↑↓ 🔲 🆎 🔲 📺

SORRENTO, *Napoli* 17

★ ★ ★ **Bellevue Syrene** (HCR)
Piazza Della Vittoria 5
☎ 081 8781024
✉ 80067

10 🍴 -/- 40 🛏 -/200000
⅄ ☕ 🅿 🍴 ↑↓ 🔲 🆎 🔲 ✕

★ ★ ★ ★ **Bristol** (HP)
Via Capo 22
☎ 081 8781436 telex 710687 fax 081 8071910

* 15 🍴 135000/165000 121 🛏 250000/280000
🆎 ⓪ 🅴 ⚡ ⅄ ☺ ◈ 🅿 ⓟ 🍴 ⚓ ⅄ ↑↓ 🔲 🆎 🔲 📺 🍽 ☺

★ ★ **Britannia** (HCR)
Via Del Capo 72
☎ 081 8782706

8 🍴 -/- 20 🛏 -/-
🅿 🍴 ↑↓ 🔲 🆎 🔲 ✕

★ ★ ★ ★ **Central** (HR)
Corso Italia 254
☎ 081 8781646 telex
721105 fax 081
8781372
✉ 80067

Hotel Central is within
walking distance of the
centre of Sorrento and
the beach. It is a tradi-
tional hotel featuring 60
rooms with en suite

SESTRI LEVANTE - East Riviera

HOTEL VIS à VIS

★ ★ ★ ★

Tel.: 0185 - 42661
Fax: 0185 - 480853

Quiet location in park overlooking sea. Heated swimming pool. Private car park. Conference hall. Beach and centre accessible within minutes by using outdoor lift. Famous à la carte cuisine. The ideal luxury hotel with the every comfort. Open throughout the year. Under the management of the De Nicolai family.

toilet, bath/shower and balcony, a restaurant and a pleasant espresso bar. At the back is a verdant garden with a swimming pool and terrace with deck chairs. The hotel features a second terrace on the roof overlooking the Bay of Naples and Mount Vesuvius. There is safe parking in the hotel car park or in the garage.

open 15.03 - 15.11
* 7 ♨ 85000/100000 53 ♨ 120000/180000
AE ⓪ E ➡ ⊙ P ⬆ ⬆ ⚓ ⇅ ⬛ 🄲 WC TV IOI 🐾

★ ★ ★ ★ ★ Best Western Grand Hotel Cocumella (HR)
Via Cocumella N. 7
☎ 081 8782933 telex 720370 fax 081 8783712
res nr 1678 20080
✉ 80065

* 10 ♨ 180000/220000 50 ♨ 320000/480000
AE ⓪ E ➡ ◆ P ⬆ ⇅ ⬛ 🄲 WC TV IOI ⊙

★ ★ ★ Villa Di Sorrento (HP)
Via Fiorimura 4
☎ 081 8781068

3 ♨ -/80000 excl. breakfast 15 ♨ -/130000 excl. breakfast
⊙ ⇅ ⬛ 🄲 WC 🐾

★ ★ ★ Bellevue (HCR)
Lungomare Adriatico 22
☎ 041 401439 fax 041 401439
✉ 30019

open 20.03 - 30.09
* 2 ♨ 50000/66000 excl. breakfast 23 ♨ 66000/90000 excl. breakfast
E ➡ ⬆ ⬆ ⊙ ◆ P ⬆ ⬆ ⚓ ⇅ ⬛ 🄲 WC IOI 🐾 🐾

★ ★ ★ Florida (HCR)
Mediterraneo 9
☎ 041 491505 telex 411376 fax 041 4966760
✉ 30019

open 01.02 - 30.11
* 6 ♨ 50000/60000 64 ♨ 90000/105000
AE E ➡ ⬆ ⬆ ◆ P ⬆ ⇅ ⬛ 🄲 WC IOI ⊙

★ ★ ★ Ritz (HCR)
Largo Europa
☎ 041 401900

1 ♨ -/- 83 ♨ -/-
⬆ ⬆ P ⚓ ⇅ ⬛ 🄲 WC 🐾

★ ★ ★ Agip (MT)
S. S. Flamina Km 127
☎ 0743 49340 fax 0743 49293
res nr 06 4821651
✉ 06049

* - ♨ 65000/80000 excl. breakfast 57 ♨ 80000/105000 excl. breakfast
AE ⓪ E ➡ P ⇅ ⬛ 🄲 TV IOI ⊙

★ ★ ★ Dei Duchi (HCR)
Viale Matteotti 4
☎ 0743 44541
fax 0743 44543
✉ 06049

AA *ANWB*

Hotel Dei Duchi is beautifully situated on the edge of the histor- ical centre, right beside the Teatro Romano and the sports park. It is a charming hotel sur- rounded by greenery, overlooking the hills of Umbria. The rooms are spacious, tastefully furnished and have a bathroom, TV and minibar. Meals can be enjoyed not only in the restaurant, but also on the cosy veranda and in the garden. There is a choice of Italian and regional Umbrian dishes.

* - ♨ 115000/140000 51 ♨ 145000/215000
AE ⓪ E ➡ ⬆ ⊙ P ⇅ ⬛ 🄲 WC TV IOI 🐾

STRESA, *Novara*   03

★ ★ ★ **Bristol** (HCR)
Corso Umberto I 75
☎ 0323 32601 telex 200217 fax 0323 924515
✉ 28049

43 ♨ -/- 201 ♨ -/-
🆎 ⓪ 🅔 🆑 👤 🌊 🚲 ⊙ ◆ 🅿 ⚯ 🍴 🛥 🚣 ⇅ 🔌 🅳 �📺 🆆 📺 🍽 ⊛

★ ★ ★ ★ **Des Iles Borromees** (HCR)
Corso Umberto I, 67
☎ 0323 30431 telex 200377 fax 0323 32405
✉ 28049

* 33 ♨ 250000/332000 139 ♨ 420000/510000
🆎 ⓪ 🅔 🆑 🌊 🚲 ⊙ 🅿 🍴 ⚯ 🛥 🚣 ⇅ 🔌 📺 🍽 ⊛

★ ★ ★ **Italie e Suisse** (HG)
Piazza Marconi 1
☎ 0323 30540 fax 0323 32621
✉ 28049

open 07.03 - 20.11
* 3 ♨ 61000/81000 25 ♨ 86000/112000
🆎 ⓪ 🅔 🆑 ⚱ ⚘ ⊙ ⇅ 🔌 🅳 🆆 📺 ⊛

★ ★ ★ **Du Parc** (HCR)
Via Gignous 1
☎ 0323 30335 fax 0323 33596
✉ 28049

open 01.04 - 31.10
4 ♨ 60000/90000 28 ♨ 85000/118000
🆎 🅔 🆑 👤 ⊙ 🅿 ⇅ 🔌 🅳 🆆 📺 🍽 ⊛

TAORMINA, *Messina*   17

★ ★ ★ **Bel Soggiorno** (HCR)
Via Pirandello 60
☎ 0942 23342 telex 980062
✉ 98039

3 ♨ -/60000 excl. breakfast 16 ♨ -/96000 excl.
breakfast
🅿 ⚯ 🔌 🅳 🆆 ✄

★ ★ ★ ★ **Bristol Park** (HCR)
Via Bagnoli Croce 92
☎ 0942 23006 telex 980005 fax 0942 24519
✉ 98039

open 01.03 - 31.10
* 12 ♨ 100000/135000 excl. breakfast 50 ♨
180000/210000 excl. breakfast
🆎 ⓪ 🅔 🆑 👤 🚲 ⊙ 🅿 🍴 ⚯ 🛥 ⇅ 🔌 🅳 🆆 📺 🍽 ↟ ⊛

★ ★ ★ **Continental** (HR)
Via Dionisio Primo
☎ 0942 23805 telex 981144 fax 0942 243284
✉ 98039

* 6 ♨ 75000/95000 37 ♨ 100000/155000
🆎 ⓪ 🅔 🆑 👤 ⊙ 🅿 ⚯ ⇅ 🔌 🅳 📺 🍽 ⊛

★ ★ ★ **Diodoro Jolly** (HCR)
Via Bagnoli Croce
☎ 0942 23312 telex 980028 fax 0942 23391

* 4 ♨ 170000/- 98 ♨ 240000/-
🆎 ⓪ 🅔 🆑 👤 ⊙ 🅿 ⚯ ⇅ 🔌 🅳 🆆 📺 🍽 ⊛

★ ★ ★ **Mediterranée** (HCR)
Via Circonvallazione 61
☎ 0942 23901 telex 980175
✉ 98039

10 ♨ -/- 40 ♨ -/-
🚲 🅿 ⚯ ⇅ 🔌 🅳 ✄

★ ★ ★ **Vello d'Oro** (HCR)
Via Fazzello
☎ 0942 23789 telex 980186
✉ 98039

9 ♨ -/70000 excl. breakfast 50 ♨ -/120000 excl.
breakfast
⇅ 🔌 🅳 🆆 ✄

★ ★ ★ **Villa Belvédere** (HP)
Via Bagnoli Croce 79
☎ 0942 23791 fax 0942 625830
✉ 98039

open 11.04 - 31.10
* 4 ♨ 73900/97000 44 ♨ 13000/178000
🅔 🆑 🚲 🅿 ⚯ ⇅ 🔌 🅳 🆆 🍽 ⊛

★ **Villa Greta** (HP)
Via Leonardo Da Vinci 44
☎ 0942 28286 telex 980062 fax 0942 24360
✉ 98039

2 ♨ -/35000 excl. breakfast 16 ♨ -/49000 excl.
breakfast
🆎 ⓪ 🅔 🆑 🅿 🅳 🆆 🍽 ↟ ⊛

TARVISIO, *Udine*   06

★ ★ ★ **Nevada** (HCR)
Via Kugy 4
☎ 0428 2332 telex 450636 fax 0428 40566
✉ 33018

* 12 ♨ 55000/60000 excl. breakfast 48 ♨ 75000/
95000 excl. breakfast
🆎 ⓪ 🅔 🆑 👤 ⊙ 🅿 🍴 ⚯ ⇅ 🔌 🅳 🆆 📺 🍽 ✄

TENNA, *Trento*   05

★ ★ **Da Remo** (HCR)
Via Albere 56
☎ 0461 706446
✉ 38050

open 01.12 - 31.10
* 2 ⌀ 25000/45000 24 ⍒ 60000/90000
⌂ 🛏 ⌖ ⊙ **P** 🛎 🝰 **P** **WC** 🍴 🐕

TENNA/TRENTO, *Trento*   05

★ ★ ★ **Le Terrazze** (HR)
Via Lago 17
TENNA
☎ 0461 707329 fax 0461 707804
✉ 38050

4 ⌀ -/- 33 ⍒ -/-
🝰 ⌂ ⌖ 🝰 ◆ **P** 🛎 🝰 🝰 **P** **WC** 🍴 🐕

TIRRÉNIA, *Pisa*   09

★ ★ ★ ★ **Continental** (HP)
Lungomare Belvedere
☎ 050 37031 telex 500103
✉ 56018

6 ⌀ -/165000 excl. breakfast 194 ⍒ -/230000 excl.
breakfast
🝰 ⊙ **P** 🝰 🛎 🝰 🝰 **P** **WC** 🍴

TÓRBOLE, *Trento*   04

★ ★ ★ **Paradiso** (HCR)
☎ 0464 505126
✉ 38069

1 ⌀ -/- 27 ⍒ -/-
⌂ **P** 🝰 **P**

TORINO, *Torino*   02

Turin's grace and charm surprise many visitors. For this delightful city wears a mantle of French influence, characterised by the wide, formal avenues, elegant squares and gardens. Turin is the capital of the Piemonte region, an important centre for trade and industry and a place of learning and culture. It has fine art collections, and its most famous sacred relic, the Holy Shroud of Turin, is housed in the vast cathedral. The Via Roma is lined with smart boutiques boasting top names in Italian fashion. The Piazza San Carlo and the Via Po are the places for antiques and books, and there is a flea market every Saturday morning in the Piazza della Republica. Local specialities include *agnolotti* - ravioli stuffed with truffles, spinach, lamb or veal; white truffles from Alba; *bolliti con salsa verde* - boiled meats with a green herb sauce; *gianduia* - chocolate pudding; *zabaglione* - whipped egg yolks

and Marsala; and *grissini* - thin breadsticks. Regional wines include the red Barolo and the sparkling white Asti Spumante. Vermouth is made in Turin using a blend of wines flavoured with Alpine herbs.

★ ★ ★ **Dock Milano** (HCR)   **AA** *ANWB*
Via Cernaia 46
☎ 011 5622622 telex
225399 fax 011 545939
✉ 10122

The Hotel-ristorante
Dock Milano is housed
in an old but architectu-
rally beautiful corner
building, with graceful
balconies and arches at
the front. All the rooms
of this traditional holiday and commercial hotel
have a private toilet, bath or shower; most of
them also have a TV, and some a balcony. The
hotel has a garage and private car park, and is
situated in the centre opposite the Porta Susa
station.

* 11 ⌀ 90000/115000 58 ⍒ 125000/145000
AE ⊙ **E** 🝰 ⌂ ⊙ **P** 🝰 🝰 🝰 **P** **WC** **TV** 🔔 😊

★ ★ ★ **Genio** (HCR)
Corso Vitt. Emanuelle 47
☎ 011 6505771 telex 220308 fax 011 6508264
res nr 1678 20080
✉ 10125

* 40 ⌀ -/125000 35 ⍒ 75000/175000
AE ⊙ **E** 🝰 ⊙ **P** **P** **WC** **TV** 😊

★ ★ ★ ★ **Jolly Principe Di Piem** (HR)
Via P. Gobetti 15
☎ 011 532153
✉ 10123

8 ⌀ -/300000 99 ⍒ -/380000
⊙ **P** **WC** **TV** 🐕

★ ★ ★ ★ **Jollyhotel Ambasciatori** (HCR)
Corso Vitt. Emanuele 104
☎ 011 5752 telex 221296 fax 011 544978
✉ 10121

* - ⌀ -/250000 151 ⍒ -/320000
AE ⊙ **E** 🝰 ⊙ **P** 🝰 🝰 🝰 **P** **WC** **TV** 🍴 🐕

★ ★ ★ ★ **Jollyhotel Ligure** (HCR)
Piazza Carlo Felice 85
☎ 011 55641 telex 220167
✉ 10100

- ⌀ -/255000 156 ⍒ -/322000
P 🝰 **P** 🐕

ITALY

Motel Agip (HCR)
Ingresso Autostrada
☎ 011 8001855
✉ 10036

- *♪* -/- 100 *♫* -/-
🅿 🖥 🖵

TORRI DEL BENACO, *Verona* 04

★ ★ ★ **Europa** (HP)
Via D'annunzio 13-15
☎ 045 9250866 fax 045 6296632
✉ 37010

open 09.04 - 15.10
* 1 *♪* 30000/59000 excl. breakfast 17 *♫* 60000/
120000 excl. breakfast
⚑ 🏠 🅿 ⚓ ✉ 🖥 🖵 🛗 ✈

TOSCOLANO MADERNO, *Brescia* 04

★ ★ ★ **Maderno** (HCR)
☎ 0365 641070
✉ 25080

1 *♪* -/85000 29 *♫* -/140000
🅿 ☂ ⚓ 🖥 🆆🅲

TREMEZZO, *Como* 03

★ ★ ★ ★ **Best Western Hotel Tremezzo Palace**
(HCR)
Via Regina 8
LAGO DI COMO
☎ 0344 40446 telex 320810 fax 0344 40201
res nr 1678 20080
✉ 22019

15 *♪* 130000/140000 85 *♫* 200000/220000
⚑ ⓘ 🅔 ⚒ ⚓ 🍽 ⊙ ◈ 🅿 ☂ 🛎 ⚓ 🛗 🖥 🆆🅲 📺 🍴 ⊛

★ ★ **Villa Marie** (HCR)
Via Regina 30
☎ 0344 40427
✉ 22019

1 *♪* -/- 12 *♫* -/-
⚑ ☂ ◈ 🅿 ☂ 🛎 🖥 🖵 🆆🅲 📺 🍴 ⊛

TRENTO, *Trento* 04

★ ★ ★ **America** (HCR)
Via Torre Verde 50
☎ 0461 23963 fax 0461 230603
✉ 38100

* 18 *♪* -/102000 excl. breakfast 30 *♫* -/144000
excl. breakfast
🆎 ⓘ 🅔 ⚒ ⊙ ◈ 🅿 ☂ 🛗 🖥 🖵 🆆🅲 📺 🍴 ⊛

★ ★ ★ **Monaco** (HG)
Via Torre D' Augusto 25
☎ 0461 983060 fax 0461 983060
✉ 38100

* 25 *♪* 100000/120000 excl. breakfast
27 *♫* 140800/170000 excl. breakfast
ⓘ 🅔 ⚒ ⚓ ⊙ 🅿 ☂ ☂ ⚓ 🛗 🖥 🆆🅲 📺 ✈

TREZZANO SUL NAVIGLIO, *Milano* 03

★ ★ ★ ★ **Eur** (HG)   *AA* *ANWB*
Uscita Sp 43 Vigevano
☎ 02 4451951
fax 02 4451075
✉ 20090

The tasteful, spacious
rooms in Hotel Eur are
all equipped with a
bath/shower and toilet.
Though the hotel only
serves breakfast, it
does have a bar; the
garden has a pleasant terrace where guests can
enjoy the sunset after sightseeing in Milan.
Parking is available.

open 25.08 - 31.07
* 2 *♪* 155000/172000 39 *♫* 195000/222000
🆎 ⓘ 🅔 ⚒ ⚓ ☂ ◈ 🅿 ☂ 🛗 🖥 🖵 🆆🅲 📺 ⊛

★ ★ ★ **Tiffany** (HR)   *AA* *ANWB*
Via Leonardo Da Vin-
ci209
☎ 02 48401178
fax 02 4450944
✉ 20090

The Hotel Tiffany has
recently been complete-
ly renovated. All the 36
rooms have their own
toilet, bath/shower,
minibar and telephone.
The restaurant has a choice of both fish and meat
specialities, and there is a relaxed atmosphere in
the bar and on the garden terrace. The hotel is
suitable as a base for visiting Milan.

open 01.10 - 31.07
* 18 *♪* 105000/- excl. breakfast 18 *♫* 148000/-
excl. breakfast
🆎 ⓘ 🅔 ⚒ ⚓ ☂ ◈ 🅿 ☂ 🛗 🖥 🖵 🆆🅲 📺 ✈

TRIESTE, *Trieste*   06

★ ★ ★ **Abbazia** (HG)
Via Della Geppa 20
☎ 040 369464 fax 040 369464
✉ 34132

9 🛏 -/80000 excl. breakfast 12 🛏 -/115000 excl.
breakfast
🚐 ⊙ ◈ ⓣ⓵ ▭ ⓟ ⓦⓒ ⓣⓥ ☺

★ ★ ★ **Agip** (HCR)
Autostrade Mestre-triest
☎ 040 208273 telex 461098 fax 040 208836
✉ 34013

6 🛏 -/- 74 🛏 -/-
ⒶⒺ Ⓓ Ⓔ ⌫ ◐ ◈ Ⓟ ⓣ⓵ ▭ ⓟ ⓣⓥ ⓘⓞⓘ ☺

★ ★ ★ ★ **Jolly** (HCR)
Corso Cavour 7
☎ 040 7694 telex 460139 fax 040 362699
✉ 34132

28 🛏 -/215000 excl. breakfast 146 🛏 -/290000
excl. breakfast
🚐 ⊙ ◈ Ⓟ ⓣ⓵ ▭ ⓟ ⓦⓒ ⓣⓥ ⓘⓞⓘ ☺

VALDAORA/BRUNICO, *Bolzano*   05

Neunhausern (HCR)
Neunhausern 1
VALDAORA
☎ 0474 46116
✉ 39030

- 🛏 -/- 15 🛏 -/-
Ⓔ 🛆 ◐ ◈ Ⓟ ⓟ ☂ ▭ ⓟ ⓦⓒ ⓘⓞⓘ

VARAZZE, *Savona*   08

★ ★ **Puntabella** (HR)
Via Genova 149
☎ 019 90894
✉ 17019

6 🛏 -/- 22 🛏 -/-
☂ 🚐 Ⓟ ☂ ⓣ⓵ ▭ ⓟ ⓦⓒ

VARENNA, *Como*   03

★ ★ **Olivedo** (HCR)
Piazza Martiri 4
☎ 0341 830115
✉ 22050

open 01.12 - 31.10
* 3 🛏 70000/95000 excl. breakfast 12 🛏 50000/
90000 excl. breakfast
☂ 🚐 ◐ ☂ ⓟ ▭ ⓘⓞⓘ ☺

VARIGOTTI, *Savona*   08

★ ★ ★ **Al Saraceno** (HCR)
Via Al Capo 2
☎ 019 698092
✉ 17029

16 🛏 -/- 50 🛏 -/-
🚐 Ⓟ ⓟ ▭ ⓟ ⓦⓒ ⅋

VENÉZIA, *Venezia*   05

Situated over a sprawling archipelago, 4km from the
Italian mainland, and split by more than 150 canals,
Venice is unique among European cities. No road
communications exist in the city. Vehicles may be
garaged in Piazale Roma at the island end of the
causeway or at open parking places on the mainland
approaches. Garages will not accept advance
bookings. Transport to hotels is by waterbus etc., and
there are fixed charges for fares and porterage.
Rooms overlooking the Grand Canal normally have a
surcharge. Venezia is built on more than 100 islands
with at least as many canals spanned by over 400
bridges. Use the *vaporetto*, the fast, cheap waterbus
to travel on the canals; water taxis or gondolas are
very expensive.
The imposing *Palazza Ducale* (Duke's Palace), stands
at the heart of the city near St Mark's Square, a superb
ensemble dominated by the Basilica of St Mark. Like
Venice, itself, the Basilica is a magnificent blend of
Eastern and Western styles, combining marble,
mosaics and glittering gold. Venice offers a wealth of
great palaces, churches, museums and galleries to
visit, notably the *Accademia*, with its definitive
collection of Venetian paintings. You can combine a
visit here with a wander round the Zattere, the stone-
flagged quay that borders the Giudecca Canal and
leads round to the Baroque Church of Santa Maria
della Salute. Among the islands to visit are San Giorgio
Maggiore, with its marvellous Palladian church;
Murano, famous for glass-making; Burano, noted for
its lace, and Torcello, which boasts a magnificent
cathedral. The Venice Lido is still one of Europe's most
fashionable beach resorts.
Excellent shops are to be found around St Mark's
Square, particulary impressive are those in Mercerie.
For budget-priced clothes, look around the Rialto
where there is also an excellent daily food market with
tantalising fruit, vegetables and fish.
Traditional Venetian cooking is largely based on
seafood. Lobster, crab, scampi and a tasty white fish
locally known as San Pietro are popular. Specialities
include *brodetto do pesce* (fish soup); *soppressa*
(Venetian sausages) and *fegato alla veneziana* - thinly
sliced calves' liver cooked with onions. Although it is
expensive, treat yourself at least once to coffee or ice
cream at one of the elegant cafés in St Mark's Square.
Venetian restaurants tend to be expensive, even by
Italian standards, especially those in the centre.

★ ★ ★ **Ala Venezia** (HG)
St.m.del Giglio 2494
☎ 041 5208333 telex 410275 fax 041 5206390
✉ 30124

* 15 ♨ 110000/160000 70 ⌷ 155000/220000
[AE] ⓪ [E] ⌷ ⅄ ☉ ➰ ↿↾ ⊟ ➪ [WC] [TV] ☺

★ ★ ★ **Best Western Albergo San Marco** (HCR)
Piazza San Marco 877
☎ 041 5204277 telex 420888 fax 041 5238447
res nr 1678 20080
✉ 30124

10 ♨ 90000/160000 50 ⌷ 120000/220000
[AE] ⓪ [E] ⌷ ☉ ↿↾ ⊟ ➪ [WC] [TV] |◎| ☺

★ ★ ★ **Ambassador Tre Rose** (HCR)
Piazza San Marco 905
☎ 041 5222490 telex 420888 fax 041 5238447
✉ 30124

1 ♨ -/- 30 ⌷ -/-
[AE] ⓪ [E] ⌷ ☉ ➰ ↿↾ ⊟ ➪ [WC] [TV] |◎| ☺

★ ★ ★ **Best Western Hotel Bisanzio** (HG)
Calle Della Pieta 3651
☎ 041 5203100 telex 420099 fax 041 5204114
res nr 1678 20080
✉ 30122

6 ♨ 100000/140000 34 ⌷ 150000/200000
[AE] ⓪ [E] ⌷ ⅄ ☉ ↿↾ ↟⊟ ⊟ ➪ [WC] [TV] ☺

★ ★ ★ **Bonvecchiati** (HCR)
Calle Goldoni 4488
☎ 041 5285017 telex 410560 fax 041 5285230
✉ 30124

22 ♨ -/- 57 ⌷ -/-
[AE] ⓪ [E] ⌷ ⅄ ☉ ↿↾ ⊟ ➪ [WC] [TV] ☺

★ ★ ★ **Boston** (HG)
Calle Dei Fabbri 848
☎ 041 5287665 telex 420307
✉ 30124

7 ♨ -/- 35 ⌷ -/-
☉ ↿↾ ➪ [WC] ✗

★ **Caneva** (HG)
Ramo Della Fava 5515
☎ 041 5228118
✉ 30120

* 2 ♨ 20000/70000 23 ⌷ 40000/100000
⅄ ➰ ☉ ⊟ ➪ [WC] ✗

★ ★ ★ **Carpaccio** (HG)
Grand Canal San Toma2765
☎ 041 5235946 fax 041 5242134
✉ 30125

2 ♨ -/- 18 ⌷ -/-
[E] ⌷ ⅄ ➰ ☉ ➰ ⊟ ➪ [WC] [TV] ☺

★ ★ ★ **Concordia** (HG)
Calle Larga San Marco367
☎ 041 5206866 telex 411069 fax 041 5206775
✉ 30124

* 6 ♨ 126000/226000 49 ⌷ 178000/336000
[AE] ⓪ [E] ⌷ ⅄ ☉ ↿↾ ⊟ ➪ [WC] [TV] ☺

★ ★ ★ **Best Western Hotel Gabrielli Sandwirth** (HCR)
R. Degli Schiavoni 41110
☎ 041 5231580 telex 410228 fax 041 5209455
res nr 1678 20080
✉ 30122

20 ♨ 130000/195000 79 ⌷ 190000/370000
⅄ ☉ ➰ ↿↾ ⊟ ➪ [WC] [TV] |◎| ☺

★ ★ ★ **Giorgione** (HG)
Ss. Apostili, 4587
☎ 041 5225810 telex 420598 fax 041 5239092
✉ 30131

9 ♨ -/- 47 ⌷ -/-
⅄ ☉ ↿↾ ⊟ ➪ [WC] [TV] ✗

★ ★ ★ **Best Western Hotel Londra Palace** (HCR)
Riv.degli Schiavoni 4171
☎ 041 5200533 telex 420681 fax 041 5225032
res nr 1678 20080
✉ 30122

17 ♨ 135000/270000 56 ⌷ 202000/435000
[AE] ⓪ [E] ⌷ ➰ ☉ ➰ ➰ ↿↾ ⊟ ➪ [WC] [TV] |◎| ☺

★ ★ ★ **Luna Hotel Baglioni** (HCR)
Piazza San Marco 1243
☎ 041 5289840 telex 410236 fax 041 5287160
✉ 30124

* 16 ♨ 180000/290000 102 ⌷ 290000/520000
[AE] ⓪ [E] ⌷ ☉ ↿↾ ⊟ ➪ [WC] [TV] |◎| ☺

★ ★ ★ **Mabapa Villa** (HCR)
Riviera S. Nicolo 16
☎ 041 5260590 telex 410357 fax 041 5269441
✉ 30126

open 15.02 - 15.11
13 ♨ 90000/160000 49 ⌷ 160000/290000
[AE] ⓪ [E] ⌷ ➰ ➰ ⓢ [P] ➰ ➰ ↿↾ ↟⊟ ⊟ ➪ [WC] [TV] |◎| ☺

★ ★ ★ **Pullman Park** (HCR)
S. Croce 245
☎ 041 5285394 telex 410310 fax 041 5230043
✉ 30135

25 🛏 160000/210000 75 🛏 240000/320000
AE ⓪ 🗲 ⚡ ⚓ ⟿ ⊙ ♨ ⫟ 🖦 🖸 WC TV 🍽 ☺

VERONA, *Verona*   04

Readers of Shakespeare are familiar with Verona,
firstly through *Two Gentlemen of Verona,* secondly as
the setting for *Romeo and Juliet,* and a stroll along Via
delle Arche Scaligere will reveal the alleged site of
Casa di Romeo and, at 23 Via Cappello, Juliet's house,
complete, of course, with balcony. But Verona has
much more to offer the visitor than its links with
Shakespeare. It became a Roman town in BC49 and
contains many reminders of those times. Perhaps
most impressive is the Arena, the 3rd- century
amphitheatre seating 22,000; unlike Rome's
Colosseum it is still in use as an opera house and
theatre. Standing on the banks of the River Adige in a
setting of cypress-covered hills, Verona has been
described as one of the country's most prosperous
and elegant cities. The Basilica of San Zeno Maggiore
is arguably the noblest Romanesque church in
northern Italy, and the *Loggia del Consiglio,* the old
town hall, one of the most beautiful of all early
Renaissance buildings. Verona is as well known for its
wines as for its food; Soave, Bardolino, and Valpolicella
are all produced in this area and make a delicious
accompaniment to the many local pasta and seafood
dishes.

★ ★ ★ ★ **Agip** (MT)
Via Unita D' Italia 346
☎ 045 972033 telex 482064 fax 045 972677
res nr 06 4821651
✉ 37132

* - 🛏 105000/130000 112 🛏 145000/175000
AE ⓪ 🗲 ⚡ ⊚ ◈ 🅿 ♨ 🖦 🖸 WC TV 🍽 ☺

★ ★ **Arena** (HP)
Stradone Porta Palio 2
☎ 045 32440

1 🛏 -/- 16 🛏 -/-
🅿 ♨ 🖦 🖸 WC 🐾

★ ★ ★ ★ ★ **Due Torri** (HCR)
Piazza S Anastasia 4
☎ 045 595044 telex
480524 fax 045
8004130
✉ 37100

The elegant, centrally
situated Hotel Due Torri
was completely rebuilt
in its original style in
1958, and can be justly
proud of an impressive
past. It has welcomed famous guests like Mozart, Goethe and King Viktor Emanuel II. The
rooms are very tastefully furnished - each in a
different style - and equipped with every comfort.
The furnishings and decoration of the restaurant
and public lounges are most attractive.

35 🛏 -/310000 excl. breakfast 47 🛏 -/490000 excl.
breakfast
AE ⓪ 🗲 ⚡ ⚓ ⊙ ♨ 🖦 🖸 WC TV 🍽

★ ★ ★ ★ **Best Western Hotel Firenze** (HCR)
Corsa Porta Nuova 88
☎ 045 590299 telex 431111
res nr 1678 20080

- 🛏 107000/118000 60 🛏 145000/162000
🅿 🖦 🖸 🐾

★ ★ ★ **Montresor Hotel San Pietro** (HG)
Via Santa Teresa 1
☎ 045 582600 telex 480523 fax 045 582149
✉ 37135

* 7 🛏 80800/151500 46 🛏 80800/202000
AE ⓪ 🗲 ⚡ ⊚ ◈ 🅿 🇵 ♨ 🖦 🖸 WC TV ☺

★ ★ ★ ★ **Montresor** (HR)
Via Giberti, 7
☎ 045 8006900 telex 482210 fax 045 8010313
✉ 37122

10 🛏 190000/- excl. breakfast 70 🛏 -/280000 excl.
breakfast
AE ⓪ 🗲 ⚡ ⊙ 🅿 🇵 ♨ 🖦 🖸 WC TV

★ ★ ★ ★ **Palace** (HR)
Via Galvani, 19
☎ 045 575700 telex 481810 fax 045 578131
✉ 37138

* 8 🛏 176000/- 56 🛏 264000/-
AE ⓪ 🗲 ⚡ ⊙ 🇵 ♨ 🖦 🖸 WC TV 🍽 🐾

VIARÉGGIO, *Lucca*   09

★ ★ ★ ★ **Astor** (HR)   AA ANWB
Viale Carducci 54
☎ 0584 50301 telex
501031 fax 0584 55181
✉ 55049

The Hotel Astor is a
holiday and 'spa hotel'
in a beautiful position
right by the beach. The
rooms have air condi-
tioning, TV and a mini-
bar; they either overlook
the sea or the Apuane Alps, which form the
beautiful backdrop to Viareggio. In addition, the
hotel offers an extensive beauty program. There
is a relaxed atmosphere in the restaurant and bar,
where a wide range of dishes and drinks are
served.

* 10 ♪ 160000/220000 58 ♫ 240000/340000
AE ① E ⌸ ⅃ ⚓ ⊙ ☂ ⅏ ⇶ ⑂ ⊟ ℗ WC ⅏ ⋈

VICO EQUENSE, *Napoli*   17

★ ★ ★ **Aequa** (HCR)
☎ 081 8798000 fax 081 8798128

7 ♪ -/- 61 ♫ -/-
℗ ⅏ ⅃ ⑂ ⊟ ℗ WC ☺

VIESTE, *Foggia*   16

★ ★ ★ ★ **Pizzomunno Vieste Palace** (HR)
Spiaggia Di Pizzomunno
☎ 0884 708741 telex 810267 fax 0884 707325
✉ 71019

10 ♪ -/343000 173 ♫ -/424000
AE ① E ⌸ ⅃ ⚞ ⚓ ⊙ ℗ ☂ ⅏ ⑂ ⊟ ℗ WC TV ⅏ ☺

VIETRI SUL MARE, *Salerno*   18

★ ★ ★ ★ **Raito Spa** (HP)
Via Nuova
☎ 089 210033 telex 770125 fax 089 211434
✉ 84010

1 ♪ 120000/160000 49 ♫ 240000/260000
⅃ ℗ ⅏ ⑂ ⊟ ℗ ⅏ ⋈

VILLABASSA, *Bolzano*   05

Emma (HCR)
Hauptplatz
☎ 0474 75122
✉ 39039

7 ♪ -/- 15 ♫ -/-
◆ ℗ ☂ ⊟ ℗ ⋔

VILLA ROSA, *Teramo*   15

Haway (HCR)
Lungomare Italia 24
☎ 0861 72649
✉ 64010

8 ♪ -/- 44 ♫ -/-
⅃ ⚓ ℗ ⅏ ⚞ ⑂ ⊟ ℗ WC ⅍ ⋈

VIPITENO, *Bolzano*   05

★ ★ ★ ★ **Schwarzer Adler** (HCR)   AA ANWB
Stadtplatz 1
☎ 0472 764064
fax 0472 766522
✉ 39049

Rich in tradition, the
Hotel Schwarzer Adler
is situated in the lively
centre of Vipiteno/
Sterzing at the foot of
the Brenner Pass. It is
an excellently well
maintained holiday and winter-sports hotel with
43 rooms, 19 of which are found in the extension. There is a relaxed atmosphere in the restaurant, and guests can enjoy a good glass of pilsner
in the Tyroler Stube. The hotel has a swimming
pool, sauna and fitness room for the energetic.

* 6 ♪ 80000/100000 37 ♫ 85000/150000
E ⌸ ⅃ ⊙ ℗ ☂ ⚞ ⑂ ⊟ ℗ WC TV ⅍ ☺

ZINGÓNIA, *Bergamo*   03

★ ★ ★ ★ **Zingonia Grandhotel** (HCR)
Corso Europa 4
☎ 035 883225 telex 300242 fax 035 885699
✉ 24040

45 ♪ -/116000 excl. breakfast 55 ♫ -/170000 excl.
breakfast
AE ① E ⌸ ⅍ ◆ ℗ ☂ ⚞ ⑂ ⊟ ℗ WC TV ⋈

Switzerland

Capital: Bern

Language: German/French/Italian depending on the region (with Romansch as a local dialect in some areas)

Currency: Swiss franc, divided into 100 centimes or rappen

Emergency numbers: Fire, telephone 118; police and ambulance, telephone 117 (144 for ambulance in some areas)

Information in Britain: Swiss National Tourist Office, Swiss Centre, Swiss Court, London W1V 8EE, telephone 071-734 1921

Motoring and general information

Additional information is in the Continental ABC *at the front of the book.*

Accidents: If there are any personal injuries, call the police immediately. It is not necessary to call the police if there is only material damage, but the driver(s) concerned should exchange particulars with the owner of the damaged property. See *Warning triangle/hazard warning lights* below.

Breakdown: The motoring association Touring Club Suisse (TCS) operates a patrol service and a 24-hour breakdown service (*secours routier*). Dial 140, ask for 'Touring Secours, Touring Club Suisse', state your location and the nature of the problem. See also *Motorways* and *Warning triangle/hazard warning lights* below.

British Embassy/Consulates: The British Embassy has its consular section at 3005 Berne 15, Thunstrasse 50, telephone 031 445021/6. Other consular offices are in Genève, Zürich, Lugano and Montreux.

Children in cars: Children under 12 are not

permitted to travel as front-seat passengers (if the car has rear seats) unless they use a suitable restraint system. Children over 12 must wear a seat belt in the front seat.

Driving licence: A valid UK or Republic of Ireland licence is acceptable in Switzerland. The minimum age at which a visitor may use a temporarily imported car is 18 years; a temporarily imported motorcycle of between 50–125cc, 16 years; a motorcycle exceeding 125cc, 20 years.

Hotels: The SHV (Schweizer Hotelier Verein) divides hotels into five star categories:
★★★★★ luxury hotel
★★★★ first-class hotel
★★★ very comfortable hotel
★★ comfortable hotel
★ modest but comfortable hotel

Lights: Driving on sidelights only and using spotlights is prohibited. Fog lamps can be used only in identical pairs. Dipped headlights must be used in tunnels (whether they are lit or not), in badly lit areas where visibility is poor and, at night, in cities and towns, 200 metres (220yds) in front of any pedestrian or oncoming vehicle (including trains parallel to the road), when reversing, travelling in lines of traffic, waiting at level crossings or near roadworks, and stopping.

Motoring club: Touring Club Suisse (TCS) has branch offices in main towns, with its head office at 1211 Genève 3, rue Pierre-Fatio 9, telephone 022 7371212.

Parking: Restricted areas are indicated by international signs, by broken yellow lines or crosses at the side of the road, or yellow markings on pavements or poles. Parking is forbidden where it would obstruct traffic or sightline on a main road, and on or within 1.5 metres (5ft) of tram lines. Stopping for unloading is forbidden, even for passengers to get in or out, in places marked by a continuous yellow line at the side of the road or red markings on pavements or poles. When parked on a slope or incline, use the handbrake and place wedges under the wheels. If you have to stop in a tunnel, you must switch off your engine. Spending the night in a vehicle or trailer on the roadside is subject to local regulations.

In some towns there are blue zones where parked vehicles must display a disc between 08.00–19.00hrs on weekdays throughout the year. Set at the time of parking, the discs show when the allotted time expires and are available free from any TCS office, petrol stations, garages, tobacconists, restaurants and police stations.

Petrol/diesel: Many petrol stations only accept Access and Visa. Leaded petrol is available in *Super* (98-99 octane) grade and unleaded petrol (*sans plomb / bleifrei / senza plombo*) in the medium (95 octane) grade. Only one grade of diesel (*diesel* or *gasoil*) is sold for automotive use. Up to 25 litres of petrol or diesel fuel may be imported duty-free in a can.

Priority: On narrow roads, lighter vehicles must try to give way to heavier, and on mountain roads, descending to acending. If two vehicles are travelling in opposite directions and both drivers want to turn left, they must pass in front of each other (not drive round). Only those bus lanes marked with a broken yellow line may be crossed. On any mountain road, the driver of a private car may be asked by the driver of a postal bus (painted yellow) to manoeuvre to allow the bus to pass.

Roads: Road surfaces are generally good, but some main roads are narrow in places. Traffic congestions may be severe at the beginning of the German school holidays in July.

On the motorway (*Autobahn* or *autoroute*), there are emergency telephones every 2km (1.25 miles) which connect to the motorway control police. All vehicles of up to 3.5 tonnes (7710lbs) total weight using Swiss motorways must display an annual tax sticker (*vignette*) – available from the AA or at the Swiss frontier for SFr30. Vehicles over 3.5 tonnes must pay a tax for all roads at the Swiss frontier.

Speed limits: In built-up areas, the limit is 50kph (31mph) for all vehicles; outside built-up

areas, it is 80kph (49mph); and on motorways, 120kph (74mph). Car/caravan or trailer combinations are restricted to 80kph (49mph) on all roads outside built-up areas.

Telephone: To call Britain from Switzerland, insert coin after lifting the receiver and listen for the continuous dialling tone. Dial 0044 (international and country codes), the area code without the first 0, and then the number.

To call Switzerland from Britain, dial 010 (international), 41 (country code), the area code without the 0, and then the number.

Traffic lights: The three-colour system is used, but the sequence in some areas is green, amber, red, green; there is no amber between red and green. It is sometimes compulsory to switch off your engine when waiting at traffic lights (or railway crossings) in aid of the campaign against pollution. Watch for signs saying `*Für Bessere Luft – Motor Abstellen*'.

Warning triangle/hazard warning lights: These are compulsory in the event of accident or breakdown. A triangle must be placed on the road at least 50 metres (55yds) behind the vehicle on ordinary roads, and at least 150 metres (164yds) on motorways and roads with fast traffic. If the vehicle is in an emergency lane, the triangle must be placed on the right of the emergency lane. Hazard warning lights may be used with the triangle on ordinary roads, but on motorways they must be switched off as soon as the warning triangle is set up.

Wheel chains: These are generally necessary on journeys to places at high altitudes. Roads with a `chains compulsory' sign (a tyre with chains on it drawn on a white board, which also includes the name of the road) are closed to cars without chains. Spiked or studded tyres may not be substituted for wheel chains when these are compulsory.

LIECHTENSTEIN

The principality is represented in diplomatic and other matters by Switzerland; traffic regulations, insurance laws and the monetary unit are the same.

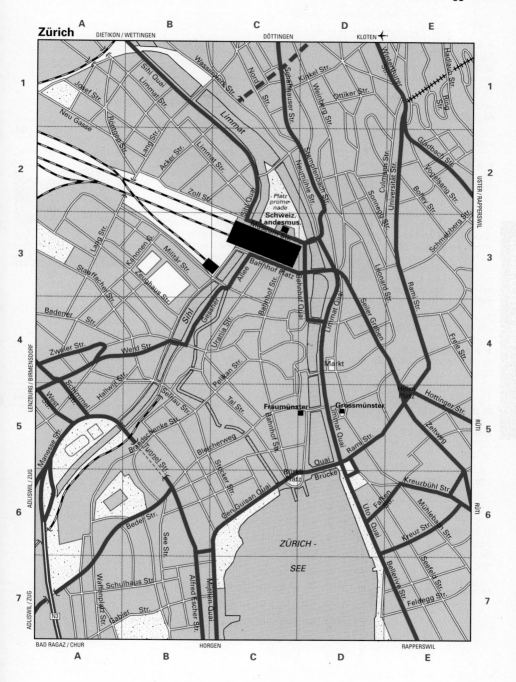

Zürich

AARAU, *Aargau* 03

★ ★ ★ ★ **Best Western Hotel Aarauerhof** (HCR)
Bahnhofstrasse 68
☎ 064 245527 telex 981192
res nr 031 234455
✉ 5000

45 🛏 -/- 22 🛏 -/-
AE ⓪ E ⚏ ☉ P ⚒ ⁑ ▭ ⬚ WC TV ⑩

ADELBODEN, *Bern* 05

★ ★ ★ ★ **Bellevue Parkhotel** (HR) AA ANWB
☎ 033 731621
fax 033 734173
✉ 3715

The Parkhotel Bellevue
is situated in a good
walking and winter-
sports area. Most of the
60 rooms have washing
facilities, and there is a
swimming pool, sauna,
solarium, terrace and
restaurant. The hotel has skis for hire in winter.

20 🛏 -/- 40 🛏 180/300
⚘ ⊙ P ⚒ ♨ ≋ ⁑ ▭ ⬚ WC TV ⑩ ⇧ ☺

★ ★ ★ **Bristol** (HG)
☎ 033 731481 fax 033 731650
✉ 3715

open 15.12 - 30.04 + 20.05 - 31.10
* 4 🛏 80/130 32 🛏 135/200
AE ⓪ E ⚏ ⚘ ☉ P ⚒ ♨ ⁑ ▭ ⬚ TV ⑩ ☺

★ ★ ★ **Crystal** (HR)
Schlegeli
☎ 033 731212 telex 922107

- 🛏 -/- 33 🛏 -/-
⚘ P ⚒ ♨ ⁑ ⬚ WC TV ⑩

ADLISWIL, *Zurich* 04

★ ★ **Jolie Ville Motor Inn** (MT)
Zuerichstrasse 105
☎ 01 7108585 telex 826760 fax 01 7109077
✉ 8134

- 🛏 89/106 60 🛏 119/136
AE ⓪ E ⚏ ◆ P ⚒ ▭ ⬚ WC TV

AIGLE, *Vaud* 02

★ ★ ★ **Du Nord** (HCR)
Rue Colomb 4
☎ 025 261055 telex 456105 fax 025 264248
✉ 1860

2 🛏 -/- 17 🛏 -/-
AE ⓪ E ⚏ ☉ ◆ P ⁑ ▭ ⬚ WC TV ⑩

ALTDORF, *Uri* 04

★ ★ ★ **Goldener Schlussel** (HR) AA ANWB
Schutzengasse 9
☎ 044 21002
fax 044 21167
✉ 6460

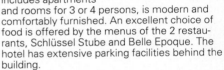

The hotel is housed in a
stylish, renovated
18th-century building, in
a peaceful position in
the town centre. The
accommodation, which
includes apartments
and rooms for 3 or 4 persons, is modern and
comfortably furnished. An excellent choice of
food is offered by the menus of the 2 restaurants, Schlüssel Stube and Belle Epoque. The
hotel has extensive parking facilities behind the
building.

* 4 🛏 75/120 20 🛏 120/195
AE ⓪ E ⚏ ⚘ ☉ P ⚒ ⁑ ▭ ⬚ WC TV ⑩

ANDERMATT, *Uri* 04

★ ★ ★ **Drei Konige und Post** (HR)
Gotthardstrasse 69
☎ 044 67203 telex 862738 fax 044 67666
✉ 6490

* 2 🛏 70/90 19 🛏 140/180
AE ⓪ E ⚏ ⚘ ☉ P ⚒ ▭ ⬚ WC ⑩ ☺

★ ★ ★ **Monopol Metropol** (HR)
☎ 044 67575 telex 868606 fax 044 67923
✉ 6490

open 15.12 - 30.04 + 01.06 - 15.10
7 🛏 80/85 30 🛏 160/170
AE ⓪ E ⚏ ☉ P ⚒ ♨ ≋ ⁑ ▭ ⬚ WC ☺

★ ★ **Schweizerhof** (HR)
☎ 044 67189

- 🛏 -/- 28 🛏 -/-
☉ ▭ ⬚

ARBON, *Thurgau* 04

★ ★ ★ ★ **Metropol** (HR)
Bahnhofstrasse 49
☎ 071 463535 telex
881747 fax 071 464701
✉ 9320

 🅰🅰 ANWB

The Best Western Hotel
Metropol is peacefully
situated on the banks of
the Bodensee and yet
only a 100m walk from
the station. This attrac-
tive holiday and confer-
ence hotel has 42 rooms (of which some are
suites) with a bathroom, TV and private loggia.
The restaurant is well known for its French
cuisine, and there is an international atmosphere
in the bar. Inside the hotel there is a sauna,
solarium and whirlpool, and outside there are
lawns for sunbathing and an attractive swimming
pool.

* 18 ♫ 125/140 24 ♨ 170/280
🆎 🄾 🄴 ⌘ ⅃ 🐾 🄿 ♈ ☃ ↾↿ ⃔ 🄿 🆆🅲 🆃🆅

ARDEZ, *Graubunden* 07

Alvertern (HP)
Hauptstrasse
☎ 084 92144
✉ 7546

- ♫ -/- 14 ♨ -/-
🆎 🄾 🄴 ⌘ ⅃ 🄼 🄿 ♈ 🄿 🆆🅲 🆃🆅 ⇧ ☺

AROLLA, *Valais* 05

★ ★ **Du Glacier** (HR)
☎ 027 831218 fax 027 831478
✉ 1961

* 2 ♫ 35/55 17 ♨ 70/110
⅃ 🄿 ♈ ⃔ 🄿 🆆🅲 🆃🆅 🏊 ☺

★ ★ ★ **Grandhotel et Kurhaus** (HCR)
☎ 027 831161
✉ 1986

6 ♫ -/- 49 ♨ -/-
⅃ 🄼 🄿 ♈ ↾↿ ⃔ 🄿 🆆🅲

Mont Collon (HCR)
☎ 027 831191 fax 027 831608
✉ 1986

open 25.12 - 25.04 + 04.07 - 19.09
* 12 ♫ 46/78 48 ♨ 92/142
🆎 🄾 🄴 ⌘ ⅃ 🄿 ♈ ↾↿ ⃔ 🆆🅲 🏊 ☺

AROSA, *Graubunden* 07

★ ★ ★ **Alpensonne** (HCR)
☎ 081 311547 fax 081 313470
✉ 7050

open 01.07 - 19.04
* 7 ♫ 75/150 28 ♨ 150/300
🆎 ⌘ ⅃ 🔴 🄿 🄿 ♈ ↾↿ ⃔ 🄿 🆆🅲 🆃🆅 🏊 ☺

★ ★ ★ ★ **Arosa Kulm** (HCR)
☎ 081 310131 telex 851679 fax 081 314090
✉ 7050

13 ♫ -/- 133 ♨ -/-
🆎 🄾 🄴 ⌘ ⅃ 🄿 ♈ ☃ ↾↿ ⃔ 🄿 🆆🅲 🆃🆅 🏊 ☺

★ ★ ★ **Bellavista** (HCR)
☎ 081 311406
open 20.12 - 05.04
24 ♫ 85/205 80 ♨ 170/350
⅃ 🄿 ♈ ↾↿ ⃔ ⃔ 🄿 🆆🅲 🏊 ⇧

★ ★ ★ **Bellevue** (HR)
☎ 081 311251 telex 851697 fax 081 314414
✉ 7050

18 ♫ -/- 47 ♨ -/-
⅃ 🄿 🄿 ♈ ↾↿ ⃔ 🄿 🆆🅲 🏊

★ ★ ★ **Merkur** (HR)
Poststrasse
☎ 081 311666 telex 851601 fax 081 314561
✉ 7050

open 05.12 - 30.04 + 19.06 - 24.10
* 7 ♫ 53/138 28 ♨ 100/252
🄾 🄴 ⌘ 🔴 🄿 ♈ ↾↿ ⃔ 🄿 🆆🅲 🏊 ☺

★ ★ ★ ★ **Park** (HCR)
☎ 081 310165 telex 74258

60 ♫ -/- 65 ♨ -/-
⅃ 🄼 🄿 🄿 ♈ ☃ ↾↿ ⃔ 🄿 🆆🅲 🏊

★ ★ ★ **Pratschli** (HR)
☎ 081 311861 fax 081 311148
✉ 7050

open 14.12 - 21.04
* 28 ♫ 119/197 68 ♨ 238/446
🄴 ⌘ ⅃ 🄼 🄿 🄿 ♈ ☃ ↾↿ ⃔ 🄿 🆆🅲 🆃🆅 🏊

★ ★ ★ ★ **Tschuggen Grandhotel** (HR)
☎ 081 310221 telex 851624 fax 081 314175
✉ 7050

open 04.12 - 28.03
* 47 ♫ 230/410 95 ♨ 360/830
⅃ 🄿 🄿 ♈ ☃ ↾↿ ⃔ 🆆🅲 🆃🆅 🏊 ☺

ASCONA, *Ticino* 06

★ ★ ★ ★ **Acapulco au Lac** (HCR)
☎ 093 354521 telex 846135 fax 093 361951
✉ 6612

open 10.03 - 08.11
- ♨ 110/170 43 ☕ 160/250
[symbols]

★ ★ ★ **Bellaria** (HP)
Via Delle Capelle
☎ 093 351121 fax 093 358957
✉ 6612

open 01.04 - 25.10
* 8 ♨ 95/150 28 ☕ 200/230
[symbols]

★ ★ ★ ★ **Borreto Sasso** (HCR)
Via Locarno
☎ 093 377115 telex 846026 fax 093 355018
✉ 6612

1 ♨ -/- 43 ☕ -/-
[symbols]

★ ★ ★ ★ **Casa Berno** (HCR)
☎ 093 353232 telex 846167
* 7 ♨ 190/210 53 ☕ 304/372
[symbols]

★ ★ ★ ★ ★ **Parkhotel Delta** (HP)
Via Delta
☎ 093 351105 telex 846101 fax 093 356724
✉ 6612

1 ♨ -/- 45 ☕ -/-
[symbols]

★ ★ ★ **Moro** (HCR)
Via Collina
☎ 093 351081
fax 093 355169
✉ 6612

The Hotel Moro is
pleasantly built against a
hill, just above Ascona,
looking out over the
town and the Lake
Maggiore. The rooms
are spacious with bath
and toilet, TV and minibar; most of them have a
balcony. The restaurant is attractively furnished.
A semi-circular swimming pool and a sauna can
be found in the basement. When the weather is
fine, guests can enjoy the sunshine in the palm
garden.

7 ♨ -/- 29 ☕ 126/166
[symbols]

★ ★ ★ **Schweizerhof** (HR)
Via Locarno 41
☎ 093 351214 fax 093 361520
✉ 6612

open 13.03 - 15.11
4 ♨ 90/120 38 ☕ 150/230
[symbols]

★ ★ ★ **Tamaro** (HCR)
☎ 093 350282 telex 846132 fax 093 352928
✉ 6612

20 ♨ -/- 41 ☕ -/-
[symbols]

★ ★ ★ **Tobler** (HP)
☎ 093 353157

1 ♨ -/- 32 ☕ -/-
[symbols]

BADEN, *Aargau* 03

★ ★ ★ ★ **Linde** (HCR)
Mellingerstrasse 22
☎ 056 225385 telex
825097 fax 056 220770
✉ 5400

The 13-floor Hotel Linde
dominates the centre of
Baden, a small and
friendly town situated
not far from Zürich. The
hotel features 60 rooms
with toilet, bath or
shower, TV, and minibar - some also have a
spacious balcony. If the weather is fine, the
restaurant prepares its specialities on the barbecue in the garden. The buns served at breakfast
are fresh from the hotel's own bakery.

* 30 ♨ 125/170 30 ☕ 175/240
[symbols]

BAD RAGAZ, *St. Gallen* 07

★ ★ ★ **Parkhotel Bad Ragaz** (HR)
☎ 081 3022244 fax 081 3026439
✉ 7310

open 01.04 - 31.10
* 31 ♨ 50/117 34 ☕ 90/225
[symbols]

★ ★ ★ ★ ★ **Quellenhof** (KH)
☎ 081 3032020 telex 855897 fax 081 3032022
✉ 7310

* 65 🛏 180/280 61 🛏 360/560
🆎 ⓐ ᴇ ⇌ ⅃ ⓝ Ⓟ 🅿 🗲 ⇅ ☜ 🔲 🄿 📺 🍽 ⊙

BAD SCUOL, *Graubunden*   07

★ ★ ★ **Bellaval** (HR)
☎ 084 91481
✉ 7550

1 🛏 -/- 22 🛏 -/-
⅃ 🅿 🗲 ⇅ 🔲 🄿 🆆🅲 🍽

★ ★ ★ **Belvédere** (HR)
☎ 084 91041 fax 084 99072
✉ 7550

open 19.12 - 17.04
* 15 🛏 95/140 40 🛏 170/340
🆎 ⓐ ᴇ ⇌ 🅿 🗲 ⅀ 🗲 ⇅ 🔲 🄿 🆆🅲 🍽

BAD TARASP-VULPERA, *Graubunden*   07

Robinson Club Schweizerhof (HCR)
☎ 084 91331 telex 85411 fax 084 90593
✉ 7552

5 🛏 -/- 123 🛏 -/-
🆎 ⓐ ᴇ ⇌ ⅃ ⓝ Ⓟ 🅿 🗲 ⅀ 🗲 ⇅ ☜ 🔲 🄿 🆆🅲 🍽 ⌂ 🏇

★ ★ ★ **Schlosshotel Chasté** (HCR)
Sparsels
☎ 084 91775
✉ 7552

4 🛏 -/- 12 🛏 80/310
⅃ 🅿 🔲 🄿 🆆🅲 🍽

★ ★ ★ **Tarasp** (HCR)
☎ 084 91445
✉ 7553

4 🛏 -/- 22 🛏 153/178
ⓐ ᴇ ⇌ ⅃ ◔ 🖴 🅿 🗲 🄿 🆆🅲 🍽 ⌂ ⊙

★ ★ ★ **Villa Maria** (HCR)
☎ 084 91138
✉ 7552

1 🛏 -/- 15 🛏 212/272
⅃ 🅿 🗲 ⅀ 🔲 🄿 🆆🅲 🍽

BAD VALS, *Graubunden*   04

★ ★ ★ **Alpina** (HP)
☎ 086 51148
✉ 7132

1 🛏 -/- 2 🛏 -/-
⊙ ⅀ ⇅ 🄿 🆆🅲 🍽 ⊙

★ ★ ★ **Thermalbad Vals** (KH)
☎ 086 50111 fax 086 51695
✉ 7132

50 🛏 -/- 100 🛏 -/-
🆎 ⓐ ᴇ ⇌ ⅃ ⓝ Ⓟ 🅿 🗲 ⅀ 🗲 ⇅ 🔲 🄿 🆆🅲 📺 🍽 ⊙

BASEL, *Basel*   03

★ ★ ★ **Admiral** (HCR)
Rosentalstr.5 Messeplatz
☎ 061 6917777 telex 963444 fax 061 6917789
✉ 4021

AA ANWB

The Hotel Admiral Basel is a comfortable hotel for a holiday or stopover. It is well situated close to the Autobahn and railway station and within walking distance of the centre. All the rooms have a TV, most are equipped with private toilet, bath or shower, and more than half have a balcony. From the deck chairs around the heated swimming pool on the roof terrace of the 9th floor, the guests are provided with a wonderful view over the city. Coming from the Autobahn, follow the signs 'Mustermesse' in order to reach the hotel.

* 60 🛏 110/150 70 🛏 150/240
🆎 ⓐ ᴇ ⇌ 🅿 🗲 ⅀ 🗲 ⇅ 🔲 🄿 🆆🅲 📺 ⊙

★ ★ ★ **City** (HR)
Henric Petristrasse 12
☎ 061 2727811 telex 962427 fax 061 2727881
✉ 4010

* 40 🛏 100/150 45 🛏 160/240
🆎 ⓐ ᴇ ⇌ ⊙ ◈ ⇅ 🔲 🄿 🆆🅲 📺 🍽

★ ★ ★ **Du Commerce** (HG)
Riehenring 91
☎ 061 6919666 fax 061 6919675
✉ 4058

open 14.01 - 14.12
* 29 🛏 100/140 20 🛏 130/220
🆎 ᴇ ⇌ ⊙ ◈ 🅿 ⇅ 🔲 🄿 🆆🅲 📺 ⊙

SWITZERLAND

★ ★ ★ ★ Europe (HCR)
Clarastrasse 43
☎ 061 6918080 telex 964103 fax 061 6918201
✉ 4005

* 100 ♨ 165/230 70 ♨ 245/330
Ⓐ🄴 ⓞ 🄴 ⌨ ⊙ 🅿 🗂 🕊 🍴 🖥 🄵 🚾 📺 🍽 👁

★ ★ ★ ★ Merian Am Rhein (HR)   Ⓐ🄰 ANWB
Greifeng. Rheing. 2
☎ 061 6810000 telex
963537 fax 061
6811101
res nr 031 234455
✉ 4005

The Best Western Hotel
Merian am Rhein is
right on the bank of the
Rhine, next to the
Mittlere Brücke and
right opposite the city centre. From the 'Rhy-
terrasse', but even more from the balconies of
the rooms, the guests have a pleasant view of
the bridge. The rooms are spacious, have stylish
modern furnishings, and are equipped with
up-to-date amenities. The restaurant's speciality
is fish dishes. The cocktail bar Schalbennest
serves drinks in a relaxed and modern atmosphere.

* 33 ♨ 160/180 30 ♨ 210/250
Ⓐ🄴 ⓞ 🄴 ⌨ ⌁ ⊙ 🅿 🗂 🕊 🍴 🖥 🄵 🚾 📺 👁

★ ★ ★ ★ Victoria Am Bahnhof (HR)
Centralbahnplatz 3-4
☎ 061 2715566 telex 962362 fax 061 2715501
✉ 4002

* 70 ♨ 180/- 40 ♨ 250/-
Ⓐ🄴 ⓞ 🄴 ⌨ ⊙ 🅿 🗂 🍴 🖥 🄵 🚾 📺 🍽

BEATENBERG, *Bern*   **03**

★ ★ ★ ★ Dorint Beatenberg (HA)
Schmocken
☎ 036 412121 telex 923203 fax 036 412144
✉ 3803

open 20.12 - 04.12
* 30 ♨ 92/113 90 ♨ 184/234
Ⓐ🄴 ⓞ 🄴 ⌨ ⌁ 🗂 🕊 🍴 🖥 🄵 🚾 📺 🍽

★ ★ Jungfraublick Beauregard (HCR)
☎ 036 411581 telex 923290 fax 036 412003
✉ 3803

* 5 ♨ 45/60 29 ♨ 80/110
Ⓐ🄴 ⓞ 🄴 ⌨ ⊙ 🅿 🗂 🕊 🍴 🖥 🄵 🚾 📺 🍽 👁

BECKENRIED, *Unterwalden*   **04**

★ ★ ★ ★ Sternen am See (HCR)
Buochserstrasse 54
☎ 041 641107 telex 78347 fax 041 646925
✉ 6375

2 ♨ -/- 37 ♨ -/-
Ⓐ🄴 ⓞ 🄴 ⌨ ⌁ ◆ 🅿 🗂 🕊 🍴 🖥 🄵 🚾 🍽

BELLINZONA, *Ticino*   **06**

★ ★ Cereda (HR)
☎ 092 272431
✉ 6514

1 ♨ -/- 21 ♨ -/-
🗂 🕊 ⌁ 🖥 🄵 🚾

BERGÜN, *Graubunden*   **07**

★ ★ ★ Weisses Kreuz (HCR)
Hauptstrasse
☎ 081 731161 fax 081 731686
✉ 7482

open 20.12 - 12.04 + 15.06 - 25.10
* 10 ♨ 73/89 19 ♨ 130/176
Ⓐ🄴 ⓞ 🄴 ⌨ ⌁ ⊙ 🅿 🗂 🖥 🄵 🚾

BERN, *Bern*   **03**

*Population*290,000 *Local tourist office* Bahnof (station)
☎ (031)221212
By European standards, Berne, the capital of
Switzerland, is not a big city. It has only 140,000
inhabitants, but it is very Swiss and picturesque. In the
past 50 years there has been enormous expansion and
wide bridges span the Aare to link the old town with
its new suburbs. While retaining its medieval
appearance, the old city has developed into an
important business centre, with ancient rows of
houses lining broad streets, and magnificent fountains
seemingly untouched by time. The principal features
of many of these streets are the arcades which are let
into the façades of buildings; no new or renovated
building can be built without one. High above the roofs
of Berne towers the cathedral, one of the finest
ecclesiastical buildings in Switzerland. Like most of
the city it dates from the 15th century; the greater part
of old Berne was reduced to ashes in 1405 by fire.
Also of special note is the clock tower *Zytglogge*,
which dates from the 12th century. In 1530 the artistic
astronomical or calendar clock showing the position of
the sun, moon, stars and planets as well as the month
and day of the week, was constructed; and at the
same time the delightful mechanical figure-play was
made. The Gerechtigkeitsgasse has many elegant
shops, and Marktgasse and Spitalgasse are both
pedestrian precincts. Typical Swiss cuisine includes
cheese fondue - a bubbling mixture of cheese and
wine which is eaten with pieces of bread - and
raclette, sliced, melted cheese served with potato.

Berne Platte is a dish of local meat, sausages, *sauerkraut* and potatoes. Among the many delicious pastries are *Zugerkirschtorte*, a cake made with kirsch.

★ ★ ★ ★ Ambassador
Seftigenstrasse 99
☎ 031 454111 telex 911826 fax 031 454117
✉ 3007

* 21 🛏 140/170 70 🍽 180/240
🆎 ⓪ 🄴 ⚌ ♨ Ⓟ ᴾ ⅋ 💷 Ⓟ WC TV ⑩ ☻

★ ★ ★ Bern (HR)
Zeughausgasse 9
☎ 031 211021 telex 911555 fax 031 211147
✉ 3011

* 10 🛏 165/175 90 🍽 230/265
🆎 ⓪ 🄴 ⚌ ⅄ ⊙ ⅋ 💷 Ⓟ WC TV ⑩

★ ★ ★ ★ Gauer Hotel Schweizerhof (HCR)
Bahnhofplatz 11
☎ 031 224501 telex 911782 fax 031 212179
✉ 3001

31 🛏 230/280 56 🍽 320/410
🆎 ⓪ 🄴 ⚌ ⊙ ᴾ ⅋ 💷 Ⓟ WC TV ⑩ ☻

★ ★ ★ Wachter Mövenpick (HCR)
☎ 031 220866 telex 912230
✉ 3011

1 🛏 -/- 29 🍽 -/-
⊙ 💷 Ⓟ

BERN/MURI, Bern   03

Krone (MT)
Thunstrasse 43
BERN
☎ 031 9511666 fax 031 9517962
✉ 3074

* - 🛏 120/160 12 🍽 150/180
🄴 ⚌ ⅄ ⊙ Ⓟ ᴾ 💷 Ⓟ WC TV

BETTMERALP, Valais   05

★ ★ Alpfrieden (HR)   🇦🇦 *ANWB*
☎ 028 272232 fax 028 272997
✉ 3992

The Hotel Alpfrieden tries to guarantee a relaxed holiday. It has 26 rooms, some of which have washing facilities, and there is a restaurant, a terrace and a TV lounge for guests to use.

open 15.12 - 18.04 + 26.06 - 24.10
* 6 🛏 70/95 20 🍽 140/245
🆎 ⓪ 🄴 ⚌ ⊙ ⅋ 💷 Ⓟ ⑩

BIASCA, Ticino   06

Albergo Della Posta (HCR)   🇦🇦 *ANWB*
Via Bellinzona
☎ 092 722121
fax 092 723147
✉ 6710

This hotel opposite the station is known for its long-standing traditions. The owner is also the chef, and his Tessiner specialities have earned his cuisine a good reputation. All renovated rooms have their own bathroom facilities, telephone, radio and TV. Guests can use the garden, terrace, 2 restaurants (Rotisserie and Grill) and private car park. The hotel is closed on Mondays.

open 01.07 - 14.06
* - 🛏 70/95 12 🍽 120/170
🆎 ⓪ 🄴 ⚌ ◆ Ⓟ ᴾ ⅋ 💷 Ⓟ WC TV
See advertisement on page 107

BIEL, Bern   02

★ ★ ★ Elite (HR)
Bahnhofstrasse 14
☎ 032 225441 telex 934101 fax 032 221383
✉ 2502

* 24 🛏 130/160 46 🍽 180/220
🆎 ⓪ 🄴 ⚌ ⊙ Ⓟ ⅋ 💷 Ⓟ WC TV ⑩ ☻

BISSONE, Ticino   06

★ ★ ★ Campione (HCR)
Via Campione 62
☎ 091 689622 telex 844700 fax 091 686821
✉ 6816

* 6 🛏 95/150 34 🍽 150/220
🆎 ⓪ 🄴 ⚌ ◉ ❄ Ⓟ ⅋ ᴾ ⚓ ⅋ 💷 Ⓟ WC TV ⑩ ☻

★ ★ ★ Lago di Lugano (HCR)
Via Campione 65
☎ 091 688591 telex 844698 fax 091 686181
✉ 6816

open 01.04 - 02.01
- 🛏 95/240 85 🍽 140/320
🆎 ⓪ 🄴 ⚌ ⅄ ❄ ⚓ ◉ Ⓟ ᴾ ⅋ ❄ ⚓ ⅋ 🛥 💷 Ⓟ WC TV ⑩ ☻

BIVIO, *Graubunden*   **07**

★ ★ ★ **Solaria** (HP)
Julierstrasse 43
☎ 081 751107 fax 081 751290
✉ 7457

open 01.01 - 30.11
- ♨ 60/105 27 ⌗ 100/160
🦶 🅿 🛎 🔌 📶 🚽 wc tv |◉| ☺

BLATTEN, *Valais*   **05**

★ ★ **Blattnerhof** (HR)
☎ 028 31741
✉ 3919

10 ♨ -/- 22 ⌗ -/-
🅿 |◉|

BÖNIGEN, *Bern*   **03**

★ ★ ★ **Schlossli** (HR)
☎ 036 222928
✉ 3806

1 ♨ -/- 30 ⌗ -/-
🦶 🚲 🎱 🎿 ↕ 🔌 📶 wc

BREGANZONA, *Ticino*   **06**

★ ★ ★ **Vita Sanotel** (KH)
Via Pradello 27
☎ 091 560341 fax 091 567183
✉ 6932

* 6 ♨ 75/95 15 ⌗ 110/190
🅿 🎱 🎿 ↕ 🔌 📶 wc |◉| 🔔 ☺

BRIENZ, *Bern*   **03**

★ ★ ★ **Baren** (HCR)
Hauptstrasse
☎ 036 512412
✉ 3855

1 ♨ -/- 20 ⌗ -/-
🦶 🚲 ◉ 🅿 🎱 🎿 ↕ 🔌 📶 wc

BRISSAGO, *Ticino*   **06**

★ ★ ★ **Brenscino** (HCR)
☎ 093 650121
✉ 6614

1 ♨ -/- 85 ⌗ -/-
◉ 🅿 🔌 📶

BRUNNEN, *Schwyz*   **04**

★ ★ ★ **Brunnerhof** (HCR)
Gersauerstrasse 3
☎ 043 311757 telex 866035 fax 043 314881
✉ 6440

open 01.03 - 15.12
8 ♨ 70/75 43 ⌗ 110/140
AE ① 🅴 🛎 ◉ ◆ 🎱 ↕ 🔌 📶 wc |◉| ☺

★ ★ ★ **Cabana** (HCR)
Gersauerstrasse 63
☎ 043 311238 fax 043 311272
✉ 6440

open 01.06 - 30.09
2 ♨ 80/90 15 ⌗ 110/150
AE ① 🅴 🛎 🦶 ◐ ◆ 🅿 🎱 🎿 📶 🔌 wc tv ☺

★ ★ ★ ★ **Best Western Hotel Waldstatterhof** (HCR)   AA ANWB
Waldstaetterquai 6
☎ 043 331133 telex 866007 fax 043 314766
res nr 031 234455
✉ 6440

The Best Western hotel Waldstätterhof is situated on the banks of the Vierwaldstättersee. The rooms of this elegant hotel are luxurious and feature all the modern comforts. The rôtisserie has a cosy and relaxed atmosphere, there are pleasant bars in which to have a drink, and the terrace on the lake provides a wonderful view of the mountain tops. The hotel offers an outdoor swimming pool, a tennis court, a sauna, a solarium and a fitness room.

30 ♨ -/- 70 ⌗ 210/320
🦶 🚲 ◉ 🅿 🎱 🎿 ↕ 🔌 📶 wc tv |◉|

BUBENDORF, *Basel*   **03**

Bad Bubendorf
Kantonsstrasse 3
☎ 61 9312595 fax 61 9313410
✉ 4416

* 4 ♨ 95/108 24 ⌗ 130/144
AE ① 🅴 🛎 🅿 ↕ 🔌 wc tv ☺
See advertisement on page 109

Hotel Restaurant Della Posta
(Fam. Piccioni) Via Stazione
CH-6710 BIASCA Tel.: 092-722121

Closed on Mondays and from 1 to 15 March.
Restaurant seating 90, banquet facilities for 20
to 60 people, conference room seating 20.
Rotisserie, grill, bar, terrace, garden, parking
area. 30 beds with bath or shower, telephone/
radio/television. Swiss Fr 60 to 100.

Single room	Swiss Fr 70-95,
double room	Swiss Fr 110-150,
3-bed room	Swiss Fr 130-170.

BUOCHS, *Unterwalden*   04

★ ★ ★ ★ **Mototel Postillon** (MT)
Ausfahrt N 2
☎ 041 645454 telex 866186 fax 041 642334
✉ 6374

- ☷ -/- 58 ☷ -/-
⧉⧉⧉⧉⧉⧉⧉⧉⧉⧉⧉⧉⧉⧉⧉⧉⧉⧉⧉⧉

★ ★ **Sonnheim** (HR)
Am Quai 5
☎ 041 641440
✉ 6374

- ☷ -/- 16 ☷ -/-
⧉⧉⧉⧉⧉⧉⧉⧉⧉⧉⧉⧉⧉

BÜRCHEN, *Valais*   05

★ ★ ★ **Silence Hotel Burchnerhof**   AA ANWB
(HCR)
☎ 028 442434 fax 028
443417
✉ 3935

This quiet and sunny
family hotel is located at
an altitude of 500m,
with good walking
country all around. The
rooms are comfortably
furnished, equipped
with colour TV, radio, telephone, safe and minibar. The hotel also has a covered swimming pool,
whirlpool, sauna, solarium and sunbathing terrace. The restaurant serves traditional food.

open 20.12 - 20.04 + 02.06 - 27.10
* 2 ☷ 88/120 17 ☷ 126/190
⧉⧉⧉⧉⧉⧉⧉⧉⧉⧉⧉⧉⧉⧉⧉⧉⧉⧉

BÜRGENSTOCK, *Unterwalden*   04

★ ★ ★ ★ **Park** (HR)
☎ 041 632545 telex 866288 fax 041 617688
✉ 6366

- ☷ -/- 60 ☷ -/-
⧉⧉⧉⧉⧉⧉⧉⧉⧉⧉⧉

BUSSIGNY, *Vaud*   02

★ ★ ★ **Novotel Lausanne** (HCR)
☎ 021 7012871 fax 021 7022902
✉ 1030

- ☷ 116/126 excl. breakfast 100 ☷ 140/155 excl.
breakfast
⧉⧉⧉⧉⧉⧉⧉⧉⧉⧉⧉⧉⧉⧉⧉

CASÁCCIA, *Graubunden*   07

Stampa (HP)
☎ 082 43162 fax 082 43474
✉ 7602

open 20.12 - 30.04 + 01.06 - 10.11
* 2 ☷ 40/45 9 ☷ 76/105
⧉⧉⧉⧉⧉⧉⧉

SWITZERLAND

CELERINA, *Graubunden*   07

★ ★ ★ ★ **Cresta Kulm** (HCR)
☎ 082 33373 fax 082 37001
✉ 7505

open 01.12 - 15.04 + 01.07 - 15.10
* 10 🛏 135/170 30 🍽 250/380
AE ⓘ E ⚡ ♨ P ☂ ⚓ ⚁ ⚒ ☎ WC TV 🍴

CHAMPÉRY, *Valais*   02

★ ★ **Des Alpes** (HCR)
☎ 025 791222 fax 025 791223
✉ 1874   /

6 🛏 50/70 24 🍽 95/130
E ⚡ ♨ P ☂ ⚒ ☎ WC

★ ★ ★ **Beau Séjour** (HCR)
☎ 025 791701 telex 456284 fax 025 792306
✉ 1874

open 01.06 - 30.09 + 15.12 - 15.04
5 🛏 52/86 15 🍽 104/172
AE ⓘ E ⚡ ⊙ ◆ P ☂ ⚒ ⚁ ☎ WC TV

★ ★ ★ **De Champéry** (HCR)
Grande Rue
☎ 025 791071 fax 025 791402
✉ 1874

open 19.12 - 13.04 + 15.05 - 31.10
* 10 🛏 93/160 62 🍽 108/180
AE ⓘ E ⚡ ⊙ P ☂ ⚒ ⚁ ☎ WC TV 🍴

Auberge Du Grand Paradis (HCR)
☎ 025 791167 fax 025 741069
✉ 1874

open 22.05 - 25.10 + 18.12 - 31.12
* 2 🛏 30/40 8 🍽 60/80
AE ⓘ E ⚡ ⚓ ♨ ⚓ P ☂ ☎ WC 🍴

CHAMPEX, *Valais*   02

★ ★ ★ **Du Gacier** (HCR)
☎ 026 41402
✉ 1938

1 🛏 -/- 30 🍽 -/-
P ⚁ ☎

CHÂTEAU-D'OEX, *Vaud*   02

★ ★ ★ **Ermitage** (HCR)
☎ 029 46003 telex 940022 fax 029 45076
✉ 1837

open 12.12 - 20.10
* 2 🛏 90/100 17 🍽 120/150
AE ⓘ E ⚡ ♨ P ☂ ☂ ⚁ ☎ WC 🍴 🐾

★ ★ ★ **Résidence la Rocaille** (HCR)
Les Bossons
☎ 029 46215 fax 029 45249
✉ 1837

open 20.12 - 20.04 + 28.05 - 30.10
3 🛏 75/105 11 🍽 135/175
AE ⓘ E ⚡ ♨ P ☂ ☂ ⚒ ⚁ ⚁ ☎ WC TV 🍴 🐾

CHIASSO, *Ticino*   06

★ ★ ★ **Movenpick Albergo Touring** (HCR)
Piazza Indipendenza 3
☎ 091 445331 telex 842493 fax 091 445661
✉ 6830

30 🛏 -/- 51 🍽 123/183
AE ⓘ E ⚡ ⊙ ◆ ☂ ⚒ ⚁ ☎ WC TV 🍴 🐾

CHUR, *Graubunden*   04

★ ★ **Drei Konige** (HR)   AA ANWB
Reichsgasse 18
☎ 081 221725
fax 081 221726
✉ 7000

The Hotel Drei Könige
can be found in the
centre of Chur, right
next to the Altstadt. It is
a well kept holiday hotel
that has 36 rooms with
TV; the furnishings vary
from tidy and functional in some rooms, to
luxurious in others with every modern comfort.
The cuisine is an important feature of this hotel; it
has an exceptionally atmospheric restaurant, and
prides itself on a historic wine cellar which includes regional wines.

* 13 🛏 63/115 23 🍽 100/160
AE ⓘ E ⚡ ⚓ ⊙ ☂ ⚒ ⚁ ☎ WC TV 🍴

LIESTAL–BUBENDORF – 4 kilometres from the N2 motorway, Liestal exit, in the direction of Waldenburg/Solothurn

Bad Bubendorf

CH-4416 Bubendorf, Kantonstrasse 3
Telephone 061-931 25 95, fax: 061-931 34 10

*** A historical hotel with a tradition going back to 1742, 52 beds (28 rooms), 120 free parking spaces

Season: Open throughout the year, single room Swiss F 102, double room Swiss F 144 & family prices, including ample buffet breakfast.

Room: Interiors of Alpen pine, shower/wc, colour television, radio alarm, minibar and telephone.

Restaurant: Various restaurants and bar, large cafe in wooded garden.

COLDRERIO, *Ticino* **06**

★ ★ ★ **Motel Mobil** (MT)
Area Di Servizio
☎ 091 464881 telex 842805 fax 091 466671
✉ 6877

- ♨ 89/109 39 ♨ 139/159
🆎 🅴 ⛯ ◆ ⇅ 🅿 📶 🆆🅲 📺 ☺

CRANS-SUR-SIERRE, *Valais* **05**

Des Alpes (HR)
☎ 027 413754
✉ 3963

5 ♨ -/- 30 ♨ -/-
🅿 🆆🅲 📺 ⇪

★ ★ ★ ★ **Alpha Residence** (HCR)
Pas De L'ours
☎ 027 431616 telex 473381
✉ 3963

5 ♨ -/- 49 ♨ -/-
⚓ 🏨 🅿 ⛱ ⛵ ⇅ ↖ ⛯ 🅿 🆆🅲 📺

★ ★ ★ **Beau Site** (HR)   🅰🅰 ANWB
☎ 027 413312 fax 027 414384
✉ 3963

The Hotel Beau Site is just outside the centre of the town in an area that is well known for its walking and skiing trails. The hotel has 34 rooms, a tennis court, a swimming pool and horse-riding facilities. There is also a bar and a good restaurant.

open 15.12 - 15.04 + 15.06 - 15.10
10 ♨ 75/90 24 ♨ 140/180
🆎 🅾 🅴 ⛯ ⚓ ⛵ 🅾 🅿 ⛱ ⛵ ⚓ ⇅ ↖ ⛯ 🅿 🆆🅲 📺 🍴 ⇪ ☺

★ ★ ★ **Mont Blanc** (HCR)
☎ 027 412343
✉ 3963

3 ♨ -/- 21 ♨ -/-
🅿 ⛱ ⛯ 🅿 🍴

★ ★ ★ **Royal** (HR)
☎ 027 413931 telex 473227 fax 027 413936
✉ 3963

open 16.12 - 10.04 + 20.06 - 10.09
29 ♨ 90/190 40 ♨ 153/323
🆎 🅾 🅴 ⛯ ⚓ 🏨 🅾 🅿 ⛱ ⇅ ⛯ 🅿 🆆🅲 📺 🍴 ☺

★ ★ ★ **Serenella** (HP)
☎ 027 413781
✉ 3963

6 *🛏* -/- 16 *🛏* -/-
🏊 ☉ **P** 🏋 ↿↾ ⬆🚪 ➖ ⬜ 🅿 WC 🍽 ⊙

DAVOS, *Graubunden*   07

★ ★ **Anna Maria** (HP)
☎ 081 453555
✉ 7270

6 *🛏* -/- 23 *🛏* -/-
🏊 🅿 ↿↾ ➖ ⬜ 🅿 WC

★ ★ ★ ★ **Schatzalp Berghotel** (HCR)   AA ANWB
☎ 081 441331 telex
853152 fax 081 431344
✉ 7270

The Berghotel Schatzalp
is beautifully situated
between woods on a
sunny mountainside,
300m above Davos, no
more than 4 minutes
from the Schatzalp
cable-car. It is a luxuri-
ous Art-Deco hotel where all the rooms are
tastefully furnished, have a private toilet, bath or
shower, and most of them feature a minibar and
a balcony with breathtaking view. The hotel
offers plenty of leisure facilities, including a
tennis court and swimming pool with sauna. The
ski lifts are right next to the hotel.

open 18.12 - 21.04 + 20.06 - 27.09
* 13 *🛏* 85/270 80 *🛏* 140/460
AE ⓪ 🅴 ➖ 🏊 ♿ ☉ **P** 🅿 🏋 🎿 ↿↾ ➖ 🅿 WC 🍽 🏠 ⊙

★ ★ ★ ★ **Centralsport** (HCR)
Promenade 62
☎ 081 421181 telex 853188 fax 081 435212
✉ 7270

20 *🛏* -/- 72 *🛏* -/-
AE ⓪ 🅴 ➖ 🏊 ☉ **P** 🅿 🏋 ↿↾ ➖ WC TV 🍽 ⊙

★ ★ ★ **Cresta** (HR)
Talstrasse 57
☎ 081 464666 telex 853101 fax 081 464685
✉ 7270

* 3 *🛏* 78/150 37 *🛏* 130/280
AE ⓪ 🅴 ➖ 🏊 ♿ **P** 🅿 🏋 🎿 ↿↾ ⬆🚪 ➖ 🅿 WC TV 🍽 ⊙

★ ★ ★ ★ **Fluela** (HCR)
Bahnhofstrasse 5
☎ 081 471221 telex 853100 fax 081 464401
✉ 7260

open 06.10 - 23.04
* 30 *🛏* 160/260 50 *🛏* 290/490
AE ⓪ 🅴 ➖ ☉ ♦ **P** 🏋 🎿 ↿↾ ➖ 🅿 TV 🍽 ⊙

★ ★ **Herrman Sporthotel** (HP)
☎ 081 451737
✉ 7270

6 *🛏* -/- 18 *🛏* -/-
🏊 **P** 🅿 🐕 🦌

★ ★ ★ ★ **Morosani Posthotel** (HR)   AA ANWB
Promenade 42
☎ 081 441161
telex 853150
fax 081 431647
open: 5/12-12/4 +
25/5-4/10

This hotel is an attrac-
tive feature of the
holiday and winter-
sports resort of Davos;
it is named after the
longstanding proprietors here. Inside the hotel is
attractively decorated in the local style, the
lounge has a welcoming open fire, and a friendly
atmosphere extends to the restaurant. All the
bedrooms have a private bathroom and TV, and
some have a balcony. There is an indoor swimming pool and sauna, and the hotel garden has a
terrace

20 *🛏* 94/230 70 *🛏* 168/450
AE ⓪ 🅴 ➖ 🏊 ☉ **P** 🅿 🏋 🎿 ↿↾ ➖ 🅿 WC KTV

★ ★ ★ ★ **Schweizerhof** (HR)
Promenade 50
☎ 081 441151 telex 853124 fax 081 434966
✉ 7270

open 22.05 - 30.09
* 36 *🛏* 102/136 57 *🛏* 184/232
AE ⓪ 🅴 ➖ 🏊 ☉ **P** 🅿 🏋 🎿 ↿↾ ⬆🚪 ➖ 🅿 TV 🍽

★ ★ ★ **Sonnenberg** (HP)   AA ANWB
☎ 081 461022 fax 081
465797
✉ 7260

Sonnenberg is a quiet
but centrally located
family hotel, known for
its light and healthy
cuisine. The rooms have
radio, telephone and
minibar. There are also
apartments for hire on a

(half board) hotel basis. The hotel features an attractive lounge, sunbathing lawn and garden with seating by the stream.
open 05.12 - 17.04 + 25.06 - 16.10
* 9 ♨ 57/80 26 ☕ 114/160
🌐📧🍴🛏️🅿️🏧♨️🍴🛁🚻📺🍽️⛄

★ ★ ★ Sunstar (HR)
☎ 081 441241 telex 853192 fax 081 431579
📧 7270

- ♨ -/- 69 ☕ -/-
🏧🌐📧🍴🛏️🅿️🏧♨️🛁🚻🗑️📺🍽️⛄⊗

DISENTIS, *Graubunden* 04

★ ★ ★ ★ Parkhotel Baur (HCR)
Sontga Catrina
☎ 086 74545 telex 74585
📧 7180

4 ♨ -/- 51 ☕ -/-
🏧🅿️♨️🛁🚻🗑️📺🍽️

★ ★ ★ Aparthotel Rhaetia (HA)   🅰🅰 ANWB
Via Sursilvana
DISENTIS
☎ 081 9475626 fax 081 9475726
📧 7180

This hotel has a beautiful mountain setting, on a south-facing slope just outside Disentis on the Chur road. Its 10 rooms are furnished as apartments, each with its own kitchen and bathroom, and all are equipped with radio, television and refridgerator; some rooms have a balcony. The hotel also has a restaurant, specialising in regional dishes. Skiing and cross-country skiing are popular winter sports here, while in summer there is tennis, fishing and walking.

open 15.12 - 01.05 + 28.05 - 31.12
* - ♨ 66/77 10 ☕ 120/140
🏧🌐📧🍴🛏️🅿️🏧♨️🛁🚻🗑️📺🍽️⊗

★ ★ ★ Sporthotel Sax (HCR)
☎ 086 9474448 fax 086 9475368
📧 7180

* 1 ♨ 50/70 19 ☕ 100/120
🏧🌐📧🍴🛏️🅿️🏧♨️🚻⊗

EGERKINGEN, *Solothurn* 03

★ ★ ★ Motel Egerkingen (MT)   🅰🅰 ANWB
Beim Autobahnkreuz
N1/n2
☎ 062 612121 telex 982856 fax 062 612853
📧 4622

The Motel Egerkingen is conveniently situated on the Gotthardt motorway, south of Basel, just before the road splits in the direction of Bern and Geneva. After a day in the car, travellers can relax in one of the motel's 68 rooms, which have a bathroom, TV and minibar. It has a pleasant restaurant, an attractive bar, and the garden contains a nice terrace and a small playground. There are also conference facilities available. The motel can be reached from the Egerkingen Olten exit.

20 ♨ 118/150 48 ☕ 169/-
🏧🌐📧🍴🛏️🅿️🏧♨️🛁🚻🗑️📺🍽️⊗

★ ★ ★ ★ Mövenpick   🅰🅰 ANWB
Konferenzzentrum (HCR)
Hoehenstrasse 666
☎ 062 626211 telex 982936 fax 062 612282
📧 4622

All rooms in the Mövenpick Konferenzzentrum have 2 king-size beds, a seating area, washing facilities and colour TV. There is a speciality restaurant and a Mövenpick restaurant, serving well known Mövenpick dishes, as well as a bistro serving products from the hotel's own bakery. The hotel also has a gym and a whirlpool; there is good access for the disabled.

* 71 ♨ 190/245 excl. breakfast 73 ☕ 230/285 excl. breakfast
🏧🌐📧🍴🛏️♨️◆🅿️♨️🚻🛁🛏️🗑️📺⊗

EINSIEDELN, *Schwyz* 04

★ ★ ★ Drei Konige (HCR)
Klosterplatz
☎ 055 532441 telex 875293
📧 8840

11 ♨ -/- 42 ☕ -/-
🛏️⊙🅿️♨️♨️🚻🗑️📺🍽️

EMMENBRÜCKE, *Luzern* 03

★ ★ ★ Landhaus (HCR)
Neuenkirchstrasse 3
☎ 041 531737 telex 862741 fax 041 531780
📧 6020

* 7 ♨ 95/125 24 ☕ 145/185
🏧🌐🍴◆🅿️♨️♨️🚻🗑️📺

ENGELBERG, *Unterwalden*   **04**

★ ★ ★ **Engelberg** (HCR)
Dorfstr. 14
☎ 041 941168 fax 041 943235
✉ 6390

open 01.01 - 31.10
* 5 ᗑ 70/90 15 ᗝ 140/180
🆎 🅾 🅴 ⊞ ☉ ♨ ⊞ ➡ 🆋 🆆🅲 🍽 😊

★ ★ ★ ★ **Regina Titlis** (HCR)
Dorfstrasse 33
☎ 041 942828 telex 866272 fax 041 942392
✉ 6390

open 11.12 - 31.10
* 96 ᗑ 125/165 128 ᗝ 200/270
🆎 🅾 🅴 ⊞ ♨ ☉ 🅿 🛖 ♨ ♨ ⊞ 🆆🅲 📺 🍽

FAIDO, *Ticino*   **06**

★ ★ ★ **Milano** (HCR)   **AA** *ANWB*
Cp 11
☎ 094 381307
fax 094 381708
✉ 6760

Just by looking at the architecture of Hotel Milano, one can sense the Italian border nearby. It is situated 100m from the St Gotthard Pass, not far from the southern entrance to the tunnel, but it is very peaceful nonetheless. Hotel Milano is surrounded by beautiful mountain scenery, and because of its position, it is very well suited to those who are travelling through. A large proportion of the rooms have a private toilet and bath/shower, and the pleasant terrace on the street-side of the hotel and the verdant garden offer plenty of relaxation.

11 ᗑ -/- 25 ᗝ -/-
♨ 🅿 🛖 ♨ ⊞ ➡ 🆆🅲

FAULENSEE, *Bern*   **03**

★ ★ ★ **Seeblick** (HCR)   **AA** *ANWB*
☎ 033 542321
fax 033 542348
✉ 3705

The Hotel Seeblick is a comfortable holiday hotel, built in traditional style. It is situated directly on the banks of the Thunersee and is surrounded by the

mountain tops of the Bernese Oberland. The fine restaurant and the pleasant terrace on the waterside overlook the lake and the surrounding area. Most of the rooms have a private bathroom and a covered balcony with a beautiful view. The hotel features a small playground for the younger ones.

open 01.02 - 15.11
* 2 ᗑ 45/76 23 ᗝ 94/138
♨ 🖐 🅿 🛖 ♨ ♨ ⊞ 🆆🅲 📺 😊

FIESCH, *Valais*   **05**

★ ★ ★ **Ideal Christania** (HCR)
☎ 028 712112 fax 028 711840
✉ 3984

open 07.05 - 24.10
* 1 ᗑ 110/140 22 ᗝ 170/200
🅴 ⊞ ♨ 🖐 🅿 ♨ ⊞ ➡ 🆋 🆆🅲 📺 🍽

FLIMS, *Graubunden*   **04**

★ ★ ★ ★ **Albana Sporthotel** (HR)
☎ 081 392333 telex 74167
✉ 7017

3 ᗑ -/- 27 ᗝ -/-
☉ 🅿 🛖 ♨ ⊞ 🆋 🆆🅲 📺

★ ★ ★ **Bellevue** (HCR)
☎ 081 393131 fax 081 393131
✉ 7017

open 06.06 - 20.04
1 ᗑ 58/85 40 ᗝ 98/100
🆎 🅾 🅴 ⊞ 🅿 ➡ 🆋

FLIMS/WALDHAUS, *Graubunden*   **04**

★ ★ ★ **Arven Waldeck** (HR)
Hauptstrasse
FLIMS
☎ 081 391228 fax 081 394384
✉ 7018

4 ᗑ -/62 25 ᗝ 58/90
🅴 ⊞ ☉ ◈ 🅿 🛖 ♨ ⊞ ➡ 🆋 🆆🅲 🍽 😊

★ ★ **Cresta**
FLIMS
☎ 081 393535 fax 081 393534
✉ 7018

open 20.12 - 20.04 + 30.05 - 10.10
* 8 ᗑ 55/85 40 ᗝ 110/160
🅴 ⊞ 🖐 🅿 🛖 ♨ ♨ ⊞ 🏧 ➡ 🆋 📺 😊

FLÜELEN, *Uri*   04

★ ★ **Weisses Kreuz** (HCR)
Axenstrasse 2
☎ 044 21717
✉ 6454

Hotel Weisses Kreuz can be found in the centre of Flüelen at the most southern point of the Vierwaltstättersee. From the hotel, and especially from the semi-circular panoramic restaurant, guests are treated to a beautiful view over the water. This quiet and comfortable hotel, where most rooms have their own toilet and shower, is suitable for a stopover during a long journey. It is only a few kilometres from the Gotthardt motorway.

5 🛏 -/- 20 🚪 35/100 excl. breakfast
AE ① E ⚏ 🏍 ⊙ ◆ 🐕 🖃 🅿 WC

FRIBOURG, *Fribourg*   02

★ ★ ★ ★ **Duc Bertold** (HCR)
Rue Des Bouchers 5
☎ 037 811121 fax 037 231587
✉ 1701

* 20 🛏 110/160 16 🚪 160/250
AE ① E ⚏ ⊙ ◆ 🅿 🐕 🍴 🖃 🅿 WC TV 🍽 ⊙

GENÈVE, *Geneve*   02

Framed by the Alps and the Jura mountains and located on the shores of the largest of the Alpine lakes, Geneva is a major hub of European cultural life, an important venue for international meetings, a popular convention and exhibitions centre, and a major financial, commercial and industrial city. Yet thanks to its cosmopolitan atmosphere, a wealth of museums, parks, excellent hotels and restaurants, Geneva also attracts more visitors each year than any other Swiss city - and has refined the art of looking after them to a high degree. Every country is represented here, from Mexican to Russian, from formal to informal. As well as traditional Swiss specialities such as fondue and *raclette*, diners are likely to find fresh fish from the lakes, especially trout, perch and pike. Many restaurants also offer hare, venison, and game birds in season, usually cooked in rich wine sauces. Regional specialities also include *saucisson vaudois*, a spicy smoked sausage. Pastries are particularly irresistible.

★ ★ ★ **Astoria** (HG)
Place Cornavin 6
☎ 022 7321025 telex 412536 fax 022 7317690
✉ 1211

* 29 🛏 100/120 33 🚪 135/160
AE ① E ⚏ ⊙ ◆ 🍴 🖃 🅿 WC TV ⊙

★ ★ ★ **Balzac** (HG)
Ancien Port 14
☎ 022 7310160 telex 412538 fax 022 7383847
✉ 1201

The Balzac Hotel, situated in the harbour district of Geneva, is a good central location for touring the city and getting to know its artistic and cultural heritage. Bedrooms are well equipped, and all have televisions, minibars, and private bath or shower rooms.

23 🛏 85/115 17 🚪 135/155
AE ① E ⚏ 🐟 ⊙ 🅿 🍴 🖃 🅿 WC TV ⊙

HOTEL ASTORIA GENEVE
☆ ☆ ☆

(Centrally Located)
Place Cornavin 6
CH-1201 GENEVE

✆ (022) 732 10 25
Fax : (022) 731 76 90
Tx. : 412 536 ASTIG CH

RATES 1993
🧍 SFr. 100,– / 120,–
🧍🧍 SFr. 135,– / 160,–
🛁 / 🚿
Direct phone – SAT-TV – Radio – Mini Bar – Sauna.
Taxes, Breakfast included.

SWITZERLAND

★ ★ ★ ★ ★ **Des Bergues** (HR)
Quai Des Bergues 33
☎ 022 7315050 telex 412540 fax 022 7321989
✉ 1201

42 🛏 -/- 81 🛏 -/-
⊙ P 🄿 🍴 🔒 🅿 wc tv ⑩ ☺

★ ★ ★ ★ **Cristal** (HG)
Rue Pradier 4
☎ 022 7313400 telex 412549 fax 022 7317078
✉ 1201

* 20 🛏 145/175 59 🛏 210/240
AE ⓪ 🄴 ⚍ ⚡ ⊙ 🍴 🔒 🅿 wc tv ☺

★ ★ ★ **Eden** (HCR)
Rue De Lausanne 135
☎ 022 7326540 telex 412551 fax 022 7315260

20 🛏 155/- 34 🛏 205/-
AE ⓪ 🄴 ⚍ 🍴 🔒 🅿 wc tv

★ ★ ★ ★ **Grand Pré** (HCR)
Rue Du Grand Pre 35
☎ 022 339150 telex 23284
✉ 1211

1 🛏 -/- 75 🛏 -/-
⊙ P 🔒 🅿

★ ★ ★ **Le Grenil** (HCR)   🄰🄰 ANWB
Av Sainte Clotilde 7
☎ 022 3283055
fax 022 3213055
✉ 1205

This tourist, business and congress hotel is situated in the centre of the city. It is, by local standards, a modestly priced hotel, but it nevertheless offers all the necessary comforts. It is a hotel that aims at a younger clientele, but of course everyone is also welcome. Forty out of the 50 modern, furnished rooms feature a private toilet and shower. In the summer the restaurant serves meals on the terrace, weather permitting.

10 🛏 95/105 40 🛏 120/130
AE ⓪ 🄴 ⚍ ⚡ ⊙ P 🍴 🔒 wc ⑩

★ ★ ★ **Marenda** (HCR)
☎ 027 652626 fax 027 652527
✉ 3901

open 19.12 - 18.04 + 12.06 - 24.10
* 5 🛏 60/95 28 🛏 110/170
AE ⓪ 🄴 ⚍ ⚡ ⚓ ⊘ ⊙ P 🄿 🍴 🔒 🅿 wc tv ⑩ ☺

★ ★ ★ ★ ★ **Mövenpick Radisson Geneve**
20, Route De Pre Bois
☎ 022 7987575 telex 415701 fax 022 7910284
✉ 1215

* 154 🛏 230/330 excl. breakfast 196 🛏 320/370 excl. breakfast
AE ⓪ 🄴 ⚍ ⚡ 🌀 P 🄿 🍴 🔒 wc tv ⑩ ☺

★ ★ ★ **Mon Repos** (HR)
Rue De Lausanne 131
☎ 022 7328010 telex 23747 fax 022 7328595

- 🛏 -/- 100 🛏 -/-
AE ⓪ 🄴 ⚍ ◈ P 🄿 🍴 🔒 🅿 wc tv ⑩

★ ★ ★ **Penta** (HCR)
Av. Louis Casai 75-77
☎ 022 7984700 telex 415571 fax 022 7987758
✉ 1216

48 🛏 190/- 260 🛏 240/-
AE ⓪ 🄴 ⚍ ⚡ 🌀 P 🄿 🍴 🔒 🅿 wc tv ⑩ ☺

★ ★ ★ ★ ★ **Du Rhone** (HCR)
Quai Turrettini
☎ 022 7319831 telex 412559 fax 022 7324558
✉ 1201

* 50 🛏 280/325 excl. breakfast 181 🛏 425/620 excl. breakfast
AE ⓪ 🄴 ⚍ ⚡ 🌀 ⊙ P 🄿 🍴 🔒 🅿 wc tv ⑩ ☺

★ ★ ★ ★ **Best Western Hotel le Warwick** (HCR)
Rue De Lausanne 14
☎ 022 7316250 telex 412731 fax 022 7389935
res nr 031 234455

* 89 🛏 240/310 excl. breakfast 80 🛏 270/365 excl. breakfast ⊙ ◈ 🄿 🍴 🔒 🅿 wc tv ⑩ ⬆ ☺

GENÈVE/VÉSENAZ, *Geneve*   **02**

★ ★ ★ **La Tourelle** (HG)
Route D' Hermance
VÉSENAZ
☎ 022 7521628 fax 022 7925493
✉ 1222

3 🛏 -/- 21 🛏 -/-
⓪ ⚍ ⚡ ⚓ 🌀 P 🄿 🔒 🅿 wc tv ☺

GERSAU, *Schwyz*   **04**

★ ★ ★ **Seehof du Lac** (HR)
☎ 041 841245 fax 041 842102
✉ 6442

open 01.04 - 15.10
* 3 🛏 86/116 17 🛏 125/140
AE ⓪ 🄴 ⚍ ⚡ 🌀 ◈ P 🄿 🍴 🔒 🅿 wc tv ⑩

GISWIL, *Unterwalden* 03

★ ★ ★ **Bahnhof** (HA)   AA ANWB
☎ 041 681161
fax 041 682457
✉ 6074

This family hotel is situated in the centre of Giswil, between high mountains in the heart of Switzerland. It is a small, traditional and well maintained holiday hotel, where half of the rooms feature a private toilet and shower, and some also have a TV. Rustic furnishings have been matched with natural stone and wrought iron to create a tasteful interior in the restaurant. The surrounding area offers plenty of recreational facilities, with plenty of walks, and cross-country and downhill skiing in winter.

open 01.02 - 31.12
* 5 ♦ 45/70 14 ⇴ 80/120
AE ⓪ E ⴲ ⤳ ◉ P ⸙ ⵟ ⵟ 🛏 ⯃ WC TV ⊛

GLATTBRUGG, *Zurich* 04

★ ★ ★ ★ **Movenpick Zurich Airport** (HR)
Walter Mittelholzerstr 8
☎ 01 8101111 telex 828781 fax 01 8104038
✉ 8152

159 ♦ 225/265 excl. breakfast 176 ⇴ 275/- excl. breakfast
AE ⓪ E ⴲ P ⵟ 🛏 ⯃ TV ⏍

GRÄCHEN, *Valais* 05

★ ★ **Abendruh** (HG)
☎ 028 561116
✉ 3925

1 ♦ -/- 9 ⇴ -/-
⤳ ◉ 🛏 WC

★ ★ ★ **Gaedi** (HP)
☎ 028 561828
✉ 3925

1 ♦ -/- 24 ⇴ -/-
◉ P ⸙ ⵟ 🛏 WC

★ ★ ★ **Montana** (HCR)   AA ANWB
Rittinen
☎ 028 561312
fax 028 563328
✉ 3925

The comfortable holiday and winter-sports hotel Montana can be found in one of the highest parts of the Alps, situated against the side of the 4545m high Dom, surrounded by sloping alpine meadows and overlooking the Ried glacier. All the 17 rooms have their own bathroom, and most feature a balcony. The hotel offers the essentials for a healthy holiday: pure air, a sauna and a fitness room.

open 15.12 - 20.04 + 10.06 - 15.10
* 4 ♦ 60/- 13 ⇴ 120/-
⤳ ⓥ P ⸙ 🛏 P WC ⏍ ⊛

See advertisement on page 117

★ ★ **Sonne** (HR)
☎ 028 561107
✉ 3925

* - ♦ -/- 13 ⇴ 125/134
◉ ⸙ P WC ⏍ ⊛

GRINDELWALD, *Bern*   03

★ ★ ★ ★ **Belvédere** (HR)   
☎ 036 545434 telex
923244 fax 036 534120
✉ 3818

The Hotel Belvédere is
an elegant and very
comfortable holiday and
leisure hotel situated in
the winter-sports resort
of Grindelwald. It lies at
the foot of the Jungfrau
massif and the spectac-
ular north side of the Eiger. Luxury and refinement characterise the public rooms and the
restaurant. There are 45 spacious rooms with
balconies, which are equipped with modern
amenities. The hotel features a beautiful swimming pool with a sauna and fitness room, and
tennis courts and an 18-hole golf course can be
found locally.

open 19.12 - 22.10
* 7 ♨ 120/150 38 ⚲ 220/400
🅰🅴 ⓪ 🄴 ⌖ ⅄ ⓢ 🅿 ⑂ ⚷ ⑂ 🔪 ⬛ 🄿 🆆🄲 🆃🆅 🍴 ☺

★ ★ **Motel Grindelwald** (MT)
☎ 036 532131 fax 036 535132
✉ 3818

open 20.12 - 15.10
* - ♨ 65/85 18 ⚲ 120/160
🄴 ⌖ ⅄ 🅿 ⑂ ⬛ 🄿 🆆🄲 ✈

★ ★ ★ **Hirschen** (HCR)
☎ 036 532777 fax 036 534894
✉ 3818

open 19.12 - 30.11
* 4 ♨ 80/115 30 ⚲ 130/192
⌖ ⅄ ⓢ 🅿 ⑂ 🔪 ⬛ 🄿 🆆🄲 🍴

★ ★ **Gasthof Panorama** (HR)
Terrassenweg
☎ 036 532010 fax 036 532089
✉ 3818

open 20.12 - 20.04 + 01.06 - 25.10
* - ♨ 60/80 11 ⚲ 100/150
🌣 🅿 ⑂ 🄿 🆆🄲 ☺

★ ★ ★ **Parkhotel Schonegg** (HR)
☎ 036 531853 fax 036 534766
✉ 3818

open 21.12 - 21.04 + 05.06 - 18.10
11 ♨ 110/150 37 ⚲ 220/300
🅰🅴 ⓪ 🄴 ⌖ ⅄ 🅿 ⑂ ⚷ 🔪 ⬛ 🄿 🆆🄲 🍴 ☺

★ ★ **Rosenegg** (HR)
☎ 036 531282
✉ 3818

1 ♨ -/- 22 ⚲ -/-
⓪ ⌖ ⅄ ⓢ 🅿 ⑂ ⚷ 🔪 ⬛ 🄿 🆆🄲 ☺

★ ★ ★ ★ **Regina** (HCR)
☎ 036 545455 telex 923263 fax 036 534717
✉ 3818

open 18.12 - 10.10
* 18 ♨ 220/260 excl. breakfast 80 ⚲ 360/400 excl.
breakfast
🅰🅴 ⌖ ⅄ ⓢ 🅿 ⑂ ⚷ ⚶ 🔪 ⬛ 🄿 🆆🄲 🆃🆅 🍴

★ ★ ★ **Schweizerhof** (HCR)
☎ 036 532202 telex 923254 fax 036 532004
✉ 3818

open 19.12 - 13.04 + 29.05 - 10.10
* 9 ♨ 126/168 42 ⚲ 230/368
🅰🅴 🄴 ⌖ ⅄ ⓢ 🅿 ⑂ 🔪 ⬛ 🄿 🆆🄲 🆃🆅 🍴 ☺

★ ★ ★ **Best Western Hotel Spinne
Guesthouse** (HR)
☎ 036 532341 telex 923297 fax 036 532341
res nr 031 234455
✉ 3818

6 ♨ -/- 46 ⚲ -/-
🅰🅴 ⓪ 🄴 ⌖ ⅄ ⓢ 🅿 ⑂ ⚷ 🔪 ⬛ 🄿 🆆🄲 🍴 ☺

★ ★ ★ **Sunstar** (HCR)
☎ 036 545417 telex 923230 fax 036 533170
✉ 3818

25 ♨ -/- 110 ⚲ -/-
⅄ ⓢ 🅿 ⑂ ⚷ ⚶ 🔪 ⬛ 🄿 🆆🄲 🆃🆅 🍴

GSTAAD, *Bern*   05

★ ★ ★ **Bellevue** (HR)
☎ 030 83171 telex 922232 fax 030 42136
✉ 3780

open 20.12 - 28.03 + 20.06 - 03.10
* 19 ♨ 140/190 36 ⚲ 240/440
🅰🅴 ⓪ 🄴 ⌖ ⅄ ⓢ 🅿 ⑂ ⚷ 🔪 ⬛ 🄿 🆆🄲 🆃🆅 🍴

★ ★ ★ ★ **Palace** (HR)
☎ 030 83131 telex 922222 fax 030 43344
✉ 3780

open 20.12 - 31.03 + 20.06 - 30.09
* 51 ♨ 300/620 82 ⚲ 520/1020
🅰🅴 ⓪ 🄴 ⌖ ⅄ ⓢ 🅿 ⑂ ⚷ ⚶ 🔪 ⬛ 🄿 🆆🄲 🆃🆅 🍴 ⬆ ☺

Hotel Montana
★★★
3925 Grächen-Rittinen

Beautiful hotel, all rooms with shower, wc,
radio, balcony, Hotel car park, sauna,
steam bath, solarium, fitness room.
A sunny settings, quiet. Bed and breakfast:
Swiss F 60 pp. Weekly half board: summer
Swiss F 490, winter Swiss F 520.
Discount for children.

Family Gruber-van der Ham.
Telephone 028-561312 Fax; 028-563328.

★★★ **Rossli Post** (HR)
☎ 030 43412 fax 030 46190
✉ 3780

* - ☗ 85/130 18 ☗ 140/230
◑ 🄴 ☎ ⊙ ◆ 🄿 ☂ 🔌 ➡ 🄵 WC TV ☻

GUNTEN, *Bern*   03

★★ **Bellevue** (HCR)
Sigriswilstrasse
☎ 033 511121
✉ 3654

open 01.03 - 31.10
12 ☗ 30/80 14 ☗ 50/120
🄿 ☂ 🄵 WC ✈

★★★★ **Best Western Hotel
Hirschen am See**
(HCR)
☎ 033 512244 telex
912100 fax 033 513884
res nr 031 234455
✉ 3654

Situated on the sunny
side of the Thunersee,
the hotel has a magnif-
icent view of the lake
and the mountains. The
rooms are comfortably furnished, and most have
a balcony. There are 2 restaurants: the Pavillon
Grill and Panorama Restaurant with (heated)
terrace. There is plenty of opportunity for walking
and water sports in the area.

open 01.03 - 30.11
* 21 ☗ 80/123 47 ☗ 155/265
🄰🄴 ◑ 🄴 ☎ 🔌 ➡ 🚠 ⊙ ◆ 🄿 ☂ 🄟 ☂ 🍴 ➡ 🄵 WC TV 🍴

★★★ **Parkhotel Am See** (HCR)
Staatsstrasse
☎ 033 512231 fax 033 512291
✉ 3654

open 01.03 - 31.01
* 24 ☗ 45/80 40 ☗ 85/132
🄰🄴 ◑ 🄴 ☎ 🔌 ⊙ 🄿 ☂ ☂ ➡ 🄵 WC TV 🍴 ✈

GUTTANNEN, *Bern*   03

★★★ **Grimsel Hospiz** (HCR)
Am Grimselpass
☎ 036 731231 telex 923257
✉ 3861

1 ☗ -/- 36 ☗ -/-
🔌 🄿 ☂ ☂ ➡ 🄵

★★★ **Handeck** (HCR)
Am Grimselpass 1400 M.
☎ 036 731131 telex 923257 fax 036 731240

open 01.03 - 31.10
12 ☗ 49/54 28 ☗ 88/98
🄰🄴 ◑ 🄴 ☎ 🔌 🐕 🄿 ☂ ☂ ➡ 🄵 WC 🍴

HERGISWIL, *Unterwalden*   03

★★★ **Pilatus Am See** (HR)
Seestrasse
☎ 041 951555 telex 866159 fax 041 953894
✉ 6052

15 ☗ -/- 45 ☗ -/-
🄰🄴 ◑ 🄴 ☎ 🔌 🚠 ⊙ 🄿 ☂ ☂ 🍴 ➡ 🄵 🍴 ☻

HETTLINGEN, *Zurich*   **04**

Sonne (HCR)   AA ANWB
Schaffhauserstrasse
☎ 052 391701.
✉ 8442

The Hotel Sonne is
situated in the centre of
the small and rural town
of Hettlingen, just north
of Winterthur and 100m
from the main road to
Schaffhausen. It is a
small, cosy hotel where
most of the well kept rooms have en suite toilet
and shower. The rustic Gaststube serves a
reasonably priced dish of the day, while the
Wyländerstube restaurant has a choice of specialities on the menu. When the weather is fine,
meals and drinks are served in the garden.

open 01.02 - 31.12
* 2 ₰ 45/85 12 ₰ 55/115
AE ➊ E ⌘ ♪ ⊙ P ⍭ ⊟ ⊡ WC TV �|○| ☺

INTERLAKEN, *Bern*   **03**

★ ★ ★ **Beau Sité** (HCR)
Seestr.16
☎ 036 228181 fax 036 232926
✉ 3800

* 2 ₰ 65/132 40 ₰ 95/215
AE ➊ E ⌘ ♪ ⊙ P ⏝ ⍭ ⊟ ⊡ WC TV ☺

★ ★ ★ **Europe** (HR)
Hoeheweg 94
☎ 036 227141 telex 923110 fax 036 229341
✉ 3800

open 11.12 - 24.10
* 11 ₰ 83/110 32 ₰ 136/172
AE ➊ E ⌘ ⊙ P ⍭ ⊟ ⊡ WC ☺

★ ★ ★ ★ **Interlaken** (HR)
Hoeheweg 74
☎ 036 212211 telex 923120 fax 036 233121
✉ 3800

* 5 ₰ 90/150 55 ₰ 140/250
AE ➊ E ⌘ ♪ ⊙ P ⍭ ⚓ ⍭ ⊟ ⊡ WC TV �|○| ☺

★ ★ ★ **Neuhaus** (HR)
Seestrasse 121
☎ 036 228282 telex 923196

17 ₰ -/- 40 ₰ -/-
♪ ⚓ P ⍭ ⚓ ⏢ ⊟ ⊡ TV �|○|

★ ★ **De la Paix** (HP)
Bernastrasse 24
☎ 036 227044 fax 036 228728
✉ 3800

open 16.04 - 01.11
* 4 ₰ 75/95 24 ₰ 98/160
AE ➊ E ⌘ ♪ ⊙ P ⍭ ⏢ ⊟ ⊡ WC TV �|○| ☂

★ ★ ★ ★ **Park Mattenhof** (HCR)
Hauptstrasse 36
☎ 036 216121 telex 923123 fax 036 222888
✉ 3800

16 ₰ 84/134 52 ₰ 148/256
AE ➊ E ⌘ ♪ ⊙ P ⍭ ⏢ ⚓ ⍭ ⊟ ⊡ TV �|○| ⬆ ☺

★ ★ ★ **Splendid** (HCR)
☎ 036 227612 fax 036 227679
✉ 3800

open 26.12 - 31.10
2 ₰ 75/100 33 ₰ 132/180
AE ➊ E ⌘ ⊙ P ⍭ ⊟ ⊡ WC TV �|○| ☺

★ ★ ★ ★ ★ **Victoria Jungfrau** (HR)
Hoeheweg
☎ 036 212171 telex 923121

20 ₰ -/- 208 ₰ -/-
♪ ⊙ P ⏢ ⍭ ⚓ ⍭ ⊟ ⊡ WC TV �|○|

ISELTWALD, *Bern*   **03**

★ ★ ★ **Bellevue** (HR)
☎ 036 451110
✉ 3807

5 ₰ -/- 11 ₰ -/-
♪ ⚓ P ⊟ ⊡ WC ⬆

JONGNY/VEVEY, *Vaud*   **02**

★ ★ ★ **Du Leman** (HCR)
Chemin De La Fontaine,2
JONGNY
☎ 021 9210544 telex 451198
✉ 1805

22 ₰ -/- 28 ₰ -/-
AE ➊ E ⌘ ♪ ⊙ P ⏢ ⍭ ⍭ ⊟ ⊡ WC �|○|

KANDERSTEG, *Bern*   **05**

★ ★ ★ **Alfa Soleil** (HR)
☎ 033 751717 fax 033 751776
✉ 3718

8 ₰ -/- 32 ₰ -/-
AE ➊ E ⌘ ♪ ⊙ P ⏢ ⍭ ⏢ ⚓ ⍭ ⊟ ⊡ WC �|○| ☺

★ ★ ★ **Blumlisalp** (HCR)
Hauptstrasse
☎ 033 751244 fax 033 751809
✉ 3718

open 12.04 - 05.10
* 1 ∅ 85/105 21 ∅ 130/150
🔟🖭🖃⊙◆🅿🅿🍹🚣🏊🍴🖃🖥 WC TV 🍽 🔾

★ ★ ★ ★ **Waldhotel Doldenhorn** (HR)
☎ 033 751818 telex 922110 fax 033 751828
✉ 3718

open 15.12 - 30.10
* 6 ∅ 80/100 26 ∅ 150/200
AE 🔟🖃🖭🚣🏠🅿🅿🍹🍴🖃🖥 WC TV 🍽 🔾

KIENTAL, *Bern*   05

★ ★ **Baren** (HCR)   AA ANWB
☎ 033 761121
fax 033 762633
✉ 3723

This family hotel is in
the centre of Kiental,
about 15km from the
Spiez junction of the
Autobahn. The rooms
and apartments have
their own bathroom
facilities, terrace and
balcony, and the kitchen is known for its many
specialities. The hotel is conveniently situated in
an area that is good for walking and winter sports
(cross-country and downhill skiing). Special terms
for families are available on request.

open 15.12 - 10.11
* 7 ∅ 38/56 15 ∅ 72/110
AE 🔟🖭🖃🚣🏠⊙🅿🅿🍹🍴🖃🖥 WC 🍽 🔾

KLOSTERS, *Graubunden*   07

★ ★ ★ ★ **Best Western Hotel Alpina** (HCR)
☎ 081 694121 telex 853347 fax 081 694710
res nr 031 234455
✉ 7250

- ∅ -/- 80 ∅ -/-
🚣⊙🅿🅿🍹🍴🖥

Pardenn (HCR)
☎ 081 41141 telex 75464

24 ∅ -/- 55 ∅ -/-
🚣🅿🅿🍹🍴🍴🖃🖥 WC 🍽

★ ★ **Silvapina** (HP)
Silvapinaweg 6
☎ 081 41468 fax 081 44078
✉ 7252

open 01.06 - 31.10
1 ∅ 50/66 14 ∅ 100/108
AE 🖃🖭🚣⊙🅿🍹🍴🖃🖥 WC 🏠 🔾

★ ★ ★ **Sport** (HP)
Alte Landstrasse
☎ 081 692921 fax 081 694953
✉ 7250

open 10.12 - 15.10
* 6 ∅ 90/170 20 ∅ 170/270
🖃🖭🅾🅿🍹🍹🏊🍴🖃🖥 WC TV 🍽 🐕

KLOSTERS-DORF, *Graubunden*   07

★ ★ ★ **Buel** (HP)
Bueelweg 1
KLOSTERS
☎ 081 692669 fax 081 694941
✉ 7252

open 19.06 - 10.10 + 19.12 - 17.04
* 2 ∅ 50/95 16 ∅ 96/160
AE 🖃🖭⊙🅿🍹🍹🍴🖃🖥 WC TV 🐕

KRIENS, *Luzern*   03

★ ★ ★ **Pilatusblick** (MT)
☎ 041 413546 telex 862905 fax 041 412062
✉ 6010

* 6 ∅ 70/94 30 ∅ 110/158
AE 🖃🖭🚣🅾◆🅿🍹🍹🍴🖃🖥 WC TV 🍽

KÜSSNACHT AM RIGI, *Schwyz*   04

★ ★ ★ **Hirschen** (HCR)
Unterdorf 9
☎ 041 811027 fax 041 816880
✉ 6403

open 15.01 - 31.12
5 ∅ 75/95 20 ∅ 150/190
AE 🔟🖃🖭⊙🅿🍹🍴🖃🖥 WC TV 🍽 🔾

LA CHAUX-DE-FONDS, *Neuchatel*   02

★ ★ ★ ★ **De la Fleur de Lys** (HCR)
Av. Leop Robert 13
☎ 039 233731 fax 039 235851
✉ 2300

* 2 ∅ 140/210 28 ∅ 210/280
AE 🔟🖃🖭◆🍹🍴🖃🖥 WC TV 🍽 🔾

★ ★ ★ Du Moulin (HCR)
Rue De La Serre 130
☎ 039 264226
fax 039 265118
✉ 2300

The Hotel du Moulin
has 19 spacious rooms,
almost all have a show-
er, but no toilet. The
hotel is situated in the
centre of La Chaux-de-
Fonds, with excellent
ski slopes nearby. It has skis for hire, and the ski
bus stops practically at the front door. There is
also a bar and restaurant.

5 ♪ -/- 14 ♫ 60/100 excl. breakfast
E ≍ ⊙ ◆ P 🅿 TV 🍽

LA NEUVEVILLE, Bern   02

★ Motel la Neuveville (MT)
Route De Bienne 31
☎ 038 511260 fax 038 513779
✉ 2520

- ♪ 80/- excl. breakfast 23 ♫ 105/-
AE ⦿ E ≍ 🕭 ◆ P 🐾 ⟵ 🅿 WC ⊛

LANGENBRUCK, Basel   03

★ ★ ★ Baren (HCR)
Hauptstrasse 10
☎ 062 601414
fax 062 601391
✉ 4438

* 6 ♪ 55/80 20 ♫ 120/
130

AE ⦿ E ≍ ⅄ ⊙ P 🅿 🐾 ⟵ 🅿 WC TV

LANGENTHAL, Bern   03

★ ★ ★ Baren (HCR)
St. Urbanstrasse 1
☎ 063 222941 telex 982507 fax 063 231624
✉ 4900

14 ♪ -/- 15 ♫ 90/160
AE ⦿ E ≍ ⊙ ◆ P 🐾 ⟵ 🅿 WC TV

LAUSANNE, Vaud   02

Lausanne, which lies about half way along the right
bank of Lake Geneva (Léman), has a strongly individual
charm. At Ouchy, the Lake Geneva steamers come
alongside and sailing boats can be hired; a mile-long
railway runs up to the city centre. Here, a covered
wooden stairway, the *Escalier du Marché* leads to the
Palais de la Palud, where a colourful market is held on
Wednesday and Saturday mornings. Many first-class
stores are to be found on the rue St François and the
rue de Borg. Lausanne is the headquarters of the
Federal Court and the International Committee for the
Olympic Games, while the Palais de Beaulieu is the
venue for exhibitions and other events. The beautiful
Château de Chillon stands on a rocky promontory in
the lake near Montreux.

See also advertisement on pages 122 and 123

★ ★ ★ ★ Agora
Av. Du Rond Point 6
☎ 021 6171211 telex 455300 fax 021 262605
✉ 1006

* 8 ♪ 150/170 75 ♫ 215/235
AE ⦿ E ≍ ⊙ P 🅿 🐾 ⟵ 🅿 WC TV 🍽

★ ★ ★ AlaGare (HCR)
Rue Du Simplon 14
☎ 021 6179252 telex 454411 fax 021 6179255
✉ 1006

open 03.01 - 23.12
* 8 ♪ 100/150 38 ♫ 150/225
AE ⦿ E ≍ ⊙ 🐾 ⟵ 🅿 WC TV 🏸

★ ★ ★ ★ Alpha (HCR)
Rue Du Petit Chene 34
☎ 021 230131 telex 454999 fax 021 230145
✉ 1003

* 32 ♪ 145/165 101 ♫ 205/225
AE ⦿ E ≍ ⅄ ⊙ P 🅿 🐾 ⟵ 🅿 WC TV 🍽

★ ★ D' Angleterre (HCR)
Place Du Port
☎ 021 6172111 fax 021 268075
✉ 1006

open 01.02 - 30.12
* 10 ♪ 60/130 25 ♫ 100/160
AE ⦿ E ≍ 🖉 🚗 P 🐾 ⟵ 🅿 WC 🍽 ⊛

★ ★ ★ ★ Best Western Hotel Carlton
(HCR)
Av. De Cour 4
☎ 021 263235 telex
454800 fax 021 263430
res nr 031 234455
✉ 1007

Situated close to Lake
Geneva and the Old
Port, the beautiful
frontage of this Best
Western Hotel Carlton
adorns the centre of Lausanne. It is a luxury hotel
with elegant furnishings in the public rooms, a

stylish restaurant, and a pleasant coffee shop/
cocktail bar. The rooms and suites are tastefully
furnished and feature TV and minibar; most have
a balcony. In fair weather, meals are served in the
garden.

* 20 🍴 158/178 30 🛏 208/248
🅰🅴 ⓪ 🄴 ➿ ⋋ ⊙ 🅿 ♉ ⇈ 🖃 🄿 🆆🅲 🆃🆅 🍴 ⊗

★ ★ ★ City
Rue De Caroline 5
☎ 021 202141 telex 454400 fax 021 202149
✉ 1007

* 15 🍴 115/135 36 🛏 160/180
🅰🅴 ⓪ 🄴 ➿ ⊙ ◈ ⇈ 🖃 🄿 🆆🅲 🆃🆅 ⊗

Mövenpick Radisson (HCR)
4, Av. De Rhodanie
☎ 021 6172121 telex 454340 fax 021 261527
✉ 1000

* 120 🍴 180/225 excl. breakfast 147 🛏 220/265
excl. breakfast
🅰🅴 ⓪ 🄴 ➿ ◔ ◈ 🅿 ☂ ♉ ⇈ 🖃 🄿 🆆🅲 🆃🆅 🍴

★ ★ ★ Des Voyageurs (HG)
Rue Grand St. Jean 19
☎ 021 231902 telex 455220 fax 021 236933
✉ 1003

Des Voyageurs is situated in a quiet area in the
heart of the town. It is a well kept, comfortable
hotel, where the Dutch owners extend a personal
welcome. There are 35 rooms, all have a TV,
telephone, radio and minibar. A babysitting
service and a central safe are available to guests.

* 13 🍴 100/150 22 🛏 150/225
🅰🅴 ⓪ 🄴 ➿ ⊙ 🅿 ⇈ 🖃 🄿 🆆🅲 🆃🆅 ⊗

LAUTERBRUNNEN, *Bern*   05

★ ★ Oberland (HCR)   🄰🄰 ANWB
☎ 036 551241
fax 036 554241
✉ 3822

Hotel Oberland lies in
the centre of the tourist
and winter-sports resort
of Lauterbrunnen, at the
foot of the Jungfrau in
the most impressive
part of the Bernese
Oberland. The rooms of
this traditional and well kept holiday hotel are
nearly all equipped with their own toilet and
washing facilities, while the rooms on the street
side of the building have a pleasant balcony as
well. The surrounding area offers plenty of oppor-

tunity for some beautiful walks, and the Jung-
fraubahn station is only 300m away.

open 01.12 - 31.10
* 4 🍴 50/78 21 🛏 85/150
🅰🅴 ⓪ 🄴 ➿ ⊙ 🅿 ♉ 🖃 🄿 🆆🅲 🍴

★ ★ ★ Staubbach (HCR)   🄰🄰 ANWB
☎ 036 551381 telex
923255
✉ 3822

The Hotel Staubbach is
situated amid some of
the most beautiful
mountain scenery to be
found in Switzerland;
steep rocks and splash-
ing waterfalls shape the
spectacular landscape
of Lauterbrunnen. The hotel has 27 rooms all
with private toilet bath/shower, and most have a
balcony as well. The Goethestube restaurant
serves excellent food, and the stylish bar has a
cosy atmosphere.
open 22.12 - 25.10
* 7 🍴 85/130 20 🛏 165/180
🅰🅴 ⓪ 🄴 ➿ ⋋ 🅿 ♉ ⇈ 🖃 🄿 🆆🅲 ⊗

LE BRASSUS, *Vaud*   02

★ ★ ★ De la Lande (HCR)
Place De La Lande
☎ 021 8454441 fax 021 8454540
✉ 1348

* 8 🍴 64/113 23 🛏 108/206
🅰🅴 🄴 ➿ ⋋ ♨ ⊙ 🅿 ♉ ⇈ 🄿 🆆🅲 🆃🆅 🍴 ⊗

LENK, *Bern*   05

★ ★ ★ Wildstrubel (HR)
☎ 030 63111 fax 030 33151
✉ 3775

open 01.01 - 12.04 + 29.05 - 10.10
* 13 🍴 80/113 32 🛏 160/226
⓪ 🄴 ➿ ⋋ ⊙ 🅿 ♉ ➿ ⇈ 🖃 🄿 🆆🅲 🆃🆅 🍴 ⊗

Lausanne

On the shores of the Lake of Geneva

(alt. 1220 ft/2110 ft)

A tourist and convention centre

- Holidays at all seasons, in an extremely varied setting composed of lake, vineyards and forests, beautiful countryside and mountains.
- Many possibilities for excursions, by road, rail or boat.
- Excellent facilities for all seminars and conventions.
- Historic buildings and museums.
- Throughout the year, a never-ending succession of cultural and artistic events.
- All sports: riding, tennis, tourist aviation, indoor swimming-pools. Starting in the spring, golf (18-hole course), swimming (beaches and swimming-pools), sailing, rowing, water-skiing. In winter, skating, curling, cross-country skiing on the outskirts of the town, Alpine skiing a few miles away in the nearby resorts of the Alps and Jura.
- Excellent road and rail connections.
- Direct railway connection from and to Geneva Intercontinental Airport (44 minutes).

Our special offers

3 days/2 nights from   Swiss Fr. 156.-
4 days/3 nights from   Swiss Fr. 214.-
7 days/6 nights from   Swiss Fr. 389.-

SWITZERLAND

HOTELS***

1 Beau-Rivage Palace
2 Lausanne-Palace

HOTELS**

3 Agora
4 Alpha
5 Carlton
6 Château d'Ouchy
7 Continental
8 Mirabeau
9 Mövenpick-Radisson
10 de la Navigation
11 de la Paix
12 La Résidence
13 Royal-Savoy
14 Victoria

HOTELS*

15 AlaGare
16 Aulac
17 Le Beau-Lieu

18 Bellerive
19 Boulevard
20 City
21 Crystal
22 Elite
23 Jan
24 des Voyageurs

HOTELS**

25 d'Angleterre
26 de la Forêt
27 Près-Lac
28 Rex

HOTELS*

29 Régina
30 du Marché

Neighbourhood

LAUSANNE-BUSSIGNY

31 Novotel***

LAUSANNE-CRISSIER

32 Ibis**

LAUSANNE-JORAT

33 Les Chevreuils***
34 des Fleurs**
35 Vert-Bois**

LAUSANNE-LAVAUX

36 de Belmont***
37 Cécil***
38 Intereurope***
39 du Raisin***
40 Auberge de Rivaz*

LAUSANNE-ROMANEL

41 A la Chotte***

LAUSANNE-ST-SULPICE

42 Débarcadère****
43 Pré-Fleuri***

For all information:
**LAUSANNE TOURIST OFFICE
AND CONVENTION BUREAU**
2, avenue de Rhodanie
CH-1000 Lausanne 6
Tel. (021) 617 73 21
Telex 454 833
Telefax (021) 26 86 47
Vidéotex * Lausanne #

Or the agency of the:
**SWISS NATIONAL
TOURIST OFFICE**
Swiss Centre
1 New Coventry Street
London W1V 8EE
Tel. 071 - 734 1921
Telex 21 295

From Swiss Fr.				
*****			225	300
****			130	180
***			100	150
**	60	95	95	130
*	50	75	70	100
Neighbourhood	45	60	80	100

SWITZERLAND

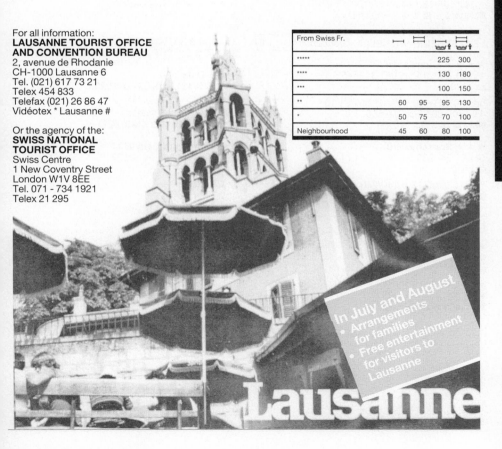

In July and August
• Arrangements for families
• Free entertainment for visitors to Lausanne

Lausanne

LENZBURG, *Aargau* 03

★ ★ ★ **Haller** (HCR) Aavorstadt 24  ⓐⓐ ANWB
☎ 064 514451
fax 064 512505
✉ 5600

Hotel Haller is situated in Lenzburg, a nice little town featuring a beautiful castle on a hill. It is a family hotel, rich in tradition and housed in an elegant and well maintained house. The furnishings are tasteful and refined, the rooms are spacious and equipped with a private bathroom, radio and TV. The restaurant's speciality is French cuisine. In sunny weather it is pleasant to relax on the terrace, which is situated on the street side of the hotel.

* 14 ♬ 105/150 14 ☎ 140/190
🆎 🖪 🖙 🍴 ⊙ 🅿 🛗 🍴 🖃 🖻 🆆🅲 📺

LENZERHEIDE-VALBELLA, *Graubunden* 07

★ ★ ★ ★ **Guarda Val** (HCR)
☎ 081 342214 fax 081 344645
✉ 7078

open 01.01 - 30.04 + 01.06 - 31.10
4 ♬ 160/180 35 ☎ 210/550
🆎 🕽 🖪 🖙 🍴 🅿 🛗 🖃 🖻 🆆🅲

★ ★ ★ **Spescha** (HR)
☎ 081 346263 fax 081 345140
✉ 7078

* - ♬ 100/160 15 ☎ 140/240
🆎 🖪 🖙 🍴 ⊙ ◆ 🛗 🍴 🖃 🖻 🆆🅲 📺

LE PRESE, *Graubunden* 07

★ ★ ★ ★ **Le Prese** (HCR)
☎ 082 50333 fax 082 50835
✉ 7746

open 15.05 - 17.10
* 8 ♬ 96/145 20 ☎ 170/270
🍴 🐾 🅿 🛗 ⚓ 🍴 🖃 🖻 📺 🍽 🛎

LES HAUDÈRES, *Valais* 05

★ ★ ★ **Les Haudères** (HCR)
☎ 027 831541 fax 027 831977
✉ 1984

open 05.12 - 23.10
* 1 ♬ 49/90 30 ☎ 98/150
🆎 🕽 🖪 🖙 ⊙ 🅿 🛗 🍴 🖃 🖻 🆆🅲 🍽

LES MARÉCOTTES, *Valais* 02

★ ★ ★ ★ **Aux Mille Étoiles** (HCR)
☎ 026 611666 fax 026 611600
✉ 1923

open 23.12 - 17.04 + 25.05 - 20.10
* 5 ♬ 85/105 22 ☎ 180/240
🖪 🖙 🍴 🅿 🛗 ⚓ 🍴 🖃 🖻 📺 🍽

LEUKERBAD, *Valais* 05

★ ★ ★ ★ ★ **Bristol Bade** (KH)
☎ 027 611833 telex 472014 fax 027 613687
✉ 3954

7 ♬ -/- 80 ☎ 309/384
🆎 🕽 🖪 🖙 🍴 ⊙ 🅿 🛗 ⚓ ⚓ 🍴 🔔 🖃 🖻 🆆🅲 📺 🍽 🛎 🍽

★ ★ ★ **Dala** (HP)
☎ 027 611213 fax 027 612929
✉ 3954

1 ♬ 120/- 29 ☎ 130/160
🆎 🕽 🖪 🖙 ⊙ 🅿 🛗 🍴 🍴 🖃 🖻 🆆🅲 📺 🍽

★ ★ ★ **Grand Bain** (HP)
☎ 027 611112 telex 38179

1 ♬ -/- 37 ☎ -/-
⚓ 🖃 🖻 🆆🅲 📺

★ ★ ★ **Heilquelle** (HCR)
☎ 027 612222

1 ♬ -/- 30 ☎ -/-
🛗 🍴 🖃 🖻 🆆🅲 🐕

★ ★ **Paradis** (HG)
☎ 027 611233

1 ♬ -/- 16 ☎ 88/96
🍴 🛗 🍴 🖃 🖻 🆆🅲 🐕

★ ★ **Waldrand** (HCR)
☎ 027 611155

14 ♬ -/- 8 ☎ -/-
🍴 🅿 🛗 ⚓ 🍽 🛎

★ ★ ★ Zayetta (HP)
☎ 027 611646 fax 027 612517
✉ 3954

21 🛏 101/108 27 🚪 168/182
AE E ⌨ ⚓ ⊙ P ☂ 🎿 ↿ ⊟ 🗝 WC IOI ☙

LEYSIN, *Vaud*   **02**

★ ★ Les Orchidees (HCR)
☎ 025 341421 fax 025 341810
✉ 1854

open 19.12 - 01.10
* 2 🛏 39/57 14 🚪 78/110
AE ⊙ E ⌨ ⚓ ⊙ P ☂ ⊟ 🗝 WC ☙

★ ★ La Paix au Vieux Pays (HR)
☎ 025 341375 fax 025 341810
✉ 1854

open 10.05 - 30.09 + 01.12 - 10.04
* 6 🛏 40/59 12 🚪 80/114
AE E ⌨ ⚓ ⊙ P ☂ 🗝 WC IOI ☙

★ ★ ★ Sylvana (HR)   *AA ANWB*
☎ 025 341136
fax 025 341614
✉ 1854

The Hotel Sylvana is
situated 1400m above
Leysin, on a steep
mountainside and
surrounded by pine
trees. All the 20 rooms
in this holiday hotel
have en suite bathroom,
radio, minibar and a balcony with a view over the
Walliser Alps. There is a good restaurant and a
pleasant terrace on the sunny side of the hotel.
The surrounding area offers plenty of recreational
facilities; a ski-lift station is nearby.

open 15.12 - 28.10
- 🛏 63/80 20 🚪 106/140
AE E ⌨ ⚓ ⛰ ⊙ P ↿ ⊟ 🗝 WC ⸙

★ ★ ★ Best Western Hotel Engel   *AA ANWB*
(HCR)
Kasernenstr 10
☎ 061 9212511
telex 966040
fax 061 9212516
res nr 031 234455
✉ 4410

This Best Western hotel
Engel is in the historical
heart of the small town
of Liestal, near Basel. It
is a well established family hotel, which offers all
modern comforts; the rooms all have a private
bathroom, radio, TV and minibar, and the Boten-
stube restaurant serves Swiss dishes, with
French cuisine on offer for gourmets. Guests can
also get a fast pizza in the Café Engel and have a
drink in the Engel bar.

open 03.01 - 23.12
* 12 🛏 120/150 21 🚪 160/200
AE ⊙ E ⌨ ⊙ P ☂ ⊟ 🗝 WC TV

★ ★ ★ Radackerhof (HCR)   *AA ANWB*
Rheinstr 93
☎ 061 9013222 fax 061 9013332
✉ 4410

Hotel Radackerhof lies just south of Basel, close
to the N2. Because of its position, the hotel is
very suitable as a comfortable stopover for those
who are travelling through to more southern
resorts. The rooms are soundproof and feature a
bathroom and a TV; some of them are also specially equipped for families with children. The
restaurant has a choice of Swiss dishes on the
menu.

* 5 🛏 49/119 21 🚪 79/179
AE ⊙ E ⌨ ⊙ ◈ P ☂ ↿ 🔄 ⊟ 🗝 WC TV IOI

★ ★ ★ Schauenburg Bad   *AA ANWB*
☎ 061 9011202
fax 061 9011055
✉ 4410

Hotel Bad Schauenburg
is somewhat remotely
situated in an area
surrounded by parks,
meadows and hills
covered with woods. It
is a peaceful holiday,
health and conference
hotel housed in a villa-like building where antique
and modern furnishings have been tastefully
combined. The rooms are elegantly furnished, all
have a bathroom, and also have a TV. The restau-

→

rant serves haute cuisine, while tasty snacks are available in the relaxed setting of the bar.

open 15.01 - 20.12
* 6 ♨ 90/100 24 ⚏ 130/160
🆎 🄌 🄴 ⇌ ⅃ ♨ 🄿 ⅏ ↥ 🔌 ⧫ WC TV ☺

LITZIRÜTI, *Graubunden*   07

★ ★ Ramoz (HR)
☎ 081 311063
✉ 7099

2 ♨ -/- 16 ⚏ -/-
⅃ 🄿 ⅏ ⅏ 🔌 ⧫ WC ↥

LOCARNO, *Ticino*   06

★ ★ Albergo Cardada (HCR)
☎ 093 315591 fax 093 319995
✉ 6600

open 06.12 - 05.11
1 ♨ 60/80 15 ⚏ 120/160
🆎 🄌 🄴 ⇌ ⅃ ⅏ 🔌 ⧫ WC

★ ★ ★ Beau Rivage (HCR)   🄰🄰 ANWB
Via Le Verbano 31
☎ 093 331355 telex 846152
✉ 6600

The Hotel Beau Rivage is a holiday hotel which has a stylish old-fash-ioned appearance. It is beautifully situated in the centre of Locarno, on the boulevard alongside Lake Maggiore. The rooms, some with a balcony and view over the lake, all have a toilet, as well as a bath or shower. The restaurant serves meals inside and on the covered terrace outside. The hotel is within walking distance of Locarno's railway station.

11 ♨ -/- 38 ⚏ 178/242
⅃ ⅃ 🄿 ⅏ ⅏ 🔌 ⧫ WC 🍽 ↥

★ ★ Camelia (HP)
Via G. G. Nessi 9
☎ 093 331767 fax 093 337415
✉ 6600

open 06.03 - 09.11
* 10 ♨ 69/79 30 ⚏ 120/140
🄴 ⇌ ◆ 🄿 ⅏ ↥ ⧫ 🔌 ⧫ WC 🍽

★ ★ ★ Du Lac (HR)
Via Ramogna 3
☎ 093 312921 fax 093 316071
✉ 6600

open 10.01 - 13.12
* 5 ♨ 80/100 26 ⚏ 130/170
🆎 🄌 🄴 ⇌ ⅃ 🄿 ⅏ ↥ 🔌 ⧫ WC TV 🍽 ☺

★ ★ ★ Orselina (HR)
☎ 093 336221 telex 846161

1 ♨ -/- 50 ⚏ -/-
⅃ 🄿 ⅏ ↥ 🔌 ⧫ WC

★ ★ ★ Piccolo
Via Buetti 11
☎ 093 330212 fax 093 332198
✉ 6600

The hotel Piccolo is situated on the outskirts of the city, only five minutes away from Lake Maggiore. It is an excellent centre for making day trips into the Alps, and in Springtime, the lake is especially beautiful when the camellias are in flower along its banks and at the same time people are still skiing on the high slopes. The hotel has all modern comforts, and good parking facilities.

* 3 ♨ 65/120 18 ⚏ 125/190
🆎 🄌 🄴 ⇌ ⅃ 🄿 ⅏ ↥ 🔌 ⧫ WC TV

★ ★ Schloss (HP)
Via San Francesco
☎ 093 312361

5 ♨ -/- 28 ⚏ -/-
⅃ ⅃ 🄿 ⅏ ↥ 🔌 ⧫ WC TV

LOCARNO/MURALTO, *Ticino*   06

★ ★ ★ Reber au Lac (HR)
Viale Verbano 55
LOCARNO
☎ 093 330202 telex 846074 fax 093 337981
✉ 6600

open 15.03 - 15.11
* 27 ♨ 115/240 63 ⚏ 200/380
🆎 🄌 🄴 ⇌ ⅃ ⅏ 🄿 🄿 ⅏ ⅏ ↥ 🔌 ⧫ WC TV 🍽 ↥

LUGANO, *Ticino*   **06**

★ ★ **Aurora** (HCR)
Via Galli 2
☎ 091 233767
✉ 6900

1 🛏 -/- 33 🛏 -/-
🅿 🍴 ⅋ ▣ 🄿 wc 🍽

★ ★ ★ **Carioca** (HP)
Via Geretta
☎ 091 543081 telex 73805

12 🛏 -/- 79 🛏 -/-
⅋ 🍴 ⅋ ▣ 🄿 wc 🍽

★ ★ ★ ★ ★ **Villa Castagnola au Lac** (HR)
Viale Castagnola 31
☎ 091 512213 telex 841200 fax 091 527271
✉ 6906

35 🛏 185/250 60 🛏 270/360
🆎 ⓐ 🄴 ⅌ ⅋ ⏚ 🄿 🍴 🛎 ⚓ 🍴 ▣ 🄿 wc 🆃 🍽 ☏

★ ★ ★ **Ceresio** (HCR)
Via Ballestra 19
☎ 091 231044 telex 73091

1 🛏 -/- 90 🛏 -/-
⊙ 🄿 ▣ 🄿

★ ★ ★ **Colorado** (HCR)
Via Cl Maraini 19
☎ 091 541631 telex 844356 fax 091 551266
✉ 6901

* 10 🛏 105/155 24 🛏 160/220
🆎 ⓐ 🄴 ⅌ ◆ 🄿 🍴 🍴 🛎 ▣ 🄿 wc 🆃 🦮

★ ★ ★ **Continental Beauregard** (HR)
Via Basilea 28
☎ 091 561112 telex 844444 fax 091 561213
✉ 6903

open 21.02 - 15.11
* 30 🛏 85/125 100 🛏 130/200
🆎 🄴 ⅌ ⏚ ⊙ 🄿 🍴 🍴 🍴 🛎 ▣ 🄿 wc 🆃 🍽 ☏

★ ★ ★ **Cristina** (HP)
Via Zorzi 28
☎ 091 543312 telex 844292 fax 091 541773
✉ 6902

open 01.04 - 31.10
10 🛏 60/100 69 🛏 90/160
🄴 ⅌ 🄿 🍴 🍴 ⚓ 🍴 ▣ 🄿 wc 🍽

★ ★ **Dischma** (HP)
Vicolo Geretta 16
☎ 091 542131 fax 091 541503
✉ 6902

open 01.03 - 20.12
* 5 🛏 48/57 30 🛏 80/110
🆎 🄴 ⅌ ⅋ ⊙ 🄿 🍴 🍴 ▣ 🄿 wc 🍽 ☏

★ ★ ★ ★ ★ **Grand Hotel Eden** (HR)
Riva Paradiso 7
☎ 091 550121 telex 844330 fax 091 542895
✉ 6902

7 🛏 200/260 123 🛏 340/440
🆎 ⓐ 🄴 ⅌ ⏚ ⊙ 🄿 🍴 🍴 ⚓ ⅋ 🍴 ▣ 🄿 wc 🆃

★ ★ ★ **International au Lac** (HR)    🅰🅰 *ANWB*
Via Nassa 68
☎ 091 227541 telex
840017 fax 091 227544
✉ 6901

On a nice little square in
the heart of Lugano lies
Hotel International au
Lac, with the lake
directly opposite. The
graceful frontage with
attractive little corner
tower has a classic appearance which extends to
the interior. All the rooms have their own toilet
and bath - some also have a TV and terrace or
balcony. The elegant restaurant is renowned for
its excellent cuisine, and there is a lush palm-tree
garden with comfortable deck chairs behind the
hotel.
open 03.04 - 25.10
* 35 🛏 100/145 45 🛏 160/240
🆎 ⓐ 🄴 ⅌ ⅋ ⏚ ⊙ 🍴 🍴 🍴 ▣ 🄿 wc 🆃 🍽 ☏

★ ★ ★ ★ **Du Lac** (HCR)
Riva Paradiso 3
☎ 091 541921 telex 844355 fax 091 546173
✉ 6902

open 01.03 - 06.01
18 🛏 110/185 35 🛏 220/314
🆎 ⓐ 🄴 ⅌ ⅋ ⏚ 🄿 🍴 🍴 ⚓ 🍴 ▣ 🄿 wc 🆃 🍽 🦮

★ ★ ★ **Lido Seegarten** (HR)
24 Viale Castagnola
☎ 091 512321 fax 091 532236
✉ 6906

10 🛏 60/90 70 🛏 110/190
🆎 ⓐ 🄴 ⅌ ⅋ ⏚ 🄿 🍴 🍴 ⚓ 🍴 ▣ 🄿 wc 🍽

SWITZERLAND

★ **Montarina** (HG)
Via Montarina
☎ 091 567272 telex 844444 fax 091 561213
✉ 6903

open 10.04 - 15.11
2 🛏 40/60 21 🛏 64/96
⏦ ⊙ 🅿 ♨ 🖃

★ ★ ★ **Nizza Parkhotel** (HCR)
Via Suidino 14
☎ 091 541771 telex 73405

1 🛏 -/- 34 🛏 -/-
⏦ 🅿 🖃 🄵

★ ★ ★ **Posthotel Simplon** (HCR)
Via Gen. Guisan 12
☎ 091 544441 fax 091 541221
✉ 6902

8 🛏 -/- 22 🛏 -/-
🄴 ⚏ ⏦ ⊙ 🅿 🄵 ♨ ⇅ ⇲ 🖃 🄵 🆆🅲 🆃🆅

★ **Regina** (HP)
Via S Salvatore 5
☎ 091 541503

1 🛏 -/- 21 🛏 -/-
⏦ 🄵 ♨

★ ★ ★ ★ ★ **Splendide Royal** (HR)
Riva A Caccia 7
☎ 091 542001 telex 73032

27 🛏 -/- 88 🛏 -/-
⊙ 🅿 🄵 ♨ ⛺ ⇅ 🖃 🄵 🆆🅲 🆃🆅

LUZERN, *Luzern*   03

Lucerne, for many the favourite Swiss city, stands in a
magnificent setting bordering the lake of the same
name, in the foothills of the St Gotthard Pass. Lake
excursions are high on the list of visitors' priorities, the
Lake Lucerne Navigation Company providing a wide
selection of half or whole-day excursions. The sights
of Lucerne, best enjoyed on foot, include the Chapel
Bridge, built in 1333, with its numerous gable
paintings and sturdy water tower. Nearby are quaint
alleys that will intrigue and fascinate, while in the city's
arcades you can enjoy the hustle and bustle of the
market crowds. Gastronomic specialities include
Brotsuppe (bread soup), and another popular starter is
Bundnerfleisch, thin slices of dried beef. Pork and veal
sausages are widely available, as are *rösti*, grated fried
potatoes.

★ ★ ★ **Astoria** (HCR)
Pilatusstrasse 29
☎ 041 244466 telex 865720 fax 041 234262
✉ 6003

* 44 🛏 120/180 99 🛏 195/285
🄴 ⓘ 🄴 ⇌ ⊙ ♨ ⇅ 🖃 🄵 🆆🅲 🆃🆅 🍽 ☺

★ ★ ★ ★ **Best Western Hotel des Balances**
(HCR)
Weinmarkt
☎ 041 511851 telex 868148 fax 041 51645,1
res nr 031 234455
✉ 6000

* 4 🛏 -/210 55 🛏 -/340
🄴 ⓘ 🄴 ⇌ ⏦ ⇶ ⊙ ♨ ⇅ 🖃 🄵 🆆🅲 🆃🆅 🍽

★ ★ ★ **Beau Séjour au Lac** (HG)
Haldenstrasse 53
☎ 041 511681
✉ 6006

* 3 🛏 95/110 23 🛏 130/160
⇌ ⚏ ◆ 🅿 ♨ ⇅ 🖃 🄵 🆆🅲 🆃🆅 ☺

★ ★ ★ ★ ★ **Best Western Carlton Hotel Tivoli**
(HR)
Haldenstrasse 57
☎ 041 513051 telex 868119 fax 041 511929
res nr 031 234455
✉ 6002

* 17 🛏 145/260 76 🛏 255/440
🄴 ⓘ 🄴 ⇌ ⇶ ◆ 🅿 🄵 ♨ ⇅ 🖃 🄵 🆆🅲 🆃🆅 🍽 ☺

★ ★ ★ ★ **Château Gutsch** (HCR)
Kanonenstrasse
☎ 041 220272 telex 868699 fax 041 220252
✉ 6000

- 🛏 230/230 31 🛏 270/295
🄴 ⓘ 🄴 ⇌ ⏦ ⚏ ⊙ 🅿 🄵 ♨ ⇶ ⚓ ⇅ 🖃 🄵 🆃🆅 ☺

★ ★ ★ **Continental und Park** (HCR)
Morgartenstrasse 4/13
☎ 041 237566 telex 865639 fax 041 233069
✉ 6002

* 10 🛏 78/128 58 🛏 133/222
🄴 ⓘ 🄴 ⇌ ⊙ 🅿 ⇅ 🖃 🄵 🆆🅲 🆃🆅 🍽 ☺

★ ★ ★ **Drei Konige** (HCR)
Bruchstrasse 35
☎ 041 41228833 telex 865511 fax 041 41228852
✉ 6003

open 01.04 - 31.12
* 10 🛏 70/120 58 🛏 130/210
🄴 ⓘ 🄴 ⇌ 🅿 ⇅ 🖃 🄵 🆆🅲 🆃🆅 🍽 ☺

★ ★ ★ ★ Best Western Hotel Flora (HP)
Seidenhofstrasse 5
☎ 041 244444 telex 865522 fax 041 238360
res nr 031 234455
✉ 6002

* 25 ⌂ 120/190 135 ⌂ 190/300
AE ⓪ E ⌷ ↘ ⊙ P ⁀ ↟ ⊟ ⁏ WC TV ⑩!

★ ★ ★ ★ Montana (HCR)
Adligenswilerstrasse 22
☎ 041 516565 telex 862820 fax 041 516676
✉ 6002

open 16.04 - 31.10
14 ⌂ 130/180 48 ⌂ 220/320
AE E ⌷ ↘ ⊙ P ⁀ ⅌ ↟ ⊟ ⁏ TV ⑩! ⤸

★ ★ ★ De la Paix (HR)
Museggstrasse 2
☎ 041 515253 telex 862762 fax 041 512550
✉ 6003

13 ⌂ -/- 20 ⌂ -/-
AE ⓪ E ⌷ ⊙ ◆ ⌲ ↟ ⊟ ⁏ WC ⑩! ☺

★ ★ ★ ★ ★ Palace (HR)
Haldenstrasse 10
☎ 041 502222 telex 865222 fax 041 516976

* 8 ⌂ 195/370 144 ⌂ 260/580
AE ⓪ E ⌷ ↘ ⇪ ⊙ P ⁀ ⅌ ↟ ⊟ ⁏ WC TV ⑩!

★ ★ ★ ★ Rebstock (HG)
St. Leodegarstrasse 3
☎ 041 513581 telex 868211 fax 041 513917
✉ 6006

6 ⌂ 130/160 16 ⌂ 210/240
AE ⓪ E ⌷ ⊜ ⊙ P ⁀ ⅌ ↟ ⊟ ⁏ WC TV ⑩! ☺

★ ★ ★ Royal (HCR)
Rigistrasse 22
☎ 041 511233 telex 862795 fax 041 528484
✉ 6006

open 01.04 - 30.09
* 8 ⌂ 100/130 42 ⌂ 160/200
AE ⓪ E ⌷ ↘ P ⅌ ⌲ ↟ ⊟ ⁏ WC TV ⑩! ⤸

★ ★ ★ ★ Schiller (HCR)
☎ 041 235155 telex 78621

2 ⌂ -/- 64 ⌂ -/-
⊙ P ↟ ⊟ ⁏

★ ★ ★ ★ Union (HCR)
Lowenstrasse 16
☎ 041 513651 telex 868142 fax 041 516776
✉ 6004

* 19 ⌂ 130/170 87 ⌂ 230/290
AE E ⌷ ⊙ ↟ ⊟ ⁏ WC TV ⑩!

MALOJA, *Graubunden*   **07**

★ ★ ★ Schweizerhaus Postli (HCR)
☎ 082 43455 fax 082 43341
✉ 7516

open 15.12 - 15.04 + 15.06 - 15.10
* 6 ⌂ 75/95 30 ⌂ 110/220
AE ⓪ E ⌷ ↘ ⊙ P ⁀ ⅌ ↟ ⊟ ⁏ WC ☺

MARTIGNY, *Valais*   **02**

★ ★ ★ Central Parc (HCR)
Place Central 5-7
☎ 026 221184 telex 38841 fax 026 221185
✉ 1920

5 ⌂ -/- 22 ⌂ -/-
AE ⓪ E ⌷ ⊙ ◆ P ⅌ ↟ ⊟ ⁏

★ ★ ★ Kluser (HCR)
Avenue De La Gare 3
☎ 026 222641 telex 473641 fax 026 227641
✉ 1920

open 26.12 - 31.10
* - ⌂ 75/95 39 ⌂ 115/150
AE ⓪ E ⌷ ⊙ P ⅌ ⊟ ⁏ WC ☺

★ ★ ★ Motel des Sports (MT)
Rue Du Forum 15
☎ 026 222078 fax 026 222348
✉ 1920

open 14.06 - 31.12
- ⌂ 63/75 30 ⌂ 98/105
⊙ ◆ P ⁀ ⁏ WC TV

★ ★ Du Vieux Stand (HCR)   AA ANWB
Av Du Gr St Bernard, 41
☎ 026 221506
fax 026 229506
✉ 1920

Besides being a holiday
hotel, the Hotel du
Vieux Stand, situated on
the outskirts of Martig-
ny, is very suitable for
an overnight stop.
Martigny is situated on
the N2, where the road forks to the St Bernard
Tunnel in the direction of Turin and Chamonix.
The well kept rooms have en suite toilet and
shower, and the restaurant has a choice of
regional dishes and wines on the menu. After a
day in the car it is nice to relax in the hotel's own
sauna.

open 15.01 - 15.12
* 6 ⌂ 55/60 24 ⌂ 80/86
E ⌷ ◆ P ⅌ ↟ ⁏ WC ⑩!

MARTIGNY/CROIX, *Valais*   **02**

★ ★ ★ ★ **Best Western Hotel la Porte d'Octodure** (HR)
Route Du Gr. St. Bernard
MARTIGNY
☎ 026 227121 telex 473721 fax 026 222173
res nr 031 234455
✉ 1921
open 27.01 - 06.01
* 15 ♨ 81/137 41 ☷ 122/233
AE ◑ 🄴 🖃 ◆ 🅿 ⛱ ⇅ 🖵 🖃 🄲 ㏃ �📺 🍽 ☺

MEIRINGEN, *Bern*   **03**

★ ★ ★ ★ **Sherlock Holmes** (HCR)
☎ 036 714242 fax 036 714222
✉ 3860

10 ♨ 81/98 42 ☷ 97/114
AE ◑ 🄴 🖃 ⬛ ● ⛱ ☎ 🖃 🖵 ☺

MENDRISIO, *Ticino*   **06**

★ ★ ★ **Morgana** (HR)   AA ANWB
Via Carlo Maderno 12
☎ 091 462355 fax 091 464264
✉ 6850

The Hotel Morgana is situated at the foot of a steep rock, just outside Mendrisio, and not far from the St Gotthard-Milan motorway. It is a cosy and comfortable stopover hotel which is also very suitable for a longer stay. The rooms feature a comprehensive range of modern amenities, and there is a pleasant restaurant that serves meals on the palm-tree terrace in summer, and there is always the swimming pool for a refreshing dip.

open 15.07 - 17.06
* 2 ♨ 90/110 14 ☷ -/140
AE ◑ 🄴 🖃 ⥯ 🔌 🅿 ⛱ ⬛ 🖃 🖵 🄲 ㏃ ☺

★ ★ ★ **Stazione** (HCR)   AA ANWB
Pza. d. Stazione
☎ 091 462244
fax 091 468227
✉ 6850

The Hotel Stazione is situated - as the name suggests - close to the station in the centre of Mendrisio, on the road from St Gotthard to Milan and close to the border with Italy. The hotel is particularly suitable as an overnight stopover for travelling tourists. All of the 26 rooms feature a private bathroom, and almost all of them have a TV. In summer, when

the weather is nice, the restaurant and bar serve meals and drinks on the pleasant garden terrace.

6 ♨ 80/90 20 ☷ 120/130
AE ◑ 🄴 ⥯ ● ◆ 🅿 ⛱ ⇅ 🖃 🖵 🄲 ㏃

MERLIGEN, *Bern*   **03**

★ ★ ★ **Motel Mon Abri** (MT)   AA ANWB
Seestrasse 580
☎ 033 511380
✉ 3658

Motel Mon Abri is an attractive suburban hotel, situated in the mountains and surrounded by greenery, on the north bank of the Thunersee. It consists of a number of buildings which are all grouped around one main building. The restaurant, which can be found on the street side of the hotel, is especially proud of its wine cellar. Most of the rooms have a private toilet and shower, and at the front of the hotel is a spacious sunny garden with lawns for sunbathing, a terrace and a barbecue. Plenty of parking facilities are available.

open 01.03 - 15.02
* 1 ♨ 35/- 21 ☷ 90/110
⥯ 🖥 🅿 ⛱ ☎ ⬛ 🄲 ㏃ ☺

MINUSIO, *Ticino*   **06**

★ ★ ★ ★ **Remorino** (HG)
Via Verbano 29
☎ 093 331033
✉ 6648

4 ♨ -/- 21 ☷ -/-
⥯ 🅿 ⛱ ⛱ ⬛ ⇅ 🖃 🖵 🄲 ㏃

MONTANA-VERMALA, *Valais*   **05**

★ ★ **Les Asters** (HCR)
☎ 027 412242
✉ 3962

3 ♨ -/- 21 ☷ -/-
🅿 ⛱ ⇅ 🖃 🖵

★ ★ ★ **Beau Regard** (HP)
☎ 027 412188 telex 38227

2 ♨ -/- 24 ☷ 112/218 excl. breakfast
🅿 ⛱ ⬛ ⇅ 🖃 🖵

★ ★ ★ ★ ★ **Crans Ambassador** (HCR)
☎ 027 415222 telex 473176 fax 027 419155
✉ 3962

10 🛏 -/- 70 🛏 285/540 excl. breakfast
🄰🄴 ⓘ 🄴 ≒ 🎿 ♠ 🕙 🅿 🍴 ♨ ☃ ↕️ 🖃 🅿 🆆🅲 🆃🆅 🍴 ⛄ ☺

★ ★ ★ **Eldorado** (HR)
☎ 027 411333 telex 473203 fax 027 419522
✉ 3962

open 15.12 - 15.10
6 🛏 58/116 28 🛏 112/204
🎿 ⓘ 🅿 ♨ ≒ ↕️ 🖃 🅿 🆆🅲 🆃🆅 🍴 ☺

★ ★ ★ **Des Grand Ducs** (HCR)
☎ 027 412822

1 🛏 -/- 20 🛏 -/-
🎿 🅿

★ ★ ★ **Mont Paisible** (HCR)
☎ 027 402161 fax 027 417792
✉ 3962

open 01.01 - 17.12
* 2 🛏 85/125 39 🛏 130/220
🄰🄴 ⓘ 🄴 ≒ 🎿 ♠ 🕙 🅿 🍴 ♨ ↕️ 🖃 🅿 🆆🅲 🍴

★ ★ ★ **Primavera** (HCR)
☎ 027 414214 telex 38414

2 🛏 -/- 24 🛏 112/218 excl. breakfast
ⓘ 🅿 ♨ ↕️ 🖃 🅿 🆃🆅

MONTE CARASSO, Ticino   06

★ ★ ★ **Mövenpick Benjamin** (HR)
Autobahn N2
☎ 092 270171 telex 846212 fax 092 277695
✉ 6513

* 1 🛏 100/- excl. breakfast 54 🛏 150/- excl.
breakfast
🄰🄴 ⓘ 🄴 ≒ ◆ 🅿 ↕️ 🅿 🆆🅲 🆃🆅 🐕

MONTREUX, Vaud   02

★ ★ ★ **Golf Hotel Rene Capt** (HP)   🄰🄰 ANWB
35 Bon Port
☎ 021 9634631
telex 453255
fax 021 9630352
✉ 1820

The hotel is right by
Lake Geneva, near the
casino and within
walking distance of the
old centre of Montreux.
It is a majestic, elegant
old-style tourist hotel, with a wonderful rose

garden which slopes to the shores of the lake.
Most of the rooms, and the panoramic restaurant, offer a magnificent view over the lake and
mountains. There is a swimming pool at the
hotel.

* 20 🛏 108/120 40 🛏 158/186
🄰🄴 ⓘ 🄴 ≒ 🎿 ♠ ⓘ 🅿 ♨ ↕️ ╬ 🖃 🅿 🆆🅲 🆃🆅 🍴 ☺

★ ★ ★ **Terminus** (HCR)
Av. De La Gare 22
☎ 021 9631071 telex 453155 fax 021 9635567
✉ 1820

* 12 🛏 110/150 39 🛏 145/210
🄰🄴 ⓘ 🄴 ≒ ⓘ 🅿 ♨ ↕️ 🖃 🅿 🆆🅲 🆃🆅 🍴

MOUDON, Vaud   02

★ ★ **Du Chemin de Fer** (HCR)   🄰🄰 ANWB
Place St. Etienne 4
☎ 021 9051251
telex 453255
fax 021 9630352
✉ 1510

The Hotel Du Chemin
de Fer is situated in the
centre of the little, old
Gallo-Roman town of
Moudon, together with
a number of medieval
buildings among which lies the beautiful Cathedral of St Etienne. Some of the tidily furnished
rooms have their own toilet and bath or shower.
There is a relaxed atmosphere in the restaurant
and a pleasant terrace outside.

8 🛏 -/- 11 🛏 -/-
🄰🄴 ⓘ 🄴 ≒ 🎿 ⓘ ◆ 🅿 ♨ 🖃 🅿 🆆🅲 🍴

MÜRREN, Bern   05

★ ★ **Belmont** (HR)
☎ 036 553535 fax 036 553531
✉ 3825

open 09.07 - 30.11 + 15.12 - 31.05
* 2 🛏 50/80 12 🛏 100/150
🄰🄴 ⓘ 🄴 ≒ 🎿 ⓘ ♨ 🖃 🍴 ☺

★ ★ ★ **Edelweiss** (HCR)
☎ 036 551312 telex 923265 fax 036 554202
✉ 3825

open 29.05 - 17.10 + 22.12 - 12.04
* 4 🛏 90/120 27 🛏 180/220
🄴 ≒ 🎿 ⓘ ♨ 🖃 🅿 🆆🅲 🍴 ☺

★ ★ ★ ★ **Eiger** (HR)
☎ 036 551331 telex 923262 fax 036 553931
✉ 3825

open 12.06 - 26.09
* 6 🛏 130/200 38 🛏 240/380
▣ ⓓ 🅴 ✆ ⚡ ☉ 🍴 🍽 ⇅ 🖳 ⬚ WC TV ♠

★ ★ ★ **Jungfrau Lodge** (HP)
☎ 036 552824 fax 036 554121
✉ 3825

open 15.06 - 15.09
4 🛏 80/120 41 🛏 140/220
▣ ⓓ 🅴 ✆ ⚡ 🅿 ⮐ 🍴 🍽 ⇅ 🖳 ⬚ WC TV 🍴 ☺

<hr>

MURTEN, *Fribourg* 02

★ ★ ★ **Krone** (HCR)
Rathausgasse 5
☎ 037 715252 fax 037 713610
✉ 3280

* 7 🛏 55/100 28 🛏 120/165
▣ ⓓ 🅴 ✆ ⚡ ☉ 🅿 ⮐ 🍴 🍽 ⇅ 🖳 ⬚ WC 🍴

<hr>

NEUCHÂTEL, *Neuchatel* 02

★ ★ ★ ★ **City** (HCR)
Place Piaget
☎ 038 255412 fax 038 213869
✉ 2000

3 🛏 90/120 23 🛏 120/160
▣ ⓓ 🅴 ✆ 🍴 ☉ 🍽 ⇅ 🖳 ⬚ WC TV ☺

<hr>

OLTEN, *Solothurn* 03

★ ★ ★ **Astoria** (HR)
Huebelistrasse 15
☎ 062 321212 fax 062 325789
✉ 4600

* 6 🛏 96/106 25 🛏 145/168
▣ ⓓ 🅴 ✆ ☉ 🍽 ⇅ 🖳 ⬚ WC 🍴

Olten (HCR)
Bahnhofstrasse 5
☎ 062 263030 telex 981788 fax 062 264004
✉ 4600

1 🛏 -/- 31 🛏 -/-
▣ ⓓ 🅴 ✆ ☉ 🍽 ⇅ 🖳 ⬚ WC TV ☺

ORSELINA, *Ticino* 06

★ **Mon Désir** (HP)
Via Consiglio Mezzano 47
☎ 093 334842
✉ 6644

open 01.03 - 06.11
18 🛏 44/73 14 🛏 88/146
✆ 🅼 🅿 ⮐ 🍽 ⇅ 🍴 🖳 ⬚ WC 🍴 🐾

<hr>

PONTRESINA, *Graubunden* 07

Atlas (HP)
☎ 082 66321

23 🛏 -/- 59 🛏 -/-
✆ ☉ 🅿 ⮐ ⚡ 🍽 🖳 ⬚ WC ♠

★ ★ ★ **Mueller** (HR)
In2
☎ 082 66341 fax 082 66838
✉ 7504

10 🛏 75/95 27 🛏 130/170
▣ ⓓ 🅴 ✆ ⚡ ☉ 🅿 ⮐ 🍽 ⇅ 🖳 ⬚ WC TV 🍴 ☺

★ ★ ★ **Pontresina Sporthotel** (HR)
Via Maistra
☎ 082 66331 telex 852594 fax 082 67785
✉ 7504

open 21.12 - 11.04 + 13.06 - 10.10
33 🛏 79/114 53 🛏 174/214
▣ ⓓ 🅴 ✆ ☉ 🅿 ⮐ 🍽 ⇅ 🖳 ⬚ TV 🍴 ☺

★ ★ ★ ★ **Schweizerhof** (HR)
Hauptstrasse
☎ 082 60131 fax 082 67988
✉ 7504

open 10.12 - 20.04 + 15.06 - 15.10
23 🛏 110/200 47 🛏 260/440
▣ ⓓ 🅴 ✆ ⚡ ☉ 🅿 ⮐ 🍽 ⇅ 🖳 ⬚ WC TV 🍴 ☺

★ ★ ★ **Steinbock** (HR)
☎ 082 66471 telex 852580 fax 082 67922
✉ 7504

7 🛏 -/- 23 🛏 190/270
🅿 ⮐ 🍽 🍴 🍴 🖳 ⬚ WC 🍴 ☺

<hr>

PROMONTOGNO/BERGELL, *Graubunden* 07

Bregaglia (HR)
PROMONTOGNO/BERGELL
☎ 082 41777 fax 082 33741
✉ 7649

open 25.05 - 25.10
8 🛏 38/55 24 🛏 76/110
· ⚡ ☉ 🅿 🍽 ⬚ WC ☺

RIGI KLÖSTERLI, *Schwyz*   **04**

★ ★ **Rigi Kulm** (HCR)
☎ 041 831312 fax 041 831114
✉ 6411

open 01.12 - 31.10
- ⊿ 45/80 33 ⊿ 80/150
AE ⅃ ⌖ ☎ ⫪ ▤ ⊡ WC ⎰ ⊙

ROLLE, *Vaud*   **02**

Rivesrolle (HCR)
Route De Lausanne 42
☎ 021 8253491 telex 458326 fax 021 8253491
✉ 1180

- ⊿ -/- 32 ⊿ -/-
AE ⓪ ▤ ⊞ ⊜ ⌖ ◈ P ⫪ ⫞ ⫪ ▤ WC TV

ROUGEMONT, *Vaud*   **02**

★ ★ ★ ★ **Viva** (HR)
☎ 029 48080 telex 940074 fax 029 49185
✉ 1838

6 ⊿ 85/170 36 ⊿ 140/350
AE ⓪ ▤ ⊞ ⅃ ⌖ ⫞ P ⫪ ⫞ ⫪ ▤ ⊡ WC TV

SAANEN, *Bern*   **03**

Résidence Cabana (HA)
☎ 030 44855 telex 922255 fax 030 45956
✉ 3792

- ⊿ -/- - ⊿ -/-
⌖ P ⫞ ⫪ ⫞ ⫪ ⎰ ⊙

★ ★ ★ ★ **Steigenberger** (HR)
Auf Der Halten
☎ 030 83388 telex 922252 fax 030 44947
res nr 01 4620825
✉ 3792

open 20.12 - 05.04 + 16.05 - 25.10
* 29 ⊿ 138/236 130 ⊿ 206/402
AE ⓪ ▤ ⊞ ⅃ ⌖ P ⫞ ⫞ ⫪ ⫞ ⎰

SAAS ALMAGELL, *Valais*   **05**

★ ★ ★ **Atlantic** (HR)
☎ 028 572020 fax 028 573527
✉ 3905

open 01.01 - 01.04 + 06.06 - 20.10
* 1 ⊿ 60/70 20 ⊿ 100/120
▤ ⊞ ⅃ ⌖ P ⫞ ⫞ ⫪ ▤ ⊡ WC ⎰ ⊙

SAAS FEE, *Valais*   **05**

★ ★ ★ **Alphubel** (HG)
☎ 028 571112 telex 472211 fax 028 571769
✉ 3906

8 ⊿ -/- 32 ⊿ -/-
AE ⓪ ▤ ⊞ ⅃ ⫪ ▤ ⊡ WC ⎰ ⊙

★ ★ ★ **Ambassador** (HCR)
☎ 028 571420
✉ 3906

- ⊿ -/- 20 ⊿ -/-
AE ⓪ ▤ ⊞ ⅃ ⊙ P ⫞ ⫞ ⫪ ▤ ⊡ WC TV ⊙

★ ★ ★ **Astoria** (HG)
☎ 028 571133 fax 028 572033
✉ 3906

open 01.01 - 30.04 + 01.07 - 15.09
3 ⊿ 85/130 27 ⊿ 160/260
▤ ⊞ ⅃ ⊙ ⫞ ⫪ ▤ ⊡ WC TV ⊙

★ ★ ★ **La Collina** (HG)
☎ 028 571938 fax 028 573349
✉ 3906

open 15.12 - 30.04 + 15.06 - 31.10
5 ⊿ 75/100 13 ⊿ 150/200
AE ⓪ ▤ ⊞ ⅃ ⫞ ⫪ ⫞ ⫪ ▤ ⊡ TV ⫯

★ ★ ★ **Derby** (HCR)
☎ 028 572345 telex 38387
✉ 3906

4 ⊿ -/- 24 ⊿ -/-
⅃ ⫞ ⫪ ▤ ⊡ WC

★ ★ ★ **Diana** (HG)
☎ 028 572705
✉ 3906

1 ⊿ -/- 22 ⊿ 158/244
⅃ ⫪ ▤ ⊡ WC ⎰

★ ★ ★ **Étoile** (HCR)
☎ 028 572981 fax 028 573229
✉ 3906

* 3 ⊿ 59/80 18 ⊿ 114/160
AE ⓪ ▤ ⊞ ⅃ ⫞ ⫪ ▤ ⊡ WC TV

★ ★ ★ **Park** (HR)
☎ 028 572446
✉ 3906

1 ⊿ -/- 20 ⊿ 144/228
⅃ ⫪ ▤ ⊡ WC

SWITZERLAND

SWITZERLAND *(vertical sidebar)*

★ ★ **Pineta** (HG)
☎ 028 571577
✉ 3906

1 ♫ -/- 11 ⌂ 94/164
⚹ ⇅ ⚞

★ ★ ★ **Soleil** (HR)
☎ 028 571233
✉ 3906

9 ♫ -/- 18 ⌂ -/-
⚹ 🅿 ⚤ ▭ 🄴 wc

★ ★ ★ **Sporthotel** (HR)
☎ 028 572044
✉ 3906

1 ♫ -/- 20 ⌂ 158/264
⚹ ⚤ ▭ 🄴 wc ⓘ

★ ★ ★ **Waldesruh** (HR)
☎ 028 572295 telex 38564
✉ 3906

12 ♫ -/- 20 ⌂ 148/246
⚹ ⚤ ⇅ ▭ 🄴 wc ⓘ

★ ★ ★ **Walliserhof** (HCR)
☎ 028 572021 telex 38821 fax 028 572910
✉ 3906

open 01.01 - 02.05 + 13.06 - 30.10
3 ♫ 308/446 37 ⌂ 290/624
🄰🄴 ⓞ 🄴 ⚌ ⚞ ⇅ ▭ 🄴 wc

SAAS GRUND, *Valais* **05**

★ ★ **Elsi** (HP)
Saastalstrasse
☎ 028 572550 fax 028 571292
✉ 3910

open 20.12 - 30.04 + 01.06 - 30.10
* 4 ♫ 51/57 13 ⌂ 92/104
🄰🄴 ⓞ 🄴 ⚌ ⚹ ⚞ 🅿 ⚤ ⇅ ▭ 🄴 wc tv ⌣

★ ★ **Monte Rosa** (HR)
☎ 028 572570
✉ 3901

8 ♫ -/- 18 ⌂ -/-
⚹ ⓞ 🅿 ⚤ 🄴 wc tv ⓘ

★ ★ **Primavera** (HCR)
☎ 028 571788
✉ 3901

open 15.12 - 30.04 + 15.06 - 15.10
* 8 ♫ 40/52 25 ⌂ 80/104
🄴 ⚌ ⚹ ⓞ 🅿 ⚤ ⇅ 🄴 wc ⓘ ⌣

★ ★ **Sporthotel** (HR)
☎ 028 572038
✉ 3910

1 ♫ -/- 22 ⌂ -/-
🄴 ⚹ ⓞ 🅿 🅿 ⚤ ⚞ ⇅ ▭ 🄴 wc

★ ★ ★ **Touring** (HCR)
☎ 028 572117 telex 38669
✉ 3901

3 ♫ -/- 30 ⌂ -/-
⚹ 🅿 ⚤ ⇅ ▭ 🄴 wc tv ⓘ ⚞

SACHSELN, *Unterwalden* **03**

★ ★ ★ **Belvoir** (HCR)   🄰🄰 *ANWB*
Bruenigstrasse 5
☎ 041 661417 telex
866466 fax 041 665926
✉ 6072

The Hotel Belvoir is situated in leafy surroundings right by the Sarnersee, a small lake in the Bernese Oberland. Because of its position - not far from the Gotthardt motorway - this holiday hotel is also well suited for an overnight stop. The rooms are well maintained and all have a bathroom; some also have a TV and balcony. When the weather is fine, the restaurant serves meals on the terrace, and there is a lively disco and a beach pool only 5 minutes from the hotel.

open 10.02 - 31.12
* - ♫ 65/80 29 ⌂ 105/120
🄰🄴 ⓞ 🄴 ⚌ ⚹ ⓣ ◆ 🅿 ⚤ ⇅ ⌂ ▭ 🄴 wc tv ⓘ

★ ★ ★ **Kreuz** (HCR)   🄰🄰 *ANWB*
Dorfstrasse 15
☎ 041 661466 telex
866411 fax 041 668188
✉ 6072

The Hotel Kreuz is in the middle of the small town of Sachseln am Sarnersee on a small and pleasant square, and is steeped in tradition. It features 54 tastefully furnished rooms - mostly with a toilet, washing facilities, TV and a minibar; there are garden rooms (equipped as apartments) which are suitable for families with children. The hotel's interior comprises beautiful historic public lounges and a rustic grill-restaurant. Entrance to the beach pool nearby is free to guests of the hotel.

* 8 🛏 85/120 46 🍴 140/170
🆎 💿 🅴 ≍ ⅄ ⊙ 🅿 ♨ ⁋ 🖳 🖭 wc tv 🍽 ⊕

SAIGNELÉGIER, *Jura*   **02**

★ ★ ★ **De la Gare et du Parc**
☎ 039 511121
✉ 2726

- 🛏 -/- 24 🍴 -/-
🅿 🍴 ♨ ⌸ 🖳 🖭 wc tv 🍽

STE CROIX, *Vaud*   **02**

★ ★ **Les Fleurettes** (HCR)
Fleurettes 3-5
☎ 024 612294
✉ 1450

open 01.05 - 31.03
* 9 🛏 43/55 11 🍴 76/96
⅄ ⊙ 🅿 ♨ 🖳 🖭 wc

ST GALLEN, *St. Gallen*   **04**

★ ★ ★ ★ **Einstein** (HCR)
Berneggstr 2
☎ 071 200033 telex 77478
✉ 9001

1 🛏 -/- 70 🍴 -/-
⊙ 🅿 🖳 🖭

★ ★ **Sporting** (HR)
Straubenzellstr. 19
☎ 071 271312
✉ 9014

1 🛏 -/- 20 🍴 -/-
⅄ 🅿 🖳 🖭

ST MORITZ, *Graubunden*   **07**

★ ★ ★ ★ **Best Western Hotel Albana** (HR)
Via Maisstrasse 6
☎ 082 33121 telex 852165 fax 082 31543
res nr 031 234455
✉ 7500

* 13 🛏 120/230 62 🍴 200/440
🆎 💿 🅴 ≍ ⅄ ⊙ 🅿 ⁋ 🖳 🖭 tv 🍽 ⊕

★ ★ ★ ★ ★ **Badrutt's Palace** (HR)
☎ 082 21101 telex 852124 fax 082 37739
✉ 7500

65 🛏 -/- 150 🍴 400/1400
🆎 💿 🅴 ≍ ⅄ ✦ ⊙ 🅿 🍴 ♨ ⚓ ⁋ 🖳 🖭 wc tv 🍽 ⌂

★ ★ ★ ★ **Baren Sporthotel** (HCR)
Via Maistra 50
☎ 082 33656 telex 852199 fax 082 38022
✉ 7500

open 08.12 - 12.04 + 28.05 - 10.10
* 17 🛏 100/140 45 🍴 180/300
🅴 ≍ ⅄ 🅿 ⚓ ⁋ 🖳 🖭 wc tv 🎿

★ ★ ★ **Bellevue** (HCR)
Via Dal Bagn 18
☎ 082 22161 telex 852128 fax 082 38163
✉ 7500

* 6 🛏 85/125 34 🍴 140/220
🆎 💿 🅴 ≍ ⊙ ◈ 🅿 🍴 ♨ ⁋ 🖳 🖭 wc tv ⊕

★ ★ ★ **Belvédere** (HCR)
☎ 082 33905 telex 74435
✉ 7500

1 🛏 -/- 60 🍴 170/290
🍴 ⚓ ⁋ 🖳 🖭 wc

★ ★ ★ ★ **Carlton** (HR)
Via Johan. Badrutt 11
☎ 082 21141 telex 852154 fax 082 32012
✉ 7500

open 15.12 - 14.04
* 26 ◪ 160/440 73 ◪ 340/880
⅃⊙🅿☂⅋⅊↿◪🆕📺🅾

★ ★ ★ ★ **Crystal** (HR)
☎ 082 21165 telex 74449
✉ 7500

20 ◪ -/- 80 ◪ -/-
⊙↿◪🆆🅲📺

★ ★ **National** (HCR)
V117 Dal C'ovagaschtra 1
☎ 082 33274
✉ 7500

13 ◪ -/- - ◪ -/-
⅃🏨🅿☂↿⅊◪🅾🛏

★ ★ ★ **Parkhotel Kurhaus** (HP)
☎ 082 22111 telex 74498
✉ 7500

80 ◪ -/- 106 ◪ -/-
⅃🅿☂↿◪⅊🅾

★ ★ ★ ★ **Best Western Hotel Steffani** (HCR)
Sonnenplatz 1
☎ 082 22101 telex 852166 fax 082 34097
res nr 031 234455
✉ 7500

* 12 ◪ 130/250 38 ◪ 220/440
🆊⓪🅴⚏⊙🅿☂⅋⅊↿◪⅊🆆🅲📺🅾☺

SAMEDAN, *Graubunden* 07

★ ★ ★ **Donatz** (HR)
☎ 082 64666 fax 082 65451
✉ 7503

open 01.06 - 30.04
9 ◪ -/- 24 ◪ 185/220
⓪🅴⚏⊙🅿☂⅋↿◪⅊🆆🅲📺☺

SAN ANTONINO, *Ticino* 06

★ ★ ★ **La Perla** (MT)
☎ 092 621538 fax 092 622597
✉ 6592

* - ◪ 98/110 24 ◪ 148/160
🆊⓪🅴⚏🅾🅿☂⅋⅌◪⅊🆆🅲📺🅾☺

SANTA MARIA, *Graubunden* 07

★ ★ ★ **Schweizerhof** (HCR) 　　　　🆊 ANWB
☎ 082 85124
fax 082 85009
✉ 7536

The Hotel Schweizerhof
lies peacefully between
meadows on the fringe
of Santa Maria. The
village is situated in the
Rätische alps, a rugged
corner of Switzerland,
where imposing moun-
tains stand out against the sky. Most of the
rooms in the hotel have en suite toilet and washing facilities, the furnishings in the public rooms
and restaurant are tasteful, and the house is very
proud of its wine cellar. There is also a sunny
garden with seats and deck chairs.

open 30.01 - 30.10
* 13 ◪ 60/100 24 ◪ 120/200
⅃🅿☂⅋↿◪⅊🆆🅲📺🅾☺

SCHAFFHAUSEN, *Schaffhausen* 04

★ ★ ★ **Kronerhof** (HCR)
Kirchhofplatz 7
☎ 053 256631 telex 897068 fax 053 244589
✉ 8200

* 12 ◪ 110/120 21 ◪ 170/190
🆊⓪🅴⚏⅃⊙⅋↿◪⅊🆆🅲📺🅾☺

SCHÖNRIED/GSTAAD, *Bern* 05

★ ★ ★ ★ **Alpin Nova** (HR)
SCHÖNRIED
☎ 030 83311 telex 922230 fax 030 42010
✉ 3778

open 17.12 - 31.10
* - ◪ 101/260 74 ◪ 202/410
🆊⓪🅴⚏⊙◆🅿☂⅋⅌↿◪⅊🆆🅲📺🅾

SEELISBERG, *Uri* 04

★ ★ ★ **Löwen** (HR)
☎ 043 311369

2 ◪ -/- 24 ◪ 50/120
⅃⊙🅿↿◪⅊🆆🅲📺

SEEWEN, *Schwyz* 04

★ ★ ★ Kristall (HCR)
Bahnhofstrasse 172
☎ 043 213474 fax 043 213406
✉ 6423

6 🛏 75/95 28 🍴 120/140
AE ⓪ E ⇌ ⊙ ◈ P ☎ ↿↾ 🖥 🖭 WC TV 🐕

SIERRE, *Valais* 05

★ ★ ★ Terminus (HCR)
Rue De Bourg 1
☎ 027 550495
telex 472995
✉ 3960

AA ANWB

The Hotel Terminus is in
the centre of Sierre,
which is situated in the
Rhône valley on the
Simplon motorway. It is
a hotel that is suitable
for an overnight stop-
over or as a base to explore the beautiful surroundings of the Matterhorn and the Monte
Rosa. All rooms have en suite toilet and washing
facilities, radio and TV. The hotel features a
restaurant, a pleasant terrace in the garden, and
the car can be parked either in the garage or in a
parking area.

2 🛏 -/- 27 🍴 124/155 excl. breakfast
↾⊙ P ☎ ↿↾ ↿🖥 🖭 WC TV 🍴

SIGRISWIL, *Bern* 03

★ ★ ★ Adler (HCR)
☎ 033 512424
fax 033 512481
✉ 3655

AA ANWB

The Hotel Adler is on
the outskirts of Sigris-
wil, a small town on the
sunny north bank of the
Thunersee. It is a
traditional holiday and
winter-sports hotel,
featuring comfortable
rooms with toilet, shower or bath and a balcony
with a beautiful view over the lake. It has a
pleasant restaurant and bar, and the surrounding
area offers plenty of recreational facilities, including swimming, surfing, walking and skiing.

- 🛏 -/- 25 🍴 140/170
⓪ E ⇌ ↾ ◈ P ☎ ↿↾ 🖥 🖭 WC 🍴 ⊙

SIHLBRUGG, *Zurich* 04

Krone (HR)
☎ 01 7299311 fax 01 7299332
✉ 8944

AA ANWB

The Hotel Krone is surrounded by woods and
situated in the hills near Sihlbrugg, halfway
between Zürich and Luzern. It is a small rural
hotel, suitable for those who are travelling
through or as a peaceful base for visiting the
nearby towns. 3 out of the 5 well kept rooms
have a shower. The rustically furnished restaurant
has fresh trout on the menu as a speciality. One
can enjoy many pleasant walks in this area.

* - 🛏 -/- 5 🍴 95/105 excl. breakfast
AE ⓪ E ⇌ ↾ ⇌ ◈ P ☎ 🖭

SILVAPLANA, *Graubunden* 07

★ ★ ★ Chesa Surlej (HCR)
☎ 082 48748 telex 852138 fax 082 48485
✉ 7513

open 06.10 - 11.04
1 🛏 -/- 35 🍴 212/320
AE ⓪ E ⇌ P ☎ ↿↾ 🖥 🖭 WC ⊙

★ ★ ★ Susom Surlej (HR)
☎ 082 48212 telex 74855

- 🛏 -/- 12 🍴 -/-
↾ P ☎ ↿↾ ↿🖥 🖭 🖭 WC TV

SION, *Valais* 05

★ ★ ★ Le Castel (HG)
Rue Du Scex 38
☎ 027 229171
fax 027 225724
✉ 1950

AA ANWB

Hotel Le Castel is a
modern tourist and
business hotel, situated
on the outskirts of Sion
in the Rhône valley. The
ruins of 2 castles are a
characteristic and
dominant aspect of the town. The rooms of this
7-floor hotel are equipped with modern comforts,
and the restaurant Les Roches Brunes, located
on the ground floor, has a choice of international
and regional dishes on the menu. The hotel is
situated on the exit road to Brig and the N9
motorway.

* 3 🛏 -/95 27 🍴 115/130
AE ⓪ E ⇌ ⊙ P ↾ ☎ ↿↾ 🖥 🖭 WC TV ⊙

SWITZERLAND

★ ★ Du Midi (HCR)
Place Du Midi 29
☎ 027 231331 fax 027 236173
✉ 1950

1 🛏 -/- 11 🛏 -/-
🅰🅴 ⓪ 🄴 ☰ ⊙ ◆ 🅿 ↕ 🄿 🆆🅲 📺 ☺

★ ★ ★ Touring (HCR)
Av De La Gare 6
☎ 027 231551 fax 027 234368

open 12.01 - 25.12
* 5 🛏 80/94 22 🛏 130/145
🅰🅴 ⓪ 🄴 ☰ ⊙ ◆ 🅿 🄿 ⅔ ↕ 🄿 🆆🅲 📺 ☺

SOGLIO, *Graubunden*   07

Pension la Soglina (HCR)
☎ 082 41608 fax 082 41594
✉ 7610

- 🛏 -/- 31 🛏 -/-
⚲ 🅿 ⅔ 🄿 🍴

SOLOTHURN, *Solothurn*   03

★ ★ ★ Astoria (HR)
Wengistrasse 13
☎ 065 227571 fax 065 236857
✉ 4500

14 🛏 85/100 18 🛏 100/150
🅰🅴 ⓪ 🄴 ☰ ⊙ ◆ ⅔ ↕ 🄿 🆆🅲 📺

SPIEZ, *Bern*   03

★ ★ ★ Des Alpes Alpenhotel (HCR)
Seestrasse 38
☎ 033 543354 fax 033 548850
✉ 3700

open 01.02 - 03.01
* 12 🛏 58/80 26 🛏 100/160
🅰🅴 ⓪ 🄴 ☰ ⊙ 🅿 🄿 ⅔ ↕ 🄿 🍴 🛗

★ ★ ★ Eden (HR)
Seestrasse 58
☎ 033 541154 fax 033 541194

open 01.05 - 30.09
* 19 🛏 85/115 37 🛏 140/230
⚲ ⊙ 🅿 🄿 ⅔ ↕ 🄿 🆆🅲 📺

★ ★ Krone (HR)
☎ 033 544131

4 🛏 -/- 7 🛏 -/-
⊙ 🅿 🄿 ⅔ 🐏

Rossli (HCR)   *AA* ANWB
Frutigenstrasse 24
☎ 033 543434
✉ 3700

The small village of Spiez is situated on the
southwest bank of the Thunersee, and a beautiful
castle which is a museum stands on a small
peninsula on the lake. The village consists of high
and low areas connected by a long road. The
hotel itself is outside the centre on the arterial
road, and features a terrace and a bowling alley.
There is a separate garage for parking.

* 8 🛏 42/70 8 🛏 75/128
🅰🅴 ⓪ 🄴 ☰ ⚲ ◆ 🅿 🄿 ⅔ 🄿 🆆🅲 📺

STEIN AM RHEIN/HEMISHOFEN, *Schaffhausen*
                                              04

★ ★ ★ Landgasthof Bacchus (HR)
Hauptstrasse 78
STEIN AM RHEIN
☎ 054 412405 fax 054 414519
✉ 8261

open 10.02 - 20.11
* - 🛏 75/115 6 🛏 120/160
⓪ ☰ ⚲ ↗ ⊙ 🅿 🄿 ⅔ ⅏ 🄿 🆆🅲 📺 🍴 ☺

SUSTEN, *Valais*   05

Susten (HCR)
☎ 027 631272
✉ 3952

4 🛏 -/- 10 🛏 -/-
🅿 ⅔

TÄSCH, *Valais*   05

★ ★ ★ Tascherhof (HR)
☎ 028 671818 fax 028 675820
✉ 3929

9 🛏 48/71 26 🛏 88/128
🅰🅴 ⓪ 🄴 ☰ ⚲ ⊙ 🅿 🄿 ⅔ ↕ 🄿 🆆🅲 📺

★ ★ ★ Walliserhof (HCR)
☎ 028 671955 fax 028 673679
✉ 3921

open 15.12 - 15.11
* 5 🛏 65/85 32 🛏 115/150
🅰🅴 ⓪ 🄴 ☰ ⚲ 🛆 🅿 🄿 ⅔ ↕ 🄿 🆆🅲 📺 🍴 ☺

THIELLE, *Neuchatel*   **02**

★ ★ ★ **Novotel Thielle** (HCR)
Route De Berne
☎ 038 335757 telex 952799 fax 038 332884
✉ 2075

- *𝄞* 90/110 excl. breakfast 60 *𝄞𝄞* 115/140 excl.
breakfast
🅰🄴 ➊ 🄴 ⭲ 🄿 🛉 ⚓ ☖ 🖥 🆆🄲 📺 🍽

THUN, *Bern*   **03**

★ ★ ★ **Alpha** (HR)
Eisenbahnstr. 1
☎ 033 369393 fax 033 369301
✉ 3604

* 10 *𝄞* 80/100 24 *𝄞𝄞* 130/170
🅰🄴 ➊ 🄴 ⭲ ⛵ 🛥 🄿 🛉 ⚓ ☖ 🖥 🆆🄲 📺 ☺

★ ★ ★ ★ **Holiday** (HCR)
Gwattstrasse 1
☎ 033 365757 telex 921357 fax 033 365704
- *𝄞* 80/120 57 *𝄞𝄞* 130/185
🅰🄴 ➊ 🄴 ⭲ 🛥 🄿 🛐 🛉 ⚓ 🖥 🆆🄲 📺 🍽 🐎

TIEFENCASTEL, *Graubunden*   **07**

★ ★ ★ **Albula** (HCR)   🆎 *ANWB*
☎ 081 711121
fax 081 712202
✉ 7450

Hotel Albula is situated
in the centre of the
beautiful and pleasant
little town of Tiefencas-
tel in the winter-sports
area of Graubünden.
The hotel gets its name
from the foaming,
swirling river on whose bank it was built. This
family-owned establishment features 43 modern
furnished rooms with attractive private bathrooms. The restaurant offers a choice of regional
and house specialities, and there is a pleasant
terrace immediately above the river.

open 20.12 - 30.10
* 6 *𝄞* 50/70 37 *𝄞𝄞* 80/120
🅰🄴 ➊ 🄴 ⭲ 🛐 ⚓ 🄿 🛐 🛉 ⚓ ☖ 🖥 🗂 🆆🄲

VERBIER, *Valais*   **05**

★ ★ ★ **Les Chamois** (HP)
☎ 026 316402 fax 026 312712
✉ 1936

* 1 *𝄞* 60/100 18 *𝄞𝄞* 120/190
🅰🄴 ➊ 🄴 ⭲ 🛐 ⚓ 🄿 🛉 🖥 🗂 🆆🄲 📺 🍽 ☺

★ ★ ★ **Le Mazot** (HP)
☎ 026 316404 fax 026 316405
✉ 1936

open 03.12 - 25.05 + 10.07 - 15.09
* 2 *𝄞* 125/240 30 *𝄞𝄞* 190/320
🅰🄴 ➊ 🄴 ⭲ 🛒 🛥 ☉ 🄿 🛐 🛋 🛉 🖥 🗂 🆆🄲 📺 🏠 🐎

★ ★ ★ **Mirabeau** (HP)
☎ 026 316335 fax 026 314806
✉ 1936

4 *𝄞* -/- 22 *𝄞𝄞* -/-
🅰🄴 ➊ 🄴 ⭲ 🛥 🛐 🄿 🛐 🛋 🛉 🖥 🆆🄲 📺 ☺

★ ★ **Le Mont Gelee** (HCR)
☎ 026 313053 fax 026 311316
✉ 1936

open 01.12 - 30.04 + 20.06 - 01.10
* 2 *𝄞* 56/78 15 *𝄞𝄞* 134/158
🛐 🄿 🛐 🗂 ☺

★ ★ ★ **Les Quatre Vallées** (HG)
☎ 026 316066 telex 473872 fax 026 313401
✉ 1936

1 *𝄞* -/- 17 *𝄞𝄞* -/-
🛐 ☉ 🄿 🛐 🛉 🖥 🗂 🆆🄲 📺 🐎

★ ★ ★ **Verluisant** (HCR)
☎ 026 316303 fax 026 314674
✉ 1963

10 *𝄞* -/- 20 *𝄞𝄞* -/-
🄿 🛋 🛉 🖥 🗂 🆆🄲 📺 🐎

VERCORIN, *Valais*   **05**

★ ★ ★ **Victoria** (HCR)
☎ 027 554055 fax 027 554057
✉ 3967

open 18.12 - 25.04 + 12.06 - 17.10
* 2 *𝄞* 65/85 13 *𝄞𝄞* 102/156
🅰🄴 ➊ 🄴 ⭲ 🛐 ☉ 🄿 🛋 🖥 🗂 🆆🄲 📺 🍽 ☺
See advertisement on page 141

SWITZERLAND

VICOSOPRANO, *Graubunden* 07

Pranzaira (HR)
☎ 082 41455
✉ 7603

3 🛏 -/- 8 🛏 -/-
◆ 🅿 🛎 🖭 WC

VIRA, *Ticino* 06

★ ★ ★ **Bellavista** (HCR)
☎ 093 611116 fax 093 612518
✉ 6574

* 15 🛏 95/110 47 🛏 150/210
⊙ 🗉 �𝄇 ⅄ 𝄞 ◑ 🅿 🛎 𝄬 ↑↓ 🔲 🖭 WC TV 🍽 ✆

VITZNAU, *Luzern* 04

★ ★ ★ ★ ★ **Park Hotel Vitznau** (HR)
☎ 041 830100 telex 862482 fax 041 831397
✉ 6354

open 24.04 - 24.10
* 23 🛏 270/380 75 🛏 420/550
🆎 🗉 �𝄇 ⅄ 🏊 🍴 🅿 🛎 𝄬 ⚓ ↑↓ 🔲 🖭 WC TV 🍽

★ ★ ★ **Rigi** (HCR)
Gotthardstrasse
☎ 041 831361 fax 041 831825
✉ 6354

4 🛏 80/100 27 🛏 120/160
🆎 ⊙ 🗉 �𝄇 ⊙ ◆ 🅿 🛎 𝄬 ↑↓ 🔲 🖭 WC TV 🍽 ✆

WALENSTADT, *St. Gallen* 04

★ ★ ★ **Curfisten** (HCR)
☎ 085 35959 fax 085 36538
✉ 8880

* 1 🛏 -/75 25 🛏 -/110
🆎 ⊙ 🗉 �𝄇 ⊙ ◆ 🅿 🛎 ↑↓ 🔲 🖭 WC TV 🍽 ✆

WALTENSBURG, *Graubunden* 04

★ ★ ★ **Grotta Sporthotel** (HR)   AA ANWB
☎ 081 9412172
fax 081 9412514
✉ 7158

Surrounded by mead-
ows, the Sporthotel
Grotta is pleasantly and
peacefully situated on a
mountain plateau, 300m
above the Rhine valley.
It is a comfortable
holiday hotel where the
rooms are tastefully decorated with light wood

and feature bathrooms. There is a large terrace
on the sunny side of the building. A true leisure
hotel, it has an attractive tennis court, a sauna
with whirlpool, and fitness facilities. The area is
good for walking and skiing.

open 20.12 - 15.11
* - 🛏 60/94 17 🛏 100/170
🆎 🗉 �𝄇 ⅄ 𝄞 🅿 🛎 𝄬 ↑↓ 🔲 🖭 WC ✆

WEGGIS, *Luzern* 04

★ ★ ★ ★ **Albana** (HCR)   AA ANWB
☎ 041 932141 telex
862463 fax 041 932959
✉ 6353

The Hotel Albana is
beautifully situated on a
steep bank of the
Vierwaltstättersee and
is surrounded by a lush
garden. An impressive
hotel, especially be-
cause of its 19th-
century mirrored hall, it offers 60 rooms with
toilet, bath or shower - most also having a TV and
balcony. From the rooms, the restaurant, and
especially from the roof terrace, the guest is
treated to a magnificent view over the lake and
the surrounding mountain scenery.

17 🛏 -/- 37 🛏 140/240
🆎 ⊙ 🗉 �𝄇 ⅄ 𝄞 ◑ 🅿 🛎 𝄬 ⚓ ↑↓ 🔲 🖭 WC TV 🍽

★ ★ ★ **Beau Rivage** (HR)
☎ 041 931422 telex 862982

12 🛏 -/- 34 🛏 140/250
⅄ 🏊 ◑ 🅿 🛎 𝄬 ⚓ ↑↓ 🔲 🖭 WC 🍽

★ ★ ★ **Central** (HCR)
Seestrasse
☎ 041 931252 fax 041 931146
✉ 6353

open 15.02 - 30.11
11 🛏 55/98 30 🛏 100/190
🆎 ⊙ 🗉 �𝄇 ⅄ 🏊 🍴 ◑ 🅿 🛎 𝄬 ⚓ ↑↓ 🔲 🖭 WC TV 🍽

★ ★ ★ **Rossli** (HCR)
Seestrasse
☎ 041 931106 telex 862931 fax 041 932726
✉ 6353

open 25.03 - 01.11
* 5 🛏 70/100 45 🛏 130/180
🆎 ⊙ 🗉 �𝄇 ⅄ ◑ 🅿 🛎 𝄬 ↑↓ 🔲 🖭 WC TV 🍽 ✆

Hotel
Victoria***

Frank Wagemakers-Jongen Family
CH-3961 VERCORIN
Telephone 027-55 40 55
Fax 027-55 40 5

Comfortable high class hotel located
in the centre of Vercorin in
the heart of Wallis. 12 kilometres
from Sierre. Ideally located for a
relaxed stay in summer and winter.
Rooms have shower, toilet and balcony
facing south. There is an attractive
lounge and a gourmet restaurant.
Dutch owners.

★ ★ ★ **Schweizerhof** (HR)   AA ANWB
Am Kurplatz
☎ 041 931114 telex
862990 fax 041 930015
✉ 6353

The Hotel Schweizerhof
is situated on the
Kurpromenade in
Weggis, on the Vier-
waltstättersee. It is a
traditional and very
comfortable holiday
hotel, where all 30 rooms have a toilet and bath
or shower, and some also have a balcony. It has a
good restaurant, but it is especially enjoyable to
pass the time indoors in the public rooms, or
outside in the large garden.

open 01.05 - 01.10
* 8 ⌿ 78/95 22 ⌿ 140/190
AE ⓞ E ⌶ ⅄ ⊛ ⬚ ⊙ P P ⅗ ⓢ ⇅ ⬛ 🄿 WC 🍽 🦌

★ ★ ★ **Best Western Hotel Waldstatten** (HCR)
Friedheimstrasse
☎ 041 931341 telex 862988 fax 041 931343
res nr 031 234455
✉ 6353

12 ⌿ -/- 30 ⌿ -/-
AE ⓞ E ⌶ ⅄ ⬚ P P ⅗ ⓢ ⇅ ⬛ 🄿 WC TV 🍽

WEISSENBURG, *Bern*   05

★ ★ **Weissenburg & Alte Post** (HR)
☎ 033 831515
✉ 3764

open 01.12 - 30.09
* 2 ⌿ 32/70 9 ⌿ 64/130
AE E ⌶ ◆ P ⅗ ⬛ 🄿

WENGEN, *Bern*   05

★ ★ **Bernerhof** (HR)
☎ 036 552721 fax 036 553358
✉ 3823

* 6 ⌿ 90/112 18 ⌿ 172/214
AE E ⌶ ⊙ P ⅗ ⬛ 🄿 TV 🍽 ⌂ ⊛

★ ★ **Bristol** (HCR)
☎ 036 551551 telex 923251

3 ⌿ -/- 30 ⌿ -/-
⅄ ⅗ ⓢ ⬛ 🄿 WC 🍽

★ ★ ★ **Falken** (HCR)
☎ 036 565121 telex 923231 fax 036 553339
✉ 3823

* 6 ⌿ 60/150 48 ⌿ 100/320
AE ⓞ E ⌶ ⅄ ⊙ ⅗ ⓢ ⇅ ⬛ 🄿 🍽 ⊛

★ ★ ★ **Silberhorn** (HCR)
☎ 036 565131 telex 923222

10 ⌿ -/- 61 ⌿ -/-
⅄ ⊙ ⓢ ⬛ 🄿 WC 🍽

★ ★ ★ ★ **Victoria Lauberhorn** (HCR)   AA ANWB
Dorfstrasse
☎ 036 565151 telex
923232 fax 036 553377
✉ 3823

The impressive façade
of the Hotel Victoria
Lauberhorn is a striking
feature at the centre of
the holiday and winter-
sports resort of Wen-
gen, situated at the foot
of the Jungfrau massif. Almost all of the rooms -
mostly tastefully furnished - have a bathroom, TV,
→

SWITZERLAND

and some have a balcony. Good food is served in the à la carte restaurant, the pizzeria, the cocktail bar and on the lively terrace in the garden.

open 19.12 - 12.04 + 29.05 - 26.09
14 ▮ -/- 56 ▦ 178/296
⚓ ☉ ♨ ⑴ ▤ ▭ ⓟ WC TV ⑩

WIESEN, *Graubunden*   07

Bellevue (HR)   AA ANWB
☎ 081 721150
✉ 7499

This robust hotel is found on a steep slope alongside the only street in the tiny village of Wiesen; the village has been built against the sides of the Graubünder Alps. The Rinerhorn, one of Switzerland's most beautiful ski areas is only a few kilometres away. The rooms are well kept, and most of them feature en suite toilet and washing facilities. The terrace in front of the restaurant provides a panoramic view of the surrounding mountain tops.

open 15.05 - 30.10
* 5 ▮ 50/55 16 ▦ -/95
AE E ▭ ☉ ♦ ⓟ ♨ ⓟ WC ⑩ ⑨

WILDERSWIL, *Bern*   03

★ ★ ★ Alpenblick (HCR)
☎ 036 220707 fax 036 228007
✉ 3812

* 3 ▮ 68/90 32 ▦ 120/190
AE ⓞ E ▭ ☉ ⓟ ♨ ⓣ ▭ ⓟ WC ⑩ ⌂ ⑨

Motel Luna (HCR)
☎ 036 228414 fax 036 228494
✉ 3812

* 2 ▮ 59/115 28 ▦ 122/126
AE E ▭ ☽ ♦ ⓟ ♨ ◀ ▭ ⓟ WC TV ⑨

WILDHAUS, *St. Gallen*   04

★ ★ ★ Toggenburg (HR)
☎ 074 52323 fax 074 53869
✉ 9658

open 17.05 - 05.04
* 5 ▮ 65/95 25 ▦ 110/170
AE ⓞ E ▭ ☉ ⓟ ♈ ♨ ⑴ ▭ ⓟ WC TV ⑩

WINTERTHUR, *Zurich*   04

★ ★ ★ ★ Best Western Hotel Garten (HCR)
Stadthausstrasse 4
☎ 052 2121919 telex 896201 fax 052 2136870
res nr 031 234455
✉ 8402

* 38 ▮ 140/150 22 ▦ 175/220
AE E ▭ ☉ ♦ ⓟ ⓟ ♨ ⑴ ▤ ⓟ WC TV ⑩

★ ★ Krone Winterthur (HCR)
Marktgasse 49
☎ 052 232521 fax 052 234808
✉ 8401

18 ▮ -/- 22 ▦ -/-
AE ⓞ E ▭ ☉ ⓟ ⑴ ▤ ⓟ WC TV ⑩ ⑨

★ ★ ★ Wulflingen (MT)
Riedhofstrasse 51
☎ 052 256721 fax 052 254972
✉ 8400

* 26 ▮ 110/120 18 ▦ 150/160
AE ⓞ E ▭ ☽ ♦ ⓟ ♨ ◀ ⓟ WC TV ⑨

WOLFENSCHIESSEN, *Unterwalden*   04

Alpina (HR)
Engelbergerstrasse
☎ 041 651114 fax 041 652343
✉ 6386

3 ▮ 45/55 6 ▦ 80/100
AE ⓞ E ▭ ☉ ♦ ⓟ ⓟ ♨ ⓟ WC TV ⑨

ZERMATT, *Valais*   05

★ ★ Admiral (HR)
I. Berg F. Plaschka
☎ 028 671555 fax 028 675058
✉ 3920

4 ▮ 82/122 20 ▦ 150/230
E ▭ ☉ ♨ ♈ ⑴ ▤ ⓟ WC TV

★ ★ ★ Allalin (HR)
☎ 028 671631 telex 38549

1 ▮ -/- 29 ▦ 134/254
☉ ♨ ⑴ ▤ TV

★ ★ ★ Alpenblick (HR)
☎ 028 671042

1 ▮ -/- 27 ▦ 172/338
☉ ⑴ ▤ 🐕

Alpenblick

Gourmet restaurant

Richard Stöckli
CH-3812
Wilderswil/Interlaken

Telephone 036-220707
Telefax 036-228007
Suisse - Switzerland

Reservations can be made
throughout the year via
Vrij Uit travel agents.

★ ★ **Alpenrose** (HR)
☎ 028 672339

1 🛏 -/- 11 🛏 -/-
⚓ ⊙ ▣ WC

★ ★ ★ ★ **Antares** (HR)
☎ 028 673664 fax 028 675236
✉ 3920

* 9 🛏 118/220 36 🛏 196/460
AE ⓓ Ⓔ ☲ ⚓ ⊙ ♨ ⇅ ▣ ▱ WC TV ⍾

★ ★ ★ **Artemis** (HR)
☎ 028 671185

1 🛏 112/217 21 🛏 224/434
⚓ ⊙ ⇅ ▣ ✈

★ ★ ★ ★ **Beau Rivage** (HR)
☎ 028 671884 telex 472127 fax 028 676510
✉ 3920

4 🛏 -/- 14 🛏 -/-
AE ⓓ Ⓔ ☲ ⚓ ⊷ ⊙ ♨ ⇅ ⬚ ▣ ▱ WC TV ⍾ ⇧ ⊛

★ ★ ★ **Bellerive** (HR)
☎ 028 671313

1 🛏 -/- 19 🛏 -/-
⚓ ⇅ ▣

★ ★ **Burgener** (HR)
☎ 028 672339 fax 028 675579

4 🛏 63/85 11 🛏 126/222
⊙ ♨ ▣ ▱

★ ★ ★ **Darioli** (HG)
☎ 028 672748

3 🛏 -/- 22 🛏 -/-
⚓ ⊙ ♨ ⇅ ▣ ▱ WC

★ ★ ★ **Dom** (HP)
☎ 028 671371 fax 028 675653
✉ 3920

open 19.12 - 17.04 + 18.05 - 10.10
13 🛏 87/- 27 🛏 74/129
AE ⓓ Ⓔ ☲ ⚓ ⊙ ♨ ⇅ ▣ ▱ WC ⍾ ⊛

★ ★ ★ **Excelsior** (HR)
☎ 028 673017

1 🛏 86/169 15 🛏 172/338
⊙ ⇅ ▣ TV

★ ★ ★ **Holiday** (HR)
☎ 028 671203 fax 028 675014

open 15.05 - 04.09 + 19.12 - 17.04
* 1 🛏 106/160 29 🛏 160/230
AE ⓓ Ⓔ ☲ ⚓ ♨ ⚞ ⇅ ▣ WC TV ⊛

★ ★ ★ **Julen** (HCR)
Steinmatterstrasse
☎ 028 672481 telex 38535

4 🛏 -/- 33 🛏 -/-
⚓ ⊙ ♨ ⇅ ▣ ▱ WC ⍾ ⇧

★ ★ ★ **Matterhornblick** (HG)
☎ 028 671010 fax 028 675093
✉ 3920

open 10.11 - 10.10
* 4 🛏 65/130 21 🛏 130/190
AE ⓓ Ⓔ ☲ ⚓ ⊙ ◈ ♨ ⇅ ▣ ▱ WC TV

★ **Le Mazot** (HR)
☎ 028 672777

1 🛏 25/50 6 🛏 50/100
⊙ ✈

SWITZERLAND

★ ★ ★ **Parnass** (HP)
☎ 028 672496 fax 028 674557
✉ 3920

open 19.12 - 02.05 + 12.06 - 10.10
* 10 ⊿ 59/95 22 ⋈ 118/220
🄰🄴 🄴 ⊏ ⊙ ⇅ ▇ 🄿 🆆🄲 🍴 ⚞

★ ★ **Primavera** (HR)
☎ 028 673013

1 ⊿ -/- 14 ⋈ 96/222
⚲ ⇅ ▇

★ ★ **Rhodania** (HP)
☎ 028 672863

1 ⊿ -/- 20 ⋈ -/-
⚲ ⊙ ⇅ ▇

★ ★ ★ ★ ★ **Seiler Hotel Mont Cervin** (HR)
Bahnhofstrasse
☎ 028 661122 telex 472129 fax 028 672878
✉ 3920

open 27.11 - 18.04 + 12.06 - 10.10
* 21 ⊿ 170/310 111 ⋈ 310/620
🄰🄴 🄳 🄴 ⊏ ⚲ ⊙ 🄿 ⋈ ⇅ ▇ 🄿 🆆🄲 🆃🆅 🍴 ⚞ ⊙

★ ★ ★ ★ **Seiler Monte Rosa** (HR)
☎ 028 661131 telex 472128 fax 028 671160
✉ 3920

open 18.12 - 17.04 + 25.06 - 23.11
* 10 ⊿ 155/230 39 ⋈ 260/460
🄰🄴 🄳 🄴 ⊏ ⊙ ⋈ ⇅ ⊩ ▇ 🄿 🆆🄲 🆃🆅 ⚞

★ ★ ★ **Sport** (HR)
☎ 028 672233

1 ⊿ -/- 20 ⋈ 156/298
⚲ ⊙ ⇅ ▇

★ ★ **Touring** (HCR)
☎ 028 671177 fax 028 674601

4 ⊿ -/- 24 ⋈ -/-
🄴 ⊏ ⚲ ⊙ 🄿 ⋈ ⊩ ▇ 🄿 🆆🄲 ⊙

ZERNEZ, *Graubunden*　　07

★ ★ ★ **Filli** (HR)
☎ 082 81223 fax 082 81430
✉ 7530

* 2 ⊿ 40/65 20 ⋈ 80/120
⚲ ⊙ 🄿 🄿 ⋈ ⊩ ▇ 🄿 🆆🄲 🆃🆅 🍴 ⊙

ZINAL, *Valais*　　05

★ ★ **Formule 1 les Erables** (HCR)
☎ 027 651881 fax 027 652414
✉ 3961

- ⊿ -/- 52 ⋈ -/-
🄰🄴 🄴 ⊏ ⚲ 🄿 🄿 ⋈ ⇅ ▇ 🄿 🆆🄲 ⊙

ZOFINGEN, *Aargau*　　03

★ ★ ★ **Engel** (HG)　　🄰🄰 ANWB
Engelgasse 4
☎ 062 515050
fax 062 519966
✉ 4800

The Hotel Engel is
peacefully situated in
the centre of Zofingen,
just around the corner
from the main street
and close to the station.
The rooms all have
modern amenities - private toilet with bath or
shower, a TV and a minibar. The Hotel Engel is
ideally suited to those who are travelling through,
and can be reached from the Basel to Zürich
motorway via the Oftringen exit, and from the
Basel to Luzern motorway, via the exit to Reiden.

* 10 ⊿ 75/110 27 ⋈ 120/160
🄰🄴 🄳 🄴 ⊏ ⚲ ⊙ ▇ 🄿 🆆🄲 🆃🆅 ⊙

★ ★ ★ **Zofingen** (HCR)
Kirchplatz 30
☎ 062 500100 fax 062 522208
✉ 4800

* 19 ⊿ 105/140 20 ⋈ 150/200
🄰🄴 🄳 🄴 ⊏ ⚲ ⊙ 🄿 ⋈ ⇅ ▇ 🄿 🆆🄲 🆃🆅 🍴

ZUG, *Zug*　　04

★ ★ ★ **Guggithal** (HR)　　🄰🄰 ANWB
Zugerbergstr
☎ 042 212821· telex
865134 fax 042 221443
✉ 6300

The Hotel Guggithal is
situated in leafy sur-
roundings on the out-
skirts of the centre of
Zug on the Zugersee. It
was originally a some-
what outmoded family
hotel, but with the construction of a new 5-storey
wing, it has been fitted out with every modern
convenience. All 33 rooms have a bathroom, TV
and minibar, and more than half have a balcony.

From the rooms, the restaurant and the pleasant terrace there is a beautiful view over the lake.

* 13 ∂ 95/140 20 ⌂ 170/220
🆎 🄴 ⚏ ⚒ 🅿 🅿 ⇞ ⇞ 📺 🄴 🄴 wc tv 🍴

ZUOZ, Graubunden 07

★ ★ ★ **Castell Zuoz** (HP)
☎ 082 70101 telex 74846
✉ 7524

1 ∂ -/- 77 ⌂ -/-
⚒ 📺 🅿 🅿 ⇞ ⇞ 🄴 🄴 wc 🍴

ZÜRICH, Zurich 04

Switzerland's largest city boasts all the advantages of an international metropolis and an attractive location at the northern end of Lake Zürich. Three old churches - the *Grossmünster*, St Peter's and the *Fraumunster* - dominate the skyline. Among more than 30 museums with a great variety of exhibitions, the Swiss National Museum provides a lively demonstration of Swiss history. The Municipal Theatre, Opera House. Concert and various smaller theatres offer a selection of cultural events. The annual June Festival presents many events based on a common theme. Fifteen minutes from Zürich lies the industrial city of Winterthur, noted for its impressive art collections. Zürich offers an enormous range of restaurants catering for most tastes and pockets. Specialities to look out for include fondue and *raclette* as well as game in season, noodle-like dumplings known as *spatzli*, and *Züri-Gschnatzlets*, diced veal with mushrooms in a cream and wine sauce.

See cityplan on page 99.

★ ★ ★ ★ **Airport** (HCR)
Oberhauserstr. 30
☎ 01 8104444 telex 825416 fax 01 8109708
✉ 8152

* 20 ∂ 150/170 24 ⌂ 200/220
🆎 🄳 🄴 ⚏ ⚒ ⊙ 🅿 🅿 ⇞ 🄴 🄴 wc tv ✈

★ ★ ★ ★ **Ascot** (HR)
Tessinerplatz 9
☎ 01 2011800 telex 815454 fax 01 2027210
✉ 8002

* 27 ∂ 180/270 46 ⌂ 260/380
🆎 🄳 🄴 ⚏ ⊙ 🅿 🅿 ⇞ 🄴 wc tv 🍴 ✈

★ ★ ★ **Basilea** (HG)
Zahringerstr. 25
☎ 01 2614250 telex 8164681 fax 01 2517411
✉ 8001

* 23 ∂ 95/130 28 ⌂ 130/180
🆎 🄳 🄴 ⚏ ⚒ ⊙ 🅿 🅿 ⇞ 🄴 wc ✈

★ ★ ★ ★ **City** (HCR)
Loewenstrasse 34
☎ 01 2112055 telex 812437 fax 01 2120036
✉ 8021

18 ∂ -/- 56 ⌂ -/-
🆎 🄳 🄴 ⚏ ⊙ 🅿 🅿 ⇞ 🄴 🄴 wc tv 🍴

★ ★ ★ ★ ★ **Dolder Grand** (HR)
Kurhausstrasse 65
☎ 01 2516231 telex 816416 fax 01 2516231
✉ 8032

* 40 ∂ 320/360 144 ⌂ 420/602
🆎 🄳 🄴 ⚏ ⚒ 📺 🅿 🅿 ⇞ ⇞ 🄴 🄴 wc tv 🍴

★ ★ ★ ★ **Best Western Hotel Engematthof** (HR)
Engimattstr. 14
☎ 01 2012504 telex 817273 fax 01 2012516
res nr 031 234455
✉ 8002

* 39 ∂ 150/180 40 ⌂ 200/290
🆎 🄳 🄴 ⚏ ⚒ ⊙ 🅿 🅿 ⇞ 🄴 🄴 wc tv

★ ★ ★ ★ **Europe** (HCR)
Dufoursstrasse 4
☎ 01 2611030 telex 816461 fax 01 2510367
✉ 8008

19 ∂ 220/250 23 ⌂ 320/430
🆎 🄳 🄴 ⚏ ⊙ ⇞ 🄴 🄴 🄴

★ ★ ★ **Florhof** (HR)
Florhofgasse 4
☎ 01 2614470 telex 817364 fax 01 2614611
✉ 8001

* 10 ∂ 150/190 23 ⌂ 210/280
🆎 🄳 🄴 ⚏ ⚒ ⊙ 🅿 ⇞ 🄴 🄴 🄴 wc tv 🍴

★ ★ ★ ★ **Best Western Hotel Glockenhof** (HCR)
Sihlstr. 31
☎ 01 2115650 telex 812466 fax 01 2115660
res nr 031 234455
✉ 8023

* 41 ∂ -/190 67 ⌂ -/280
🆎 🄳 🄴 ⚏ ⊙ ◆ 🅿 ⇞ 🄴 🄴 wc tv 🍴

★ ★ ★ ★ **International** (HCR)
Am Marktplatz
☎ 01 3114341 telex 823251 fax 01 3124468
✉ 8050

100 ∂ -/- 250 ⌂ -/-
🆎 🄳 🄴 ⚏ ⊙ 🅿 🅿 ⇞ 🄴 🄴 wc tv 🍴 ✈

SWITZERLAND

★ ★ **Jolie Ville Motor Inn** (HR)
Zurichstr. 105
☎ 01 7108585 telex 52507
✉ 8134

2 🛏 -/- 60 🛏 -/-
◆ **P** **WC** **TV**

★ ★ ★ **Krone Unterstrass** (HCR)
Schaffhauserstrasse 1
☎ 01 3611688 telex 815068 fax 01 3611967
✉ 8006

30 🛏 -/- 27 🛏 -/-
AE ⓘ **E** ⚡ ⊙ ◆ **P** ⌔ ↥ ⊟ ⌂ **WC** **TV** ☺

★ ★ ★ **Limmat** (HCR)
Limmatstrasse 118
☎ 01 2715240 telex 823161 fax 01 2728676
✉ 8005

8 🛏 120/150 48 🛏 150/220
AE ⓘ **E** ⚡ ☽ ◆ ⌔ ↥ ⊟ ⌂ **WC** **TV** |◎| ☺

★ ★ ★ **Montana** (HCR)
Konradstr. 39
☎ 01 2716900 telex 822640 fax 01 2723070
✉ 8000

* 20 🛏 130/190 54 🛏 190/280
AE ⓘ **E** ⚡ ⊙ **P** ⌔ ↥ ⊟ ⌂ **WC** **TV**

★ ★ ★ ★ **Nova Park** (HCR)
Badenerstrasse 420
☎ 01 4912222 telex 822822 fax 01 4912220
✉ 8040

* - 🛏 185/360 excl. breakfast 365 🛏 235/360 excl.
breakfast
AE ⓘ **E** ⚡ ◆ **P** ⌔ ⌔ ↥ ⊟ **WC** **TV** |◎| ☺

★ ★ ★ ★ **Pullman Continental** (HCR)
Stampfenbachstr. 60
☎ 01 3633363 telex 817089 fax 01 3633318
✉ 8035

* 30 🛏 210/240 excl. breakfast 150 🛏 250/280
excl. breakfast
AE ⓘ **E** ⚡ ↿ ⊙ ⌔ ⌔ ↥ ⊟ ⌂ **WC** **TV** |◎| ☺

★ ★ ★ **Seegarten** (HCR)
Seegartenstrasse 14
☎ 01 3833737 telex 817868 fax 01 3833738
✉ 8008

17 🛏 -/- 11 🛏 -/-
AE ⓘ **E** ⚡ ☽ ◆ ⌔ ↥ ⊟ ⌂ **WC** **TV**

★ ★ ★ ★ **St. Gotthard** (HCR)
Bahnhofstrasse 87
☎ 01 2115334 telex 812420 fax 01 2112419
✉ 8023

* 70 🛏 210/310 excl. breakfast 70 🛏 340/430 excl.
breakfast
AE ⓘ **E** ⚡ ⊙ ⌔ ↥ ⊟ ⌂ **WC** **TV** ☺

★ ★ ★ ★ ★ **Zürich** (HCR)
Neumuehlequai 42
☎ 01 3636363 telex 817587 fax 01 3636015
✉ 8001

* 90 🛏 220/335 167 🛏 270/385
⊙ ◆ **P** ⌔ ⌔ ⌁ ↥ ⊟ ⌂ **WC** **TV** |◎| ☺

ZÜRICH-AIRPORT, *Zurich*   **04**

★ ★ ★ **Welcome Inn** (HCR)
Holbergstr. 1
KLOTEN
☎ 01 8140727 telex 825527 fax 01 8135616
✉ 8302

2 🛏 98/- excl. breakfast 94 🛏 135/- excl. breakfast
AE ⓘ **E** ⚡ ⊙ ◆ **P** ⌔ ⌔ ↥ ⌂ **WC** **TV** ☺

ZÜRICH-GLATTBURG, *Zurich*   **04**

★ ★ ★ ★ **Mövenpick Zurich airport** (HCR)
W. Mittelholzerstr. 8
ZÜRICH
☎ 01 8101111 telex 828781 fax 01 8104038
✉ 8058

* - 🛏 230/270 excl. breakfast 335 🛏 280/320 excl.
breakfast
AE ⓘ **E** ⚡ ⊙ **P** ⌔ ↥ ⊟ ⌂ **WC** **TV** |◎| ☺

ZWEISIMMEN, *Bern*   **05**

★ ★ ★ **Résidence** (HCR)
☎ 030 21715 telex 923243
✉ 3770

1 🛏 -/- 15 🛏 -/-
⌔ ↥ ⊟ ⌂ **WC** |◎|

★ ★ ★ **Sportmotel** (HCR)   AA ANWB
Saanenstrasse
☎ 030 21431
✉ 3770

Zweisimmen lies in a mountainous area which is
a good base for walking and skiing. The Sportmotel is situated in the centre of the town and has
20 rooms with good facilities. There is a bar as
well as a good restaurant and disco. Parking
facilities are available.

open 01.06 - 31.03
* - ♫ 50/80 20 ♨ 100/150
🔲 🚽 ⅄ ⌣ ⊙ ◈ 🄿 ☂ ♨ 📠 🄿 🆆🅒 ☺

Index